D1274092

ANTI-SLAVERY SENTIMENT IN AMERICAN LITERATURE PRIOR TO 1865

ANTI-SLAVERY SENTIMENT IN AMERICAN LITERATURE PRIOR TO 1865

BY

LORENZO DOW TURNER, Ph.D.
Professor of English
Fisk University

KENNIKAT PRESS, INC./PORT WASHINGTON, N. Y.

ANTI-SLAVERY SENTIMENT IN AMERICAN LITERATURE
PRIOR TO 1865

Originally published in 1929
Reissued in 1966 by Kennikat Press

Library of Congress Catalog Card No: 66-28052

To
My Wife and Mother

PREFACE

This study, with the exception of the Appendix and the discussion of a few anti-slavery productions to which the author did not have access in 1926, was completed in that year and submitted to the Faculty of the Graduate School of Arts and Literature of the University of Chicago in candidacy for the degree of Doctor of Philosophy. The author is under obligation to several persons for suggestions that have been of great value to him in making this study. To the librarians and their assistants at the Universities of Chicago and Pennsylvania, at Harvard, Yale, Columbia, Brown, and Howard, as well as to those at the Library of Congress, the New York Historical Society, the New York and Boston Public Libraries, the Boston Athenaeum, and the Newberry and John Crerar Libraries, of Chicago, he is indebted for generously making accessible material without which this volume would have been impossible. He wishes also to express deep appreciation to Professors Percy H. Boynton, John M. Manly, William E. Dodd, T. P. Cross, and James Napier Wilt, of the University of Chicago, to Dr. Carter G. Woodson, Editor of the Journal of Negro History, and to Mr. Arthur A. Schomburg, of New York, for suggestions which led to his finding several important anti-slavery productions. Especially is he grateful for the friendly and scholarly criticism of Professor Boynton, under whose direction this study was made.

LORENZO DOW TURNER

Nashville, Tennessee
September, 1929

CONTENTS

CHAPTER V

CHAPTER VI

ANTI-SLAVERY SENTIMENT IN AMERICAN LITERATURE PRIOR TO 1865

ANTI-SLAVERY SENTIMENT IN AMERICAN LITER-ATURE PRIOR TO 1865

INTRODUCTION

The purpose of this study has been to discover the extent to which anti-slavery sentiment found expression in American literature prior to 1865, to trace the growth of this sentiment, to ascertain its nature, and to indicate the extent to which it was influenced by the spirit of the time in which it appeared.

The chief sources of information have been novels, poems, plays, short narratives, essays, sketches, magazine and newspaper articles having literary value, and a selected number of orations, sermons, letters, diaries, journals, biographies, and books of travel.

The long period during which opposition to slavery was expressed in the literature of America has been divided into five shorter periods, each one indicating a definite stage in the development of the anti-slavery movement, which had a continuous growth up to the end of the Civil War. The first period ended in January, 1808, when the Slave-Trade Act, abolishing the African slave-trade, became effective; the second, in 1831, when William Lloyd Garrison published the first number of the *Liberator* and became the leader of the anti-slavery movement; the third, in 1850, the year of the passage of the Fugitive Slave Act, which was responsible for the conversion of thousands of persons to the cause of abolition; the fourth, in 1861, when the Civil War began; and the fifth, in 1865, when it ended.

A study of the literature of these periods has revealed the fact that opposition to slavery was based upon a variety of grounds. During the seventeenth and the first half of the eighteenth centuries, when the literature of America was essentially didactic and religious, the basis of opposition was chiefly moral and religious, though at this time such authors as Samuel Sewall, William Byrd, John Woolman, and Benjamin Franklin were advocating the abolition of slavery upon social and economic grounds as well. During the latter part of the eighteenth century, when the doctrine of the natural and inalienable rights of man was being proclaimed so widely, anti-slavery arguments frequently showed the influence of the political philosophy of the time. It was also during this time that opposition to slavery on sentimental grounds became considerable. Even though there were manifestations of the humanitarian spirit in the earliest anti-slavery literary productions, there was no considerable opposition to slavery on sentimental grounds until between 1770 and 1800, when the sentimentalism of European writers had begun to influence American authors.

Throughout the remaining four periods of the abolition movement, as revealed in American literature, the anti-slavery arguments based upon moral, religious, and sentimental grounds were the most numerous and the most effectively presented, though convincing appeals for the abolition of slavery as a social, economic, and political necessity found frequent expression. The social and economic arguments, for example, were very effectively used in many literary productions during the third and fourth periods, which extended from 1831 to 1861. These various grounds of objection to slavery—moral, religious, sentimental, social, economic, and political—have determined the method here employed for the study of anti-slavery sentiment.

THE ANTI-SLAVERY MOVEMENT PRIOR TO THE ABOLITION OF THE AFRICAN SLAVE-TRADE (1641-1808)

I. MORAL AND RELIGIOUS ARGUMENTS

A. *The Puritans and the Quakers*

Prior to January 1, 1808, when the Slave-Trade Act prohibiting the importation of slaves into the United States became effective, opposition to slavery as recorded in the literature of America was based most often upon moral and religious grounds. It appeared first in the writings of the Puritans and the Quakers.

The majority of the Puritans who showed interest in the welfare of the slave were concerned primarily with his moral and religious instruction. Consequently, seeing in slavery a hindrance to this instruction, they opposed slavery. Few of them, however, appear to have foreseen any very serious consequences that might result from the continuance of such a system, and none of them effected any permanent plan for abolishing it.[1] John Eliot, one of the authors of the *Bay*

---

[1] Between 1641 and 1652 statutes were enacted by the Puritans to limit Negro slavery in Massachusetts and Rhode Island, but they were not long enforced. See A. B. Hart, *Slavery and Abolition*, pp. 50-51. The Massachusetts "Body of Liberties" (1641), compiled chiefly by Nathaniel Ward, contained a provision to the effect that there should "never be any bond slaverie, villinage or captivitie amongst us unles it be lawful captives taken in just warres, and such strangers as willingly selle themselves or are sold to us." See *Old South Leaflets*, VII, 273. An attempt was made to enforce this regulation, for in 1646 the General Court ordered that certain Negroes unlawfully brought from Africa be returned at the charge of the country, and that a letter be sent with them expressing the indignation of the Court. See *Records of the Massachusetts Bay Colony*, II, 168. In 1652 a statute was enacted in Rhode Island limiting the period during which Negroes might be held in slavery. The commissioners of Providence and Warwick ordered that no man, black or white, should be forced "to serve any man or his assignes longer than ten yeares, or untill they come to bee twentie, from the time of their cominge within the liberties of this Collonie. . . . And that man that will not let them goe free, or shall sell them away elsewhere, to that end that they may bee enslaved to others for a long time, hee or they shall forfeit to the Collonie forty pounds." See *Records of the Colony of Rhode Island*, I, 243. By the beginning of the eighteenth century,

Psalm Book, lamented the fact that the Negroes were used as if they were horses or oxen, and considered it a prodigy "that any wearing the name of Christians, should so much have the heart of Devils in them, as to prevent and hinder the Instructions of the poor Blackamoores, and confine the Souls of their miserable Slaves to a destroying ignorance, meerly for fear of thereby loosing the benefit of their Vassalage."[2] He offered to meet the slaves once a week for instruction, but he did not live to make much progress in the undertaking.[2] Cotton Mather's views on slavery were practically the same as Eliot's. In 1706 he wrote an essay entitled "The Negro Christianized," a copy of which was to be placed in every family of New England owning a Negro; and many copies were to be sent to the West Indies.[3] Four years later, in an essay entitled "On Doing Good in our Domestic Relations," he expressed the belief that God had brought the Negroes to America for a good purpose:

"What if they should be the elect of God, fetched from Africa and the Indies that, by means of their situation, they may be brought home to the Shepherd of Souls?"[4]

He said that the Americans could not pretend to Christianity until they did more to Christianize their slaves; and he hoped that an act might be obtained from the British Parliament for the Christianizing of the slaves in the plantations. Yet, in the meantime, the slave-trade, said he, was a spectacle that shocked humanity:

"The harmless natives basely they trepan,
And barter baubles for the souls of men;
The wretches they to Christian climes bring o'er,
To serve worse heathens than they did before."[5]

A better example from the Puritans of the moral and religious argument and the first really significant one in the

---

however, this law was no longer enforced.—DuBois, *The Suppression of the African Slave-Trade,* p. 34.

[2] Mather, *The Life and Death of the Renown'd Mr. John Eliot,* p. 125.

[3] *Diary of Cotton Mather,* in *Mass. Hist. Soc. Coll.,* 7th Ser., VII, Part I, 565.

[4] Mather, *Essays to Do Good,* p. 94.

[5] *Ibid.,* p. 95.

history of the anti-slavery movement in America was Judge Samuel Sewall's pamphlet "The Selling of Joseph," published June 24, 1700. Sewall had long intended to write something against the slave-trade. A visit from a friend who showed him a petition he intended to present to the General Court for the freeing of a Negro and his wife unjustly held in bondage was said to be in part the occasion of his writing "The Selling of Joseph." Here his opposition to slavery was considerably in advance of any that had appeared previously in American literature. He referred to temptations that confronted masters "to connive at the Fornication of their Slaves; lest they should be obliged to find them Wives or pay their Fines," and said it was "most lamentable to think, how in taking Negroes out of Africa, and selling them here, That which God has joyned together men do boldly rend asunder; Men from their Country, Husbands from their Wives, Parents from their children."[6] He answered most of the pro-slavery arguments based upon passages from the Scriptures; and in reply to the argument that the opportunity which the Negro in America had of becoming a Christian justified his being brought from Africa, he said that evil must not be done in order that good might result from it.[7] In 1705 he made inquiry of the Athenian Society "Whether trading for Negroes, i.e., carrying them out of their own country into perpetual slavery, be in itself unlawful, and especially contrary to the great Law of Christianity."[8] Sewall's moral and religious argument anticipated that of the latter eighteenth century writers, for it called attention to the detrimental effect of slavery upon the master as well as upon the slave.

The anti-slavery arguments of the Quakers during this period were also based most often upon moral and religious grounds, but they revealed a more democratic spirit than those of the Puritans, for they embodied the doctrine of

[6] Sewall, "The Selling of Joseph," in *Mass. Hist. Soc. Coll.*, 5th Ser., VI, 18.

[7] *Ibid.*, 19.

[8] "Letter-Book of Samuel Sewall," in *Mass. Hist. Soc. Coll.*, 6th Ser., I, 322.

human brotherhood and frequently contained definite plans for the emancipation of the slaves.[9] The often cited John Woolman (1720-1772) was by no means the earliest of the Quakers in America who opposed slavery. In 1688 German Quakers in Germantown, Pennsylvania, issued a protest against slavery.[10] The work of George Keith, John Hepburn, Ralph Sandiford, Benjamin Lay, and others antedates Woolman's and that of Anthony Benezet exerted a greater influence upon the general anti-slavery movement in America than his;[11] but Woolman was the most important of the Quakers who won a place in the American literature of this period. As a traveling preacher he spent the greater part of his life in advocating the cause of the poor and oppressed. This humanitarian spirit was manifested throughout his works, yet there was no bitterness shown toward his opponents. In his twenty-third year while employed at Mount Holly, New Jersey, he was asked by his employer, who had sold a slave, to write a bill of sale. The request was sudden and came from one who employed him by the year; consequently, he wrote it, but told his employer that he believed "slave-keeping to be a practice inconsistent with the Christian religion."[12] He afterwards refused to comply with similar requests. In "Some Considerations on the Keeping of Negroes" (1754), he said that all nations were of one blood:

"To consider mankind otherwise than brethren, to think favours are peculiar to one nation, and exclude others, plainly supposes a darkness in the understanding: for as God's love is universal, so where the mind is sufficiently influenced by it, it begets a likeness of itself, and the heart is enlarged towards all men."[13]

[9] See below, p. 26.

[10] See Hart, *American History Told by Contemporaries*, II, 291-293.

[11] For an account of the activities of the Quakers in the anti-slavery movement in America during this period, see Thomas Clarkson, *The History of the Rise, Progress, and Accomplishment of the Abolition of the African Slave. Trade* (1808), I, 108-156. For an excellent account of Benezet, see also C. G. Woodson, "Anthony Benezet," in the *Journal of Negro History*, II, 37-50.

[12] "The Life and Travels of John Woolman," in *Works*, pp. 15-16.

[13] Woolman, "Some Considerations on the Keeping of Negroes," in *Works*, pp. 258-260.

Masters, he contended, were not competent to be the owners
of men, for the human mind was not naturally fortified with
that firmness in wisdom and goodness necessary to an independent ruler. Furthermore,

"Placing on men the ignominious title slave . . . . tends gradu-
ally to fix a notion in the mind, that they are a sort of people below
us in nature, and leads us to consider them as such in all our conclu-
sions about them."[14]

Woolman could conceive of the enslavement of persons guilty
of such crimes as would unfit them to be at liberty; yet the
children of such persons, he thought, ought not to be enslaved
because their parents sinned.[15] With such arguments he
attacked the evils of slavery without antagonizing the slaveholder or losing the respect and sympathy of any of his contemporaries. He told the slaveholder that his wicked specu-
lations in human lives should be stopped, and he was received hospitably by him. He persuaded many of his own
group, the Friends, to desist from holding slaves, even
though to do so was detrimental to their own interests. The
success of the emancipation movement among the Quakers
who in the Middle and Northern States had freed practically
all of their slaves before the close of the Revolutionary War,
is said to have been due very largely to his influence.[16]

B. Latter Eighteenth Century Writers

Like the Puritans and the Quakers, writers of the latter
eighteenth century made frequent use of the moral and religious argument, but they were more severe in their condemnation of slavery and dwelt more at length upon its demoralizing effect upon the slaveholder and the slave.

By this time, because of the growing complexity of the
slave problem due to the rapid increase in the number of
slaves, the question of the effect of slavery upon the morals
of the master and the slave was one of graver concern to

[14] *Ibid.*, pp. 296-297.
[15] *Ibid.*, p. 282.
[16] Locke, *Anti-Slavery in America, 1619-1808*, pp. 30-36.

anti-slavery writers than in the colonial period, and accordingly received more detailed treatment. In his *Notes on the State of Virginia,* issued at Paris in 1784 and at Philadelphia in 1788, Thomas Jefferson spoke of the commerce between master and slave as a "perpetual exercise of the most boisterous passions, the most unremitting despotism on the one part, and degrading submissions on the other."[17] He lamented the fact that the children of masters saw this and learned to imitate it. "The man must be a prodigy," said he, "who can retain his manners and morals undepraved by such circumstances. . . . . Indeed I tremble for my country when I reflect that God is just; that his justice cannot sleep forever!"[17] Benjamin Franklin, Sarah Wentworth Morton, and Timothy Dwight were also greatly alarmed over these conditions. In "An Address to the Public; from the Pennsylvania Society for Promoting the Abolition of Slavery, and the Relief of Free Negroes unlawfully held in Bondage" (1789), Franklin said that slavery was such an "atrocious debasement of human nature" that its very extirpation, if not performed with solicitous care, might open a source of serious evils, for

"The unhappy man, who has long been treated as a brute animal, too frequently sinks beneath the common standard of the human species. The galling chains, that bind his body, do also fetter his intellectual faculties, and impair the social affections of his heart . . . . reason and conscience have but little influence over his conduct, because he is chiefly governed by the passion of fear."[18]

In Mrs. Morton's novel entitled *The Power of Sympathy* (1789), one of the characters (Harrington) noticed on his tour through the United States that those inhabitants "accustomed to a habit of domineering over their slaves" were "haughtier, more tenacious of honour," and more aristocratic in temper[19] than those where slavery did not exist; but he anticipated the happy time when the sighs of the slave should "no longer expire in the air of freedom."[20] Probably

---

[17] Jefferson, *Notes on the State of Virginia,* pp. 172-174.
[18] Franklin, *Works,* ed. Sparks, II, 515-516.
[19] Morton, *The Power of Sympathy,* II, 74.
[20] *Ibid.,* 30.

the most bitter attack upon slavery on moral grounds to be
found in the poetry of the period was made by Timothy
Dwight in *Greenfield Hill* (1794), in which he stressed the
immoral effect of slavery upon the African youth, who

> "Thus, shut from honour's path .... turns to shame,
> And filches the small good, he cannot claim.
> To sour, and stupid, sinks his active mind;
> Finds joy in drink, he cannot elsewhere find;
>
> . . . .
>
> Sees from himself his sole redress must flow,
> And makes revenge the balsam of his woe.
> "Thus slavery's blast bids sense and virtue die;
> Thus lower'd to dust the sons of Afric lie.
>
> . . . .
>
> "O thou chief curse, since curses here began;
> First guilt, first woe, first infamy of man;
> Thou spot of hell, deep smirch'd on human kind,
> The uncur'd gangrene of the reasoning mind;
> Alike in church, in state, and household all,
> Supreme memorial of the world's dread fall;
> O slavery! laurel of the infernal mind,
> Proud Satan's triumph over lost mankind!"[21]

The literature of this period contained also a great many
anti-slavery arguments based upon religious grounds. Many
of these were replies to the argument that slavery was not
forbidden in the Scriptures; some pointed to the teachings of
Christ as the strongest possible argument against slavery;[22]
and others were directed definitely toward the religion of the
slaveholders. Thomas Paine, in 1775, said that Africans
would be filled with abhorrence of Christians and be led to
think that the Christian religion would make them more inhuman savages if they embraced it.[23] In a novel by Mrs.
Susanna Rowson, called *The Inquisitor; or, Invisible Rambler* (1794), the leading character possessed a ring which,
when on his finger, rendered him invisible, so that he could
visit at will habitations of vice and luxury and give aid and

[21] Dwight, *Greenfield Hill*, pp. 37-38.
[22] Rush, *An Address to the Inhabitants of the British Settlements in America
upon Slave-Keeping* (pub. 1773), pp. 2-3.
[23] Paine, "African Slavery in America," in *Writings of Thomas Paine*, ed.
Conway, I, 6, 7.

protection to persons in distress. Among those for whom he had great sympathy was the slave. After describing a scene in Africa where a native was stolen by the European slave-trader, he followed the enslaved African to the West Indies; saw him in his suffering there until age, sickness, and bitter grief were his only companions. The slave died, and was thrown into a grave "without one tear of effection or regret being shed upon his bier." But his soul, said the narrator, "shall appear white and spotless at the throne of Grace, to confound the man who called himself a Christian, and yet betrayed a fellow-creature into bondage."[24]

An effective attack upon the religion of the slaveholder, extremely ironical in method and apparently in imitation of Swift's "A Modest Proposal," was John Trumbull's eighth essay in "The Correspondent," published in the *Connecticut Journal and New Haven Post-Boy* on July 6, 1770.[25] Trumbull began by saying that since the whole world was the property of the righteous, the Africans, being infidels and heretics, might rightly be considered lawful plunder. He spoke of the boundless charity and benevolence of the Americans who, with no other end in view than to bring "those poor creatures" within hearing of the gospel, spared no expense of time or money, and endured the greatest fatigues of body and trouble of conscience in carrying on this "pious design"; and asked if the Africans were not, therefore, bound by the ties of gratitude to devote their whole lives to the service of their enslavers as the only reward that could be adequate to such superabundant charity. He was aware that some persons doubted whether the sole purpose of Americans in enslaving Africans was to teach them the principles of Christianity, but he was able to prove that this was their purpose by the many instances of learned, pious Negroes; for, said he:

"I myself have heard of no less than three, who know half the letters of the alphabet, and have made considerable advances

[24] Rowson, *The Inquisitor; or, Invisible Rambler,* p. 90.

[25] See Appendix, pp. 123-125, for a reprint of the entire essay.

in the Lord's prayer and catechism. In general, I confess they are scarcely so learned; which deficiency we do not charge to the fault of any one, but have the good nature to attribute it merely to their natural stupidity, and dullness of intellect."[26]

He called attention to many other nations in the world whom Americans had equal right to enslave, and who stood in as much need of Christianity as the Africans, and suggested, in particular, that the Turks and Papists should thus be transformed into Christians:

"I propose at first and by way of trial, in this laudable scheme, that two vessels be sent, one to Rome, and the other to Constantinople, to fetch off the Pope and the Grand Signior; I make no doubt but the public, convinced of the legality of the thing, and filled to the brim with the charitable design of enslaving infidels, will readily engage in such an enterprise. For my part, would my circumstances permit, I would be ready to lead in the adventure, and should promise myself certain success, with the assistance of a select company of seamen concerned in the African trade. But at present, I can only show my zeal, by promising when the affair is concluded and the captives brought ashore, to set apart several hours in every day, when their masters can spare them, for instructing the Pope in his creed, and teaching the Grand Signior to say his catechism."[26]

II. ARGUMENTS BASED UPON NATURAL AND INALIENABLE RIGHTS

In American literature as early as 1700 the theory that all men were born free and had equal rights was used in reference to the African slave.[27] Samuel Sewall contended that "all Men, as they are the Sons of Adam, are Coheirs, and have equal Right unto Liberty, and all other outward Comforts of Life"; that Joseph was "rightfully no more a Slave to his Brethren, than they were to him"; and that they had "no more Authority to *Sell* him, than they had to *Slay* him."[28] It was not until the latter part of the eighteenth

---

[26] Trumbull, "The Correspondent, No. 8," in the *Connecticut Journal and New Haven Post-Boy*, July 6, 1770.

[27] For an account of the beginnings of this doctrine among English-speaking peoples in the seventeenth century and of the extent to which the writings of John Locke influenced eighteenth century authors, including Americans, in their use of it, see Charles A. Beard, *The Economic Basis of Politics*, pp. 82-85; Harold J. Laski, *Political Thought in England from Locke to Bentham*, pp. 29-76; and D. G. Ritchie, *Natural Rights*, pp. 3-19.

[28] Sewall, "The Selling of Joseph," in the *Mass. Hist. Soc. Coll.*, 5th Ser., VI, 16-17.

century, however, that opposition to slavery based upon the theory of the natural and inalienable rights of man found fullest expression in American literature. During the period of the American Revolution, when all loyal Americans were asserting their own rights against the claims of England, this doctrine became a convenient means of advancing the cause of freedom generally. The more liberal-minded writers applied it without distinction as to race or condition; whereas others allowed considerations of expediency to determine the nature and extent of their defense and practical application of the theory.[29] In 1764 James Otis contended that by the law of nature all men, whether white or black, were born free; and inquired whether any logical inference in favor of slavery could be drawn from a flat nose and a long or short face.[30] Thomas Paine, in 1775, argued that inasmuch as the Africans were not convicted of forfeiting freedom, they had a "natural, perfect right to it"; and he entreated the Americans to consider with what "consistency or decency" they complained so loudly of attempts to enslave them, while they held so many hundred thousands in slavery and annually enslaved more "without any pretence of authority, or claim upon them."[31] Again, in 1807, in William Dunlap's play entitled *The Father of an Only Child*,[32] this

[29] Patrick Henry, for instance, thought it was amazing that at a time when the rights of humanity were defined with precision, in a country above all others fond of liberty, there should be so many men (including himself) holding slaves. "I am drawn along," said he, "by the general inconvenience of living without them. I will not, I cannot justify it. However culpable my conduct, I will so far pay my devoir to virtue, as to own the excellence and rectitude of her precepts, and to lament my own want of conformity to them."—"Letter of Patrick Henry of Virginia, to Robert Pleasants, of the Society of Friends" (1773), in L. M. Child, *The Evils of Slavery and the Cure of Slavery*, p. 3. Thomas Jefferson also advanced the theory of natural rights, but remained an owner of slaves until his death. In 1785, however, he gloried in the fact that in Virginia young men were coming into office who had "sucked in the principles of liberty, as it were, with their mother's milk," and said that it was to them that he looked with anxiety to turn the fate of slavery. See Jefferson, *Writings*, ed. Washington, I, 377.

[30] Otis, *The Rights of the British Colonies Asserted and Proved*, p. 43.

[31] Paine, *Writings*, ed. Conway, I, 6, 7.

[32] It should be noted that the anti-slavery speech here concerning the hero did

kind of sentiment found expression in a description of
Colonel Campbell, the hero, who, on his estate in Virginia,
said one of the characters, "liberated all those unhappy
Africans, who had been doomed by his predecessors to a
hopeless life of slavery. He not only liberated, but protected, and placed them in the way, and with the means, of
becoming useful to themselves and to others. 'No,' said my
gallant colonel, 'it never shall be said that I shed the blood
of my English brethren for a theoretic principle, which I
violate myself in practice.' "[33] But the strongest of these
arguments based upon the theory of the natural rights of
man was made by Joel Barlow in *The Columbiad* (1807).[34]
After dwelling somewhat at length upon the peace America
enjoyed as a result of her "victories, virtues, wisdom, weal,"
the author had Atlas, the guardian of "old Afric's clime,"
inquire of his brother Hesper, guardian of the Western Continent, why the African tribes were enslaved. He censured
Hesper's proud sons for preaching faith, justice, liberty, and
the rights of man, without practicing these virtues, and
urged that the rights of man be asserted:

> "Prove plain and clear how nature's hand of old
> Cast all men equal in her human mould!
> Their fibres, feelings, reasoning powers the same,
> Like wants await them, like desires inflame.
> .   .   .   .
> Equality of Right is nature's plan;
> And following nature is the march of man.
> Whene'er he deviates in the least degree,
> When, free himself, he would be more than free,
> The baseless column, rear'd to bear his bust,
> Falls as he mounts, and whelms him in the dust."[35]

Many minor writers of the latter eighteenth century were
also ardent advocates of this theory. Much in the manner of
the authors already discussed, but with less effectiveness,

---

not appear in the earliest edition of this play, called *The Father, or American
Shandyism* (1789).

[33] Dunlap, *The Father of an Only Child*, p. 44.

[34] The first edition of this poem, entitled *The Vision of Columbus* (1787),
did not contain this appeal for the slave.

[35] Barlow, *The Columbiad* (ed. 1809), Book VIII, pp. 258-264.

they called attention to the inconsistency between the love of liberty which prevailed in America and the practice on the part of many persons of enslaving the African,[36] and contended that the quality of his hair, the color of his skin, and the uncultivated state in which he lived were not sufficient warrant for his being made a slave.[37] George Buchanan argued that God created men after his own image and granted them liberty and independence, and that if varieties were found in their "structure and colour," these were to be attributed to the nature of their diet and habits and to the soil and climate of the land they inhabited, and served as "flimsy pretexts" for enslaving them.[38] Using the same argument that Thomas Paine had used in 1775, Enos Hitchcock in 1790 and Jonathan Edwards[39] in 1791 contended that Americans had no right to deprive the Africans either of their liberty or of their lives, for, neither had God given them this right nor had the Africans by their own voluntary conduct forfeited their liberty or their lives.[40] In 1791 also Benjamin Banneker, the Negro astronomer, sent to Thomas Jefferson a copy of his Almanac, in which was enclosed a letter entitled "An Appeal on Behalf of the African Race." Here, after calling Jefferson's attention to the doctrine that "all men are created equal; that they are endowed by their creator with certain unalienable rights; and that among these are life, liberty, and the pursuit of happiness," he asked how Jefferson could detain "by fraud and violence" so many Negroes "under groaning captivity and cruel opression"

[36] Othello, "Essay on Negro Slavery" (1788), in the *American Museum*, IV, 414-415.

[37] Enos Hitchcock, *Memoirs of the Bloomgrove Family* (pub. 1790), II, 233-235.

[38] Buchanan, "An Oration upon the Moral and Political Evil of Slavery" (1791), p. 7, in W. F. Poole, *Anti-Slavery Opinions Before the Year 1800*.

[39] Jonathan Edwards was born in 1745 and died in 1801. He should not be confused with the author of *The Freedom of the Will*, who died in 1758.

[40] Hitchcock, *op. cit.*, 240; Edwards, *The Injustice and Impolicy of the Slave-Trade*, p. 5.

and be found guilty of "that most criminal act" which he himself professedly detested in others.[41]

More in the spirit of defiance than Banneker, Hitchcock, Buchanan, or Edwards, the author of an anonymous poem entitled *The American in Algiers, or the Patriot of Seventy-Six in Captivity* (1797), asserted that the unmerited wrongs of the slave would proclaim with shame America's "boasted rights, and prove them but a name."[42] Then addressing the Fathers of the American republic, inquiring whence they obtained the right to enslave Africans, he related his own sufferings at the hands of slave owners and concluded the passage with the following impassioned lines:

> "Eternal God! and is this freedom's land,
> Where whip is law, and mis'ries' wings expand?
> Are these the men who spurn'd despotic pow'r?
> And drench'd their swords in haughty Albion's gore?
> Freedom, avaunt! your sweets I'll never crave,
> If this is Liberty, oh! let me be a slave."[43]

III. SOCIAL AND ECONOMIC ARGUMENTS

The institution of slavery touched life in so many different ways that early in the literature of America there appeared a great variety of arguments against its continuance. During the eighteenth century the abolition of slavery was regarded by many writers as a social and economic necessity.[44] One condition that disturbed them was the high cost

[41] Banneker, "An Appeal on Behalf of the African Race," in *The Negro's Friend,* No. 17, p. 4.

[42] *The American in Algiers,* p. 21.

[43] *Ibid.,* p. 32.

[44] As early as 1624, five years after slavery was introduced into Virginia, opposition to American slavery on social and economic grounds was made in Sweden by William Usselinx, a native of Antwerp. In a proposition to King Gustavus Adolphus for the establishment of the Swedish Trading Company, Usselinx urged that slaves be not introduced into the Swedish colonies, "because they cost much, work reluctantly, require nothing from mechanics, as they go almost without clothes, and through ill-treatment soon die"; whereas the people from different parts of Europe, being free, intelligent, and industrious, have wives and children and require all kinds of merchandise and mechanics.—J. J. Mickley, "Some Account of William Usselinx and Peter Minuit," in *Hist. and Biog. Papers of the Del. Hist. Soc.,* I, No. III, 10-11.

of slave labor. Slave labor, they said, made slaves unwilling workmen.[45] The slaves had no inducement to be industrious, because they had no prospect of being other than slaves during life.[46] Free labor, on the other hand, was a stimulus to industry and made workmen careful of their apparel and their instruments of husbandry.[47] The argument that America might compete with Great Britain in cheapness of manufactures Franklin considered untenable. In 1751 he said:

"Interest of money is in the colonies from six to ten per cent. Slaves, one with another, cost thirty pounds sterling per head. Reckon then the interest of the first purchase of a slave, the insurance or risk on his life, his clothing and diet, expenses in his sickness and loss of time, loss by his neglect of business, ... expense of a driver to keep him at work, and his pilfering from time to time, ... and compare the whole amount with the wages of a manufacturer of iron or wool in England, you will see that labor is much cheaper there than it ever can be by negroes here."[48]

Slave labor also worked a hardship upon the white people. It made them "proud and disdainful of work,"[49] because they feared that to do the work commonly assigned to slaves would "make them look like slaves."[50] Franklin contended that the importation of Negroes deprived the poor whites of employment, while a few families acquired enormous wealth, which they spent on foreign luxuries and in educating their children in the habit of those luxuries; consequently, the same income was needed for the support of one that might maintain one hundred.[51] Thomas Jefferson was

[45] Sewall, "The Selling of Joseph" (1700), in the *Mass. Hist. Soc. Coll.*, 5th Ser., VI, 17; Jonathan Boucher, *A View of the Causes and Consequences of the American Revolution* (1797), pp. 38-39.

[46] Woolman, *Works* (ed. 1774), p. 58.

[47] Buchanan, "An Oration upon the Moral and Political Evil of Slavery" (1791), p. 16, in W. F. Poole, *Anti-Slavery Opinions Before the Year 1800*.

[48] Franklin, "Observations Concerning the Increase of Mankind and the Peopling of Countries," in *Works*, ed. Bigelow, II, 227.

[49] Byrd, "Letter to General Oglethorpe" (1736). See *Writings of Colonel William Byrd*, ed. Bassett, p. lxxxv.

[50] Byrd, "Letter to Lord Egmont" (1736), in the *American Historical Review*, I, 89.

[51] Franklin, *op. cit.*, 228-229.

convinced that in a warm climate no man would labor for himself who could make another labor for him. "This is so true," said he, "that of the proprietors of slaves a very small proportion indeed are ever seen to labour. And can the liberties of a nation be thought secure when we have removed their only firm basis, a conviction in the minds of the people that these liberties are of the gift of God?"[52] Thomas Branagan, in 1805, said that in the South, where one citizen by "fraud or force" had gained the sovereignty over a thousand slaves and sent his "imperial commands over as many acres of land," fifty poor whites were in low circumstances; the consequence being that a few of the citizens were furnished with the means of corruption and the many were put into such a condition that they could not avoid being corrupted.[53]

Some attention was also given by these early anti-slavery writers to the question of the effect of slavery upon the growth of population. Franklin said that the birth rate among slave-holders and slaves was small, because the former, not laboring were enfeebled, and, therefore, not so generally prolific; whereas the latter, overworked and ill-fed, were soon broken in health, the result being that there were more deaths among them than births.[54] Gilbert Imlay, in 1793, attributed to slavery the tardiness with which the population of the South increased, and suggested, as a means of improving the economic status of the South, that the slaves be attached to the land of their respective masters for a certain number of years as tenants. Afterwards they should be at liberty to change their positions as their circumstances or pleasure might direct. This method, he said, would benefit the slaves by enabling them to educate their children and acquire property. It would also be of great advantage to the state, especially a state like Virginia, where, as a result of the parcelling out of immense waste

[52] Jefferson, *Notes on the State of Virginia*, p. 173.
[53] Branagan, *Avenia*, Notes (ed. 1810), p. 125.
[54] Franklin, *op. cit.*, 234.

tracts of land into little farms, the low country, which had been impoverished by the "pernicious cultivation of tobacco, would become fertilized, and restored to its pristine fecundity."[55]

Though not greatly elaborated upon at this time, nor used with great frequency, these social and economic arguments at least suggested the character which this kind of opposition was to assume in the periods to follow; for the question of the effect of slavery upon agriculture, commerce, manufactures, accumulation of wealth, living conditions, growth of population, and so forth, which in the years immediately preceding the Civil War assumed such great importance, had its beginning in this period.

IV.   SENTIMENTAL ARGUMENTS

Many writers opposed slavery out of sheer sympathy for the slave. Indications of this humanitarian spirit were observed in connection with moral and religious arguments from the first appearance of anti-slavery sentiment in American literature. During the latter part of the eighteenth century, however, as American authors came more and more under the influence of the sentimentalism of European writers, this spirit became more prevalent, and between 1770 and 1800 colored much of the anti-slavery literature of America. Opposition to slavery on purely sentimental grounds was not, in the strict sense of the term, argument, for it was generally devoid of the intellectual element; yet, what it lacked in this respect, it more than supplied in its strong emotional appeal, and thus became an effective means of promoting the anti-slavery cause. These sentimental appeals for the slave fell into two general classes: those mild in tone with no suggestion of malice or bitterness toward the slaveholder, and those written in a spirit of defiance, and partaking of the nature of bitter invective.

Several of the milder appeals for the slave were utter-

---

[55] Imlay, *A Topographical Description of the Western Territory of North America*, pp. 203-204.

ances of the Negroes themselves who had had kind masters.[56]
For instance, in her poem entitled "To the Right Honorable
William, Earl of Dartmouth" (1773), Phillis Wheatley, the
Negro poetess, explained the source of her love of freedom
without any manifestation of ill-will toward those responsi-
ble for her being made a slave:

> "Should you, my lord, while you peruse my song,
> Wonder from whence my love of Freedom sprung,
> Whence flow these wishes for the common good,
> By feeling hearts alone best understood,
> I, young in life, by seeming cruel fate
> Was snatch'd from Afric's fancy'd happy seat:
> What pangs excruciating must molest,
> What sorrows labour in my parents' breast?
> Steel'd was that soul and by no misery mov'd
> That from a father seiz'd his babe belov'd:
> Such, such my case. And can I then but pray
> Others may never feel tyrannic sway?"[57]

The same was true of the author of an anonymous poem entitled "A Poetical Epistle to the Enslaved Africans" (1790).
This author wrote "in the character of an ancient Negro,"
born a slave but later liberated, and showed deep sympathy
for the slaves; but he urged them to use no violence in their
efforts to gain freedom:

> "Be patient, humble, diligent, and true,
> In hope of coming freedom, as you can—
> Commend your righteous cause to God and Man.
>   .   .   .   .
> Meanwhile—in silence let us wait the hour
> That shall to civil-life our Race restore—
> To God let Afric's dusky Sons sing praise,
> His works are marvelous and just his ways.'"[58]

Of the other sentimental appeals of this class—some of
which, such as John Woolman's essay "On Loving our
Neighbors,"[59] described rather touchingly the condition of

---

[56] Jupiter Hammon, a slave poet who had been treated kindly by his master,
delivered "An Address to the Negroes of the State of New York" (1787), in
which he expressed keen sympathy for the younger slaves, whom he longed to
see freed, but showed little concern about his own freedom.

[57] Wheatley, *Poems on Various Subjects*, p. 74.

[58] *A Poetical Epistle to the Enslaved Africans*, pp. 21-22.

[59] See Woolman, *Works* (ed. 1774), p. 398.

the slave—probably the strongest from an emotional point
of view appeared in John Murdock's comedy, *The Triumph
of Love; or, Happy Reconciliation* (1795); in Sarah W. Morton's poem *Beacon Hill* (1797); and in Henry Sherburne's
novel, *The Oriental Philanthropist* (1800). In *The Triumph
of Love*, one of the earliest American plays containing anti-
slavery sentiment, Sambo, a slave belonging to George
Friendly, soliloquized upon his condition and the uncertainty
of his fate should his kind master die, remarking that "the
great somebody above" did not so order things. His master
overheard the soliloquy, and was made to realize, as he had
never done before, the great injustice of slavery:

> "Be softened as thou wilt, still, slavery, thy condition is hard.
> The untutored, pathetic soliloquy of that honest creature, has more
> sensibly affected me, than all I have read, or thought, on that bar-
> barous, iniquitous slave-trade. . . . . It is cruel. It is unjust, for
> one creature to hold another in a state of bondage for life. Sambo,
> thou shalt be free."[60]

He accordingly gave Sambo his freedom, allowing him either
to remain in his own employ upon a salary or to go where he
might be happy. In *Beacon Hill* Mrs. Morton extolled the
work of the several states and their commanding officers in
the Revolutionary War, but inquired of Carolina how she
could contend for freedom without heeding the scourge that
inflicted suffering upon her shackled slave. She further inquired:

> "What boots the fleecy field, and ricy mead,
> If mid their bloom the culturing captive bleed!
> Or what avails, that many a sumptuous dome
> To every traveller yields a generous home,
> If the rich banquet, and costly cheer
> Are fan'd by sighs, and moisten'd with a tear!"[61]

Henry Sherburne's *The Oriental Philanthropist* revealed
even greater sympathy for the slave than *The Triumph of
Love* or *Beacon Hill*, for the hero, the Chinese Prince Nytan,
visited the home of a rich Turk who owned African slaves,
persuaded him to free his slaves, and offered him a supply

⁶⁰ Murdock, *The Triumph of Love*, p. 52.
⁶¹ Morton, *Beacon Hill*, p. 35.

of money to defray the expense of their journey back to their
native land. To a remark of one of the slaves that his
sovereign in Africa was an enemy of every species of slavery, and that God would avenge slavery by a dreadful punishment, Prince Nytan replied:

"Yes, ... the emancipation of the human race from every
species of slavery is not far distant. The mists of ignorance are fast
dispersing. You, Zaddquin, shall carry a letter from me to your
sovereign. He is the friend of humanity, and will become an instrument of much good in the African world."[62]

The authors of sentimental arguments of the second class
did not stop with a mere expression of sympathy for the
slave, but assumed a more defiant attitude, many of them
employing the most bitter invective against slavery and the
slave-trade.

Some of these writers exposed the cruelties that the
slave suffered in America and the West Indies at the hands
of overseers or other persons placed over him; as, for
example, Robert Munford, in a poem entitled "A Letter from
the Devil to his Son" (1798), and St. John Crèvecoeur, in
Letters from an American Farmer (1782).[63] In Munford's
poem the intimation was that more sympathy was shown the
slave in hell than on earth. Satan, pleased with the evil
deeds of his son, promised to give him a position in hell. He,
accordingly, summoned his crew to inquire what position
best suited his son's abilities. A Negro offered the suggestion that he be not made an overseer,

"For dat man, he been killey me."

Whereupon Satan decided to build another hell for his son
to govern, noting meanwhile, with respect to the slave, that

"His back, his head, his meagre face,
    Drew pity from the hellish race;
A murmur ran from shore to shore,
    And hell was instant in a roar."[64]

[62] Sherburne, The Oriental Philanthropist, pp. 163-164.
[63] Philip Freneau did likewise in his poem "To Sir Toby" (1792). See
Poems, ed. Pattee, II, 258-260.
[64] Munford, "A Letter from the Devil to his Son," in Plays and Poems, p.
194.

Crèvecoeur gave a more horrible picture of slavery than this. After a severe arraignment of the people of the South for their treatment of the slave, he described a scene he had witnessed in the South in which a slave, who had been accused of killing an overseer, was suspended from a tree in a cage and left there to be tortured to death by the birds of prey:

"I shudder when I recollect that the birds had already picked out his eyes; his cheek bones were bare; his arms had been attacked in several places, and his body seemed covered with a multitude of wounds. From the edges of the hollow sockets and from the lacerations with which he was disfigured, the blood slowly dropped, and tinged the ground beneath."[65]

Then he related the brief conversation which took place between himself and the slave when he gave the latter water to drink:

" 'Tankè, you whitè man, tankè you, putè some poison and give me.'
" 'How long have you been hanging there?' I asked.
" 'Two days, and me no die; the birds, the birds; aaah me!'
"Oppressed with the reflections which this shocking spectacle afforded me, I mustered strength enough to walk away, and soon reached the house at which I intended to dine."[66]

More often, however, the sentimental arguments of this second class dealt more specifically with the slave-trade, the source of the evil, and demanded the most severe punishment imaginable for those engaged therein.[67] In *The Beauties of Santa Cruz* (1776), in which ten stanzas (70-79) were devoted to the subject of slavery, Philip Freneau made a bitter attack upon this traffic. Beginning with an appeal to the sympathy of the reader, his lines quickly assumed the nature of an invective against greed for gold at the sacrifice of the lives of human beings:

"See yonder slave that slowly bends his way,
    With years, and pain, and ceaseless toil opprest,

[65] Crèvecoeur, "Thoughts on Slavery," in *Letters from an American Farmer*, pp. 233-235.
[66] *Ibid.*, p. 235.
[67] See Gilbert Imlay, *The Emigrants; or The History of an Expatriated Family* (1793), I, 136-138.

> Though no complaining words his woes betray,
> The eye dejected proves the heart distrest.

> "Perhaps in chains he left his native shore
> Perhaps he left a helpless offspring there,
> Perhaps a wife, that he must see no more,
> Perhaps a father, who his love did share.

> "Curs'd be the ship that brought him o'er the main,
> And curs'd the hands who from his country tore,
> May she be stranded, ne'er to float again,
> May they be shipwreck'd on some hostile shore."[68]

Royall Tyler's opposition to the slave-trade was of the same nature as Freneau's. In *The Algerine Captive* (1797), the narrator, Dr. Updike Underhill, after a series of adventures in America and England, became a surgeon on a ship bound for Africa, where slaves were to be secured and conveyed to the British West Indies and South Carolina. The narrator was shocked to hear men talk of purchasing human beings as if they were so many head of cattle or swine. But when, said he,

"I suffered my imagination to rove to the habitation of these victims to this infamous, cruel commerce, and fancied that I saw . . . . the fond husband torn from the embraces of his beloved wife, the mother from her babes . . . . and all the tender, endearing ties of natural affection rended by the hand of avaricious violence, my heart sunk within me. I execrated myself for even the involuntary part I bore in this execrable traffic: I thought of my native land, and blushed . . . .

"I cannot even now reflect on this transaction without shuddering. I have deplored my conduct with tears of anguish; and I pray a merciful God . . . . that the miseries, the insults, and cruel woundings I afterwards received when a slave myself,[69] may expiate for the inhumanity[70] I was necessitated to exercise toward my brethren of the human race."[71]

The two most effective attacks upon the slave-trade of all those made during this period were made by Thomas Branagan in 1805, when he published at Philadelphia two epics entitled *Avenia; or a Tragical Poem* and *The Peniten-*

---

[68] Freneau, "The Beauties of Santa Cruz," in *Poems*, ed. Pattee, I, 262-263.
[69] He was later enslaved by the Algerines.
[70] As a surgeon he had to inspect the bodies of the slaves.
[71] Tyler, *The Algerine Captive*, pp. 98-101.

tial Tyrant; or Slave Trader Reformed. Branagan had already been employed on vessels engaged in the slave-trade and had served as overseer on a plantation in Antigua. These poems, written in the heroic couplet, depicted slavery in its worst form. They contained a frontispiece intended to contrast slavery with liberty. The Goddess of Liberty was seated before her temple, viewing with sad countenance a group of African slaves, "in order to demonstrate," said the author, "the hypocrisy and villainy of professing to be votaries of liberty, while at the same time, we encourage or countenance, the most ignoble slavery."[72] In *Avenia* were described the bloody struggles in Africa between the natives and the Christian slave-traders, culminating in the capture, importation, and preparation for the sale of those Africans who were neither killed in battle nor drowned in their passage over the sea. Avenia, the heroine, attacked by one of the planters and grieved by the constant thought of the fate of her husband and of her own condition, ascended a high rock and committed suicide by plunging into the sea. The intensity of the author's feeling regarding such events as he described was shown in the following lines:

> "Give ear ye tyrants, distant nations hear,
> And learn the judgments of high heaven to fear,
> Your children yet unborn shall blush to see,
> Their predecessors' guilt and villany,
> Their impious thirst for gold, while fierce in arms,
> Their cruel breasts no tender pity warms;
> Should heathens but one virtuous Christian find,
> Name but the slave-trade; they will curse your kind."[73]

In *The Penitential Tyrant,* after contrasting the luxury and pleasures of the idle rich with the sufferings of the slaves, and describing a vision in which the unhappy slaves rose before his view, charging him with being negligent in exhibiting their wrongs, the author confessed his guilt—he had been a slave-trader and overseer himself—became a real Christian, and urged his readers to live in truth the Christian life.

[72] Branagan, *The Penitential Tyrant,* p. iii; *Avenia* (ed. 181 , p. ii.
[73] Branagan, *Avenia; or a Tragical Poem* (ed. 1810), p. 205.

Branagan was fully aware of his short-comings as a writer of verse, but felt that he was justified in publishing these poems because of the worthy cause they defended. Appearing just before the prohibition of the African slave-trade by Congressional action, *Avenia* and *The Penitential Tyrant* must have done much by way of influencing the public sentiment of the time. On May 11, 1805, Thomas Jefferson, then President of the United States, in a letter to Dr. George Logan, wrote as follows of having received a letter from Thomas Branagan asking for his subscription to *Avenia:*

"The cause in which he [Branagan] embarks is so holy, the sentiments he expresses in his letter so friendly that it is highly painful to me to hesitate on a compliance which appears so small. But that is not its true character, and it would be injurious even to his views, for me to commit myself on paper by answering his letter. I have most carefully avoided every public act or manifestation on that subject."[74]

On December 12, 1805, the same year in which *Avenia* and *The Penitential Tyrant* appeared, Senator Bradley of Vermont gave notice of a bill to prohibit the introduction of slaves after 1808.[75] On December 2, 1806, Jefferson himself, in his message to Congress, urged his fellow-citizens to interpose their authority constitutionally "to withdraw the citizens of the United States from all further participation in those violations of human rights which have been so long continued on the unoffending inhabitants of Africa, and which the morality, the reputation, and the best interests of our country, have long been eager to proscribe."[76] A bill was subsequently passed, becoming on March 2, 1807, the "Act to prohibit the importation of Slaves into any port or place within the jurisdiction of the United States, from and after the first day of January, in the year of our Lord one thousand eight hundred and eight."[77]

[74] Jefferson, *Writings,* ed. Ford, X, 141.
[75] DuBois, *Suppression of the African Slave-trade,* p. 105.
[76] Jefferson, *op. cit.,* 315-316.
[77] DuBois, *op. cit.,* p. 108.

V. PLANS FOR THE EMANCIPATION OF THE SLAVE[78]

The first definite plans for the emancipation of the slaves in America originated during the early part of the eighteenth century among the Quakers, who in the Middle and Northern States had freed practically all of their slaves before the close of the Revolutionary War, and who continued thereafter to exert an important influence upon the emancipation movement in America.[79] So far as American literature is concerned, however, it was not until the latter part of the eighteenth century that elaborate schemes for emancipation began to appear.[80] Nearly all of these called for

[78] For a detailed account of the plans initiated before 1808 for the emancipation of the slaves, see M. S. Locke, *Anti-Slavery in America, 1619-1808.*

[79] As early as 1714 and 1737 John Hepburn and Benjamin Lay published respectively definite plans for the emancipation of the slaves. The plan published by Hepburn provided that those Negroes whose freedom masters would grant be returned to Africa; that money be raised for this purpose; and that those not desiring their freedom be retained in America as slaves. Lay's plan provided that the slaves be first educated and then set free. See M. S. Locke, *Anti-Slavery in America, 1619-1808,* pp. 30-31. Anthony Benezet urged that further importation of slaves be prohibited; that those already in America, after serving as ''long as may appear to be equitable,'' be declared free, be enrolled in the county courts, and be compelled to live ''a certain number of years within the said county under the care of the overseers of the poor''; that the children be given instruction; and that a small tract of land be assigned to every family of Negroes, who should be compelled to live upon and improve it. See Benezet, *Some Historical Account of Guinea* (ed. 1771), pp. 140-141. John Woolman, the most important of the Quakers who won a place in the American literature of this period, offered no definite scheme of emancipation, but saw no insurmountable difficulties in the way of attaining it. See Woolman, ''Some Considerations on the Keeping of Negroes'' (1754), in *Works,* p. 324. For a detailed account of the part played by the Quakers in the emancipation of the slaves, see S. B. Weeks, *Southern Quakers and Slavery,* pp. 198-244.

[80] This interest in emancipation was greatly stimulated by the formation of anti-slavery societies between 1775 and the close of the century. The first anti-slavery society was formed on April 14, 1775, in Philadelphia. It was called ''The Society for the Relief of Free Negroes unlawfully held in Bondage.'' With its reorganization in 1787, the ''Abolition of Slavery,'' as well as the ''Relief of Free Negroes,'' was included in its program, and Benjamin Franklin was chosen president. Similar societies were formed between 1775 and 1792 in New York, Delaware, Maryland, Rhode Island, Connecticut, Virginia, and New Jersey. See W. F. Poole, *Anti-Slavery Opinions before the Year 1800,* pp. 42-51.

gradual emancipation. There were very few advocates of immediatism during this period.

The belief that the Negro would be unable to care for himself if freed and the fear lest immediate emancipation would work too great a hardship upon the master led many writers to advocate gradual in preference to immediate emancipation.[81] This belief was more fully expressed in the works of Thomas Jefferson than in those of any other writer of the period. He was doubtful of the Negro's ability to care for himself if freed. "This unfortunate difference of color," he said, "and perhaps of faculty, is a powerful obstacle to the emancipation of these people."[82] Yet on several occasions, he publicly advocated emancipation. While a member of the legislature of Virginia, which he entered in 1769, he proposed an act permitting masters to free their slaves, but his effort was unsuccessful.[83] The original draft of the Declaration of Independence contained a bitter arraignment of the King of Great Britain for not prohibiting the slave-trade:

". . . . Determined to keep open market where men should be bought and sold, he has prostituted his negative for suppressing every attempt to prohibit or restrain this execrable commerce; and that this assemblage of horrors might want no fact of distinguished die, he is now exciting those very people to rise in arms among us, and to purchase that liberty of which he has deprived them by murdering the people on whom he has also obtruded them: thus paying off former crimes committed against the liberties of one people, with crimes which he urges them to commit against the lives of another."[84]

Jefferson said that this clause was removed from the original draft "in compliance to South Carolina and Georgia, who had never attempted to restrain the importation of slaves,

[81] John Woolman, in 1754, answered the argument that if slaves were freed they could not care for themselves properly, by saying that "to deny people the privilege of human creatures, on the supposition that, being free, many of them would be troublesome, is to mix the condition of good and bad men together, and treat the whole as the worst of them deserve."—"Some Considerations on the Keeping of Negroes," in *Works*, p. 324.

[82] Jefferson, *Notes on the State of Virginia*, p. 154.

[83] Jefferson, *Writings*, ed. Washington, I, 3.

[84] *The Papers of James Madison*, I, 24.

and who on the contrary still wished to continue it.''[85]   He
said that certain Northerners also ''felt a little tender under
those censures,'' for though their people had very few slaves
themselves, yet they had been pretty considerable carriers of
them to others.[85]   Shortly after this, in 1778, a bill which he
introduced in the legislature to prevent the further importation of slaves into Virginia was passed without opposition.[86]
Seven years later he expressed the desire that a way might
be prepared for total emancipation ''with the consent of the
masters, rather than by their extirpation.''[87]   To the question of what should be done with the Negro when freed Jefferson also gave considerable thought.   In a letter from
Paris to Dr. Edward Bancroft, dated January 26, 1789, he
said that on his return to America he would endeavor to
import as many Germans as he had grown slaves:

''I will settle them and my slaves, on farms of fifty acres each,
intermingled, and place all on the footing of the Metayers . . . .
of Europe.   Their children shall be brought up, as others are, in
habits of property and foresight, and I have no doubt but that they
will be good citizens.''[88]

He also advocated that all slaves born after a given day
should be freed and educated, and after a given age sent out
of the country.   ''This,'' he said, ''would give time for a
gradual extinction of that species of labour and substitution
of another, and lessen the shock which an operation so funda-
mental cannot fail to produce.''[89]   The West Indies or Africa,
he thought, would be a desirable location for the liberated
slaves.[90]   Finally, in December, 1806, as President of the
United States, Jefferson recommended to Congress the prohibition of the African slave-trade.   Shortly after, a law to
that effect was passed which became operative on January 1,
1808.

A great many other advocates of gradual emancipation,
whose plans appeared in the literature of America before

[85] *Ibid.*, 18.
[86] Jefferson, *Writings*, ed. Washington, I, 38.
[87] *Ibid.*, 377.
[88] Jefferson, *Writings*, ed. Ford, V, 448.
[89] *Ibid.*, XI, 418.
[90] Jefferson, *Writings*, ed. Washington, IV, 421.

1808, unlike Jefferson, had genuine faith in the Negro's ability to care for himself if freed and contemplated no disastrous results from emancipation either for the master or the slaves, provided the slaves were first prepared for freedom through training and experience;[91] and they included in their plans specific suggestions as to how this training and experience might be given. Thomas Paine, who has been called "the first American abolitionist,"[92] and Benjamin Rush suggested that those Negroes in America who, from vices of slavery or from age and infirmities, were unfit to be freed should remain the property of those with whom they grew old and from whom they contracted vices; but that the young Negroes should be taught to read and write, instructed in some business, paid for their labor, and after a limited time liberated.[93] William Dunlap, the dramatist, went further in his advocacy of gradual emancipation than the authors just mentioned, for he put his theories into practice. After his father's death he actually liberated the family slaves, some of whom he afterwards hired as servants,[94] and became an active member of the Manumission Society and a trustee of the free school for African children, founded in 1789 by the same society.[95] He was also a deputy to the convention of the abolition societies of the several states which met at Philadelphia in 1797. Even though Dunlap liberated his own slaves, he was doubtful as to the expediency of sudden abolition; but, said he, "this subject is

[91]Franklin, "An Address to the Public; from the Pennsylvania Society for Promoting the Abolition of Slavery, and the Relief of Free Negroes unlawfully held in Bondage" (1789), in *Works*, ed. Sparks, II, 515-516.

[92] See *Writings of Thomas Paine*, ed. Conway, I, 2. This designation, based upon the assumption that Paine was the first person in America to offer a definite scheme of emancipation, is hardly justifiable when one considers the work of Hepburn, Lay, Benezet, and Rush, all of whom before 1775, the year in which Paine's plan appeared, had offered plans for the liberation of the slaves. See above, p. 26.

[93] Rush, *An Address to the Inhabitants of the British Settlements in America upon Slave-Keeping* (1773), pp. 18-20; Paine, "African Slavery in America" (1775), in *Writings*, ed. Conway, I, 8.

[94] In Dunlap's play, *The Father of an Only Child* (1807), the hero, Colonel Campbell, liberated his slaves and furnished them with the means of "becoming useful to themselves and to others." See above, p. 13.

[95] O. S. Coad, *William Dunlap*, p. 23.

better understood now, and colonization societies are super-
seding the abolitionists, who are to be blessed for beginning
the good work.''[96]

These advocates of gradual abolition during this period
were far more numerous than those of immediatism. Of the
comparatively few appeals for immediate emancipation that
appeared in the literature of the period that by Theodore
Dwight, in *An Oration* (1794) delivered before ''The Connecticut Society for the Promotion of Freedom and the Relief of Persons Unlawfully Holden in Bondage,'' and that by
Hugh H. Brackenridge, in his novel entitled *Modern Chivalry* (1792), were the most significant. Dwight made a
strong plea for immediate emancipation by governmental
action, and expressed the belief that the master would not
experience any disadvantage in obtaining from the government the value of the slave.[97] Brackenridge's plea for immediate emancipation took the form of a bitter satire on a
law passed in Pennsylvania in 1780 for the gradual abolition
of slavery. The hero, Captain Farrago, having lost his
servant, Teague O'Regan, who had become an actor, considered purchasing a Negro in his place. Before doing so,
he conversed with a Quaker on the subject of slavery. Much
in the manner of Swift, the author put into the mouth of the
Captain many of the pro-slavery arguments of the time, and
gave himself, in the chapter that followed, the remainder of
these. Both passages were highly ironical and so skilfully
handled that, taken together, they formed probably the most
bitter satire of the period on Negro slavery. The Captain
began with the argument that force governed all things;
the strong man had as much right to invade the liberty of
the African as he had to invade the liberty of a horse or an
ox; the natural rights of men were resolvable into power on
the one hand and weakness on the other. ''I should think
myself justifiable,'' said he, ''in making any man a slave to
answer my purpose, provided, I treated him well while he
was such.''[98] Some persons were by nature fitted only to be

[96] Dunlap, *A History of the American Theater*, p. 170.
[97] Dwight, *An Oration*, pp. 8, 22.
[98] Brackenridge, *Modern Chivalry* (ed. 1815), I, Book IV, 140.

slaves; others to be masters. As it was difficult to determine
a priori who were intended for slavery and who for freedom,
the rule should be "catch, who catch can,"[99] and every man
should have a slave who can get one. It was not of so
much consequence who the slave was as it was that there
should be one.

This irony was continued with even greater effect by the
author himself, who satirized the attitude of the churches
and the courts toward slavery. He said that there was no
religious denomination, "except the fanatical people called
Quakers," that went so far as to insist that its members
should not hold slaves.[100] It could not, therefore, be a matter
of conscience. He approved of gradual abolition of slavery,
for "numbers being embarked in this trade, it must ruin
them all at once to desist from it; just as it would greatly inconvenience thieves and cut-throats, who have run risks in
acquiring skill in their profession, to be obliged all at once
to desist from this and apply themselves to industry in other
ways for a livelihood."[101] The author feared that some
young lawyers in the courts, knowing that it was established
by the constitution of the state that all men were born
equally free and independent, might show the illegality of
gradual abolition. But he hesitated to say more on this
topic, lest he should "furnish hints to pettifoggers," who
might make ill use of their information.[102]

A backward glance at the anti-slavery literature in America prior to 1808, as discussed in this chapter, will reveal the
fact that sentiment against slavery during this period had a
gradual and consistent growth. At every stage in its development it reflected the prevailing spirit of the time.
Though many writers began early and continued throughout
the period to look upon slavery as a great social and economic danger, the principal arguments against slavery from
the time of the Puritans until the latter part of the eight-

[99] *Ibid.*, 142.
[100] *Ibid.*, 144.
[101] *Ibid.*, 145.
[102] *Ibid.*, 146-147.

eenth century were based upon moral and religious grounds. American literature itself at this time was essentially didactic and religious. The Puritans, being concerned primarily with the moral and religious instruction of the slave, offered no permanent plan for universal emancipation; yet, one of their productions, Samuel Sewall's pamphlet, *The Selling of Joseph,* became really significant in the history of anti-slavery literature. The Quakers, on the other hand, were interested not only in the slave's moral and religious welfare, but also in his being accorded every privilege of an American citizen; and with this end in view, they liberated their own slaves and urged others to follow their example. With the formation of anti-slavery societies between 1775 and the close of the century, the efforts of the abolitionists were united and the production of anti-slavery literature was greatly stimulated. Up to this time the chief forms through which this sentiment had been expressed were poetry and the essay. Now the novel and drama supplemented these, giving to the opponents of slavery additional means with which to disseminate their ideas. From the latter part of the eighteenth century until the abolition of the slave-trade in 1807 by Congressional action, many arguments against slavery were strongly colored by the political philosophy of the time. These were based upon the theory of the natural and inalienable rights of man. During the latter part of the eighteenth century also, with the spread of sentimentalism in literature, American authors were given an additional weapon with which to combat the evil and they made effective use of it in advancing the cause of abolition. With few exceptions, plans for the emancipation of the slaves during the first period provided for gradual emancipation. Many of these also included suggestions for colonizing the freed Negroes in Africa, the West Indies, or elsewhere. There was little opposition at this time to colonization.[103] Of the appeals for immediate emancipation, that of Hugh H. Brackenridge in *Modern Chivalry* was the most significant.

[103] Gilbert Imlay, in *A Topographical Description of the Western Territory of North America* (1793), p. 203, opposed the colonization of Negroes.

CHAPTER II

THE TRANSITION PERIOD (1808-1831)

During the years immediately following the passage of the Slave-Trade Act in 1807 arguments against slavery, so far as American literature is concerned, were less frequent and on the whole milder in tone than those of the preceding period. The African slave-trade, to the abolition of which many writers of the first period had solely directed their efforts, had, in theory, at least, been abandoned. This period from 1808 to 1831 has been termed the period of preparation for Garrisonian abolitionism,[1] when the opponents of slavery were fitting themselves for the struggle which was to begin in 1831 with William Lloyd Garrison as leader. The chief arguments at this time were moral and religious, social and economic, and sentimental. These, however, differed somewhat in their nature from those already discussed.

I. MORAL AND RELIGIOUS ARGUMENTS

The general tone of the moral and religious arguments against slavery during this period is best illustrated in the "Vision of Slavery," written in 1822 by Ralph Waldo Emerson.[2] Compared with similar arguments before 1808, the "Vision of Slavery" is mild. Emerson here considered slavery philosophically. He said that he was unable to reconcile the idea of the slave's toiling and suffering from birth to death without any conception of God kindled in his mind, with the idea "that a merciful Lord made man in his benevolence to live and enjoy his works and worship him forever."[3] He considered two questions: first, whether any individual had a right to deprive any other individual of freedom without his consent; and second, whether he might continue to withhold the freedom which another had taken away. The

---

[1] A. B. Adams, *The Neglected Period of Anti-Slavery in America*, p. 252.

[2] Though not published until 1909, this work is mentioned here as merely indicative of a contemporary young man's opinions.

[3] Emerson, *Journals*, I, 180.

weakness and incapacity of the Africans, he said, would seem
to have no bearing on the first, though they might affect the
second. He called slavery an assault upon reason and common sense, and said that if man was himself free—and it
offended the attributes of God to have him otherwise—it was
manifestly a bold stroke of impiety to wrest the same liberty
from his fellow. And if he was not free, then this "inhuman
barbarity ascends to derive its origin from the author of all
necessity."[4] Four years later (1826) he wrote concerning
the slave-trade:

"To stop the slave traffic the nations should league themselves
in indissoluble bands, should link the thunderbolts of national power
to demolish this debtor of all Justice human and divine."[5]

The minor writers of this period made considerable use
of the moral and religious argument, but they too, with few
exceptions, were mild in their opposition to slavery, in most
cases making only a brief reference to it.[6] Two exceptions to
this were Anne Royall and David Walker, both of whom
made very bitter attacks upon the religion and morals of
slaveholders. On her visit to Alexandria, D.C. (now Virginia), in the winter of 1823-1824, Anne Royall was shocked
to see so many mulattoes. The presence of so many slaves
of this type drew from her a severe condemnation of slaveholders:

"To one unaccustomed to see human nature in this guise, it
excites feelings of horror and disgust..... Strange that a nation who
extol so much, who praise themselves in such unqualified terms, as
possessing in the highest degree, both moral and political virtue,

[4] Emerson, *Journals*, I, 185-186.
[5] *Ibid.*, II, 80.
[6] For example, the Reverend William Miller, of the African Methodist Epis-
copal Church, delivered on January 1, 1810, "A Sermon on the Abolition of the
Slave Trade." It was written in the spirit of thanksgiving, yet the author
touched upon the brutality of those engaged in the slave trade. David Darling,
also, in a play performed at the Fredericksburg Theater and published at Charlottesville, Virginia, in 1820, had one of his characters lament the fact that
fortunes were not made so rapidly then as formerly, because people living in a
civilized country and professing Christianity had "sacrificed the honour of
human nature and moral justice by buying and selling their fellow-creatures."—
Beaux Without Belles, or, Ladies We Can Do Without You, pp. 11-12.

should afford no better proof of it than this before me. . . . . There is a measure even in crime. There is a point, beyond which the most daring will not venture. History affords us many examples, amongst the most barbarous nations, in the most barbarous ages, where the most lawless ruffians become softened at the sight of human distress, to which they were impelled by no law, but that of common humanity. But for man in this free, and (as they say) enlightened country to doom his own children, to a state (to say the least of it) fraught with every species of human misery, we want no better evidence to prove, that such men must not only be void of virtue; but guilty of the most indignant crime.''[7]

David Walker's work, entitled *Appeal* (1829), was even more severe. Walker was a free Negro, who, dissatisfied with conditions in North Carolina, his native state, moved to Boston, and in 1827 is said to have begun preparations for an insurrection of the slaves.[8] In 1829 he published his *Appeal,* which ran through three editions within twelve months, and was widely distributed throughout the United States. His work fell into four sections, called ''Articles'': 1. ''Our wretchedness in consequence of slavery''; 2. ''Our wretchedness in consequence of ignorance''; 3. ''Our wretchedness in consequence of the preachers of the religion of Jesus Christ''; 4. ''Our wretchedness in consequence of the colonizing plan.'' The entire work was written in a spirit of defiance. The Americans, he said, made the Negroes the *''most wretched, degraded* and *abject* set of beings that *ever lived* since the world began.''[9] He urged the Negroes to acquire an education and make ''tyrants quake and tremble on their sandy foundation.''[10] He was most severe upon pro-slavery clergymen, concerning whom he wrote as follows:

''Can anything be a greater mockery of religion than the way in which it is conducted by the Americans? It appears as though they are bent only on daring God Almighty to do his best—they chain and handcuff us and our children, ... drive us around the country like brutes, and go into the house of the God of justice to return Him thanks for having aided them in their infernal cruelties inflicted

---

[7] Royall, *Sketches of History, Life, and Manners in the United States,* p. 101.

[8] A. D. Adams, *The Neglected Period of Anti-Slavery in America,* p. 93.

[9] Walker, *Appeal* (3rd ed., 1830), p. 9.

[10] *Ibid.,* p. 37.

upon us. Will the Lord suffer this people to go on much longer, taking his Holy name in vain? Will he not stop them, preachers and all? O Americans!! Americans!! I call God—I call angels—I call men, to witness, that your destruction *is at hand,* and will be speedily consummated unless you Repent."[11]

When Walker's *Appeal* was distributed throughout the South, it provoked considerable alarm. A reward of $1,000 was offered for the author's "head, and ten times as much for the live Walker."[12] The Mayor of Savannah requested Mayor Otis of Boston to suppress the work, but the Mayor replied that he had not the power to do so.[13] Walker was advised by friends to flee to Canada, but he refused to leave Boston. He died there in 1830.

II.   SOCIAL AND ECONOMIC ARGUMENTS

In the literature of this period social and economic arguments against slavery occurred less frequently than the other types. They dealt principally with the cost of free as compared with slave labor and with the effect of slavery upon the growth of population.

Slave labor, it was said, was far more costly than that of free men.[14] It was so costly that the income from it was hardly sufficient to maintain the slaves.[15] Where slavery existed farm labor would not be sufficiently varied in quantity. There were many conditions, it was said, which demanded such variety: the changes of the seasons prevented the farmer from conveniently or profitably employing as much labor in winter as in summer; the fluctuations of commerce also induced the farmer to vary the quantity of his labor; and the soil itself required frequent changes in the kind of husbandry. The advantages of free over slave labor

[11] *Ibid.,* p. 49.

[12] H. H. Barnet, *Walker's Appeal, With a Brief Sketch of His Life,* p. vii.

[13] George W. Williams, *History of the Negro Race in America,* II, 554.

[14] "Views of the Benevolent Society of Alexandria for Ameliorating and Improving the Condition of the People of Color," in *Freedom's Journal,* May 25-June 22, 1827.

[15] Mathew Carey, *A Short Account of the Malignant Fever and Miscellaneous Essays* (1829), pp. 218-219.

in meeting this situation were probably best stated by James Raymond of Frederick, Maryland, in an essay which appeared in the *African Observer* in 1828:

"The good northern farmer, after tilling his lots a few years, lays them down to grass. This he calls letting his lands rest. But if he cultivated with slave labour, whilst his lands were resting, most of his labourers would also be resting at his expense. . . . . A farmer who should purchase a large number of slaves, to perform the labour of his farm in summer, and who should sell them again when winter approaches, and so on from year to year, would be denied a respectable standing in the community. But where labour is free, and, therefore, the subject of contract between the employer and the labourer, these changes are frequently taking place throughout the year."[16]

Mathew Carey was among those who were alarmed over the low birth rate among the white people in the South. He called attention to the fact that in Maryland, Virginia, North Carolina, South Carolina, and Georgia between the years 1790 and 1820 the white population increased only 57 per cent, as opposed to an increase of 81 per cent among the slaves; whereas in the Middle and Eastern States between those years the white population increased 112 per cent. "These facts," he said, "ought to arouse the citizens of the Southern States to a sense of the necessity of affording a cordial co-operation in the Colonization scheme, as they regard not merely their own welfare, but the interests, welfare, and safety of their children."[17]

III. SENTIMENTAL ARGUMENTS

During the early part of this period authors of the sentimental argument were usually not very severe in their condemnation of slavery. They revealed strong fellow-feeling for the slave, and hoped and were even confident that sooner or later his condition would be ameliorated; but at this time they seldom manifested any bitterness toward his oppressors. As the end of the period approached, however, the

[16] Raymond, "A Prize Essay on the Comparative Economy of Free and Slave Labour in Agriculture," in the *African Observer*, p. 142.

[17] Carey, *op. cit.*, pp. 218-219.

authors of this type of argument revealed, on the whole, a keener and more forceful resentment toward slavery. They showed, at times, an attitude of defiance and used bitter invective against slaveholders, not hesitating to suggest even a resort to arms in behalf of the slave.

The best examples of the earlier and milder sentimental appeal were *The Africans; or, War, Love, and Duty* (1811), a play attributed to William Dunlap,[18] *Letters from the South* (1816), by James Kirke Paulding, and "The African Chief," a poem by William Cullen Bryant, written in 1825 and published in the *United States Review and Literary Gazette*, December, 1826.[19]

The play dealt with the activities of European slave merchants in Africa and the struggles of the natives for freedom. Berissa, the daughter of the African priest, Farulho, was asked by her father what she wished for a wedding gift. She replied that she would have all of his slaves made free and happy. Farulho would have granted her wish; but while her marriage to Selico, another African, was in progress, the town was attacked by a hostile tribe, and Berissa disappeared. The conquering king offered four hundred ounces in gold for the capture of the person who tried to escape with

[18] Considerable doubt has been expressed as to the authorship of this play. In many of the lists of Dunlap's plays that have been consulted it did not appear at all. J. N. Ireland in his *Records of the New York Stage from 1750 to 1860*, I, 267, attributed it to Colman. O. S. Coad in his "William Dunlap," p. 293, attributed it to Dunlap with doubt. Dunlap himself in *A History of the American Theater*, p. 408, included it among his works.

[19] Among the anti-slavery productions of this type by Negro writers of the period may be mentioned the following: "An Oration on the Abolition of the Slave Trade" (1808), by Peter Williams; "An Oration Commemorative of the Abolition of the Slave Trade in the United States" (1809), by Joseph Sidney; "An Address, Delivered on the Celebration of the Abolition of Slavery in the State of New York" (1827), by Nathaniel Paul; and "An Oration in Commemoration of the Abolition of Domestic Slavery in New York," by William Hamilton, in *Freedom's Journal*, October 12, 1827. There were also published in *Freedom's Journal* during this period many anonymous productions of this type, among which were: "The Sorrows of Angola," a poem (June 8, 1827); "Theresa—A Haytien Tale" (January 18, 1828), in which was related the escape of three women from French barbarity in Haiti to the camp of Toussaint L'Ouverture; and "Letters from a Man of Colour, on a Late Bill before the Senate of Pennsylvania" (February 22-March 21, 1828).

Berissa. Selico, supposing Berissa dead, and desirous of providing means for the support of his mother, offered himself as the guilty person. The king, thereupon, decided to have both Berissa and her lover executed. Before the time for the execution, however, Farulho insisted that he tried to escape with Berissa and demanded Selico's release. The mother of Selico also fell at the king's feet and made a plea for her son's life. The king was so much moved by these circumstances that he gave all of them their freedom and presented Berissa with a thousand crowns. The leading African characters were depicted as noble, self-sacrificing persons with a strong sense of duty and reverence for home and family, and with such other characteristics as would insure for them the sympathy of the reader. Throughout the play there was a slight undercurrent of satire on slavery and the slave trade. To a remark of one of the slave merchants that a bill was being passed in London which "would kick their business to the devil," Augustus Mug, a Londoner, and secretary to the African King, replied:

"I am very glad to hear it. The work begins in the natural quarter; and the stream of freedom flows from the very fountain head of true, natural liberty."[20]

James Kirke Paulding, during a visit in the South in 1816, expressed keen sympathy for the slave. He wished it understood that he was not an advocate of slavery, for, said he, "I hate it: and wish most sincerely and ardently, that there was not a man in our country that could stand up, and with his black finger point to the preamble of our Constitution, which declares—all men are born free and equal—and swear it was not true. . . . . Wo to those, who, tempted by avarice, or impelled by vengeance, shall divide the parent from its offspring, and sell them apart in distant lands! A cruel and inhuman act;—for it is seldom we see the ties of kindred or of conjugal affection, stronger than in the poor Negro."[21] Then he described a scene he had witnessed in the South in

[20] Dunlap, *The Africans*, p. 142.
[21] Paulding, *Letters from the South*, I, 119-120.

which slaves were treated with such cruelty by a white man
that he wished to see the man hunted by bloodhounds.[22]   In
the third of these examples of the milder sentimental appeal,
"The African Chief,"[23] Bryant related the experiences of an
African chief captured and exhibited in the market-place, his
ankles still adorned with the rings of gold which he wore
when captured. His offer to buy his freedom was promptly
refused. The last three stanzas, consisting partly in a dialogue between the African and his captor, were as follows:

> " 'Look, feast thy greedy eye with gold
>   Take it—thou askest sums untold,
>   And say that I am freed.
>   Take it—my wife, the long, long day
>   Weeps by the cocoa-tree,
>   And my young children leave their play,
>   And ask in vain for me.'
>
> " 'I take thy gold—but I have made
>   Thy fetters fast and strong,
>   And ween that by the cocoa shade
>   Thy wife will wait thee long.'
>   Strong was the agony that shook
>   The captive's frame to hear,
>   And the proud meaning of his look
>   Was changed to mortal fear.
>
> "His heart was broken—crazed his brain:
>   At once his eye grew wild;
>   He struggled fiercely with his chain,
>   Whispered, and wept, and smiled;

[22] *Ibid.*, 128-129. It is interesting to note that by 1836 Paulding's attitude
toward slavery had changed completely, for in that year he published his *Slavery
in the United States,* in which he contended that Negroes were morally, intellec-
tually, and in all other ways unfitted for freedom. He made a virulent attack
upon the advocates of immediate emancipation and termed all abolitionists dangerous enemies of religion, morals, liberty, patriotism, and all the social relations of life. A contemporary of Paulding's, Theodore Tilton, later attributed
this change of attitude to Paulding's having become an aspirant for political
advancement. For a discussion of this see the *National Anti-Slavery Standard,*
April 21, 1860.

[23] In a poem by Sarah W. Morton, also entitled "The African Chief" and
published in 1823, but less effective from an emotional point of view than Bryant's poem, the author described the capture and murder of an African chief by
slave-traders, showed profound sympathy for the slave, and urged her readers
to feel for "bleeding Africa" and "hate oppression's mad control."—Morton,
Sketches, Fragments, and Essays, pp. 202-203.

> Yet wore not long those fatal bands,
> And once at shut of day,
> They drew him forth upon the sands,
> The foul hyena's prey.''[24]

On the other hand, a play by Robert Montgomery **Bird** entitled *The Gladiator* (1831), which was a more severe arraignment of slavery than that made by Dunlap, Paulding, or Bryant, was typical of the sentimental appeals of the latter part of the period. Though depicting the struggles of the oppressed in Italy in the year 73 B.C., it very probably was intended to influence the abolition movement in this country, for the author was reported as saying that if the play had been produced in a slave state, the manager, actors, and author as well would probably have been rewarded with the penitentiary.[25] It described the struggles of foreign slaves with Rome for their freedom. Two enslaved Thracian gladiators, Pharsarius and Spartacus, were called upon to meet each other in deadly combat, in the arena, for the amusement of the Roman nobility. Spartacus at first refused to fight a Thracian, but, on being promised freedom for his wife and child, he agreed to meet Pharsarius. Soon, however, discovering that he and Pharsarius were brothers, he not only refused to fight, but immediately organized the gladiators for the purpose of defeating Rome and winning their freedom. Spartacus hoped that death might overtake the Roman fiends who made their mirth

> "Out of the groans of bleeding misery!
> Ho, slaves, arise! it is your hour to kill!
> Kill and spare not—for wrath and liberty!
> Freedom for bondmen—freedom and revenge.''[26]

In the conflicts which ensued the gladiators were successful as long as they fought as a unit. They began to meet reverses when they refused to obey the orders of Spartacus,

---

[24] Bryant, *Poems* (ed. 1890), pp. 77-79.

[25] C. E. Foust, *The Life and Dramatic Works of Robert Montgomery Bird*, p. 51.

[26] Bird, ''The Gladiator,'' in C. E. Foust, *The Life and Dramatic Works of Robert Montgomery Bird*, pp. 354-355.

their leader.   One by one the followers of Spartacus were
struck down, including his brother, wife, and child.   In his
attempt to reach Crassus, the Roman Praetor, he himself
was killed, but not until Bracchius and Lentulus, promoters
of the gladiatorial combats, had been slain.   The anti-slavery
sentiment here was best shown in the author's treatment of
Spartacus, who was portrayed quite sympathetically
throughout the play.   His aim was merely to win his freedom
and that of his comrades.

> ".... We do not fight for conquest,
> But conquer for our liberties....."[27]

Pharsarius deserted him because he would not surrender to
Pharsarius the niece of the Roman Praetor whom he held as
a prisoner.   The closing speech of Crassus, the Roman Praetor, whose life Spartacus was seeking when he fell, gave
some idea of the impression Spartacus had made upon his
enemies:

> "Thy bark is wreck'd but nobly did she buffet
> These waves of war, and grandly lies at last,
> A stranded ruin on this fatal shore.
> Let him have burial; not as a base bondman,
> But as a chief enfranchised and ennobled.
> If we denied him honour while he lived,
> Justice shall carve it on his monument."[28]

The sentimental appeals by many minor writers of the
latter part of this period also showed very bitter resentment
toward slaveholders and their abettors.   One of these contrasted the happiness the African enjoyed in his native land
with the cruelties he suffered in America;[29] another inquired
of masters how they could witness the slave's condition without feeling sympathy and guilt;[30] and still another urged
emancipation to avoid insurrection among the slaves.[31]

[27] Ibid., p. 363.

[28] Ibid., p. 440.   For an account of the success of this play in New York,
Philadelphia, and Boston, see ibid., pp. 39-44.

[29] James B. Walker, The Slaves; A Poem (1831), pp. 1-4.

[30] Benjamin Hine, "The Slave Holder" (1829), in Miscellaneous Poetry:
or, The Farmer's Muse, pp. 208-209.

[31] "New Year's Eve" (1831), in the Genius of Universal Emancipation, ed.
Lundy, II, 3rd Ser., 149.

Many of these appeals were made by a slave poet, George Horton, of Chatham County, North Carolina, who wrote several poems in which he keenly resented being deprived of his freedom. In 1829 many of his poems were published in order that a sum of money sufficient for his emancipation might be obtained. He was to be emancipated, however, only on condition that he sailed forthwith for Liberia. The project was not successful, however, for in 1837 he was still the slave of James Horton and was employed as a servant at Chapel Hill, North Carolina. The following stanzas were taken from his poem entitled "On Liberty and Slavery" (1829):

> "Alas! and am I born for this,
> To wear this slavish chain?
> Deprived of all created bliss
> Through hardship, toil and pain!
>
> .   .   .   .
>
> "Oh, Heaven! and is there no relief
> This side the silent grave—
> To soothe the pain—to quell the grief
> And anguish of a slave?
>
> .   .   .   .
>
> "Come Liberty, thou cheerful sound,
> Roll through my ravished ears!
> Come, let my grief in joys be drowned,
> And drive away my fears.
>
> "Say unto foul oppression, Cease:
> Ye tyrants rage no more,
> And let the joyful trump of peace,
> Now bid the vassal soar.
>
> .   .   .   .
>
> "Bid Slavery hide her haggard face,
> And barbarism fly;
> I scorn to see the sad disgrace
> In which enslaved I lie."[32]

The same impatient yearning, but with less bitterness toward his oppressors, characterized Horton's poem called "The Slave's Complaint" (1829):

[32] Horton, "Poems by a Slave," in *Memoir and Poems of Phillis Wheatley* (ed. 1838), pp. 130-132.

"Am I sadly cast aside,
  On misfortune's rugged tide?
  Will the world my pains deride
      Forever?

"Must I dwell in Slavery's night,
  And all pleasure take its flight,
  Far beyond my feeble sight,
      Forever?

"Worst of all, must hope grow dim,
  And withhold her cheering beam?
  Rather let me sleep and dream
      Forever!

.   .   .   .

"Heaven! in whom can I confide?
  Canst thou not for all provide?
  Condescend to be my guide
      Forever:

"And when this transient life shall end,
  Oh, may some kind, eternal friend
  Bid me from servitude ascend,
      Forever!"[33]

IV. PLANS FOR THE EMANCIPATION OF THE SLAVE[34]

During this second period of the anti-slavery movement
in America there were advocates of both gradual and immediate abolition. Many of those who favored gradual abolition considered colonization the best method of attaining
it. Thomas Jefferson, in 1814, saw no proposition "so expedient, on the whole, as that of emancipation of those born
after a given day, and of their education and expatriation
after a given age."[35] In 1816 the American Colonization
Society was organized for the purpose of colonizing free
Negroes in Africa or such other place as Congress might
"deem most expedient."[36] Regarding the effect that such
an organization might have upon slavery there was great

[33] *Ibid.*, p. 133.

[34] For a detailed account of the plans initiated during this period for the
emancipation of the slaves, see A. D. Adams, *The Neglected Period of Anti-
Slavery in America, 1808-1831.*

[35] Jefferson, "Letter to Edward Coles," in *Writings*, ed. Ford, XI, 418.

[36] See "The Formation of the American Colonization Society," by Henry
Noble Sherwood, in the *Journal of Negro History*, II, 209-228.

difference of opinion. Many pro-slavery men opposed it because they thought it would lead ultimately to abolition. Many advocates of gradual abolition favored it for the same reason. They thought they saw in it a means whereby their plan to free the slaves might be greatly facilitated.[37] The most bitter opponents of colonization, however, were the advocates of immediate emancipation. They contended that colonization strengthened the hold of the master upon the slaves by ridding the country of the free Negroes whose presence in America was causing the slaves to become dissatisfied with their condition.[38] The utterances of William Lloyd Garrison during the latter part of this period furnished the most significant example of this attitude. In the year 1826 his writings began to reveal his growing interest in the anti-slavery movement. In May of that year, as editor of the *Free Press,* at Newburyport, Massachusetts, he commented favorably upon an anti-slavery poem entitled "Africa."[39] In 1828 as editor of the *National Philanthropist,* at Boston, and of the *Journal of the Times,* at Bennington, Vermont, he took a very active part in the anti-slavery controversy, recommending, while filling the latter position, that petitions be sent to Congress for the abolition of slavery in the District of Columbia. On July 4, 1829, he delivered an anti-slavery address in Boston in which he expressed the desire that the overthrow of slavery might be accomplished without resort to coercive measures, spoke of the inadequacy of the colonization plan as a cure for the evil, and advocated gradual emancipation.[40] Six weeks later, however, he was convinced that nothing short of immediate and unconditional emancipation would suffice; and on September 2, 1829, writ-

[37] Matthew Carey, *A Short Account of the Malignant Fever and Miscellaneous Essays,* pp. 218-219. See also A. D. Adams, *The Neglected Period of Anti-Slavery in America, 1808-1831,* pp. 199-207.

[38] David Walker, *Appeal* (3rd ed., 1830), p. 62; James B. Walker, *The Slaves; a Poem* (1831), p. v.

[39] For this comment, together with an excerpt from the poem, see W. P. and F. J. Garrison, *William Lloyd Garrison,* I, 64-65.

[40] Garrison, "First Anti-Slavery Address in Boston," *Old South Leaflets,* II, 85.

ing in the *Genius of Universal Emancipation,* in the editing of which he was at that time associated with Benjamin Lundy, he said that the slaves were entitled to immediate and complete emancipation; consequently, to hold them longer in bondage was both "tyrannical and unnecessary."[41] His utterances shortly afterwards regarding the domestic slave-trade led to his being imprisoned in Baltimore for seven weeks.

The years from 1808 to 1831 served to connect the first period of the anti-slavery movement, which had culminated in the abolition of the African slave-trade in 1808, with the more significant period leading up to the Civil War. Throughout these years there was a continuous flow of anti-slavery sentiment which increased in force as it approached the end of the period. At first it was milder in spirit than it had been during the years immediately preceding the passage of the Slave-Trade Act; but as the years passed it developed with increasing severity, reaching its height between 1829 and 1831. It found rather full expression in all the important literary forms of the day. Nor was it confined to any one section, but appeared in the works of writers from Northern, Middle, and Southern States. The moral, religious, and sentimental arguments were used chiefly, though the social and economic were not lacking. Colonization and gradual emancipation were still the rallying cry, yet many advocates of immediatism could be found, chief among whom was William Lloyd Garrison, who, in 1831, became the leading figure in a struggle that did not cease until the close of the Civil War.

" W. P. and F. J. Garrison, *William Lloyd Garrison,* I, 143.

CHAPTER III

THE FIRST PERIOD OF MILITANT ABOLITIONISM
(1831-1850)

On January 1, 1831, after having given a series of stirring lectures on behalf of the slave, William Lloyd Garrison published the first number of the *Liberator*. Here in a spirit of bold defiance he declared his position with respect to slavery:

> "Oppression! I have seen thee face to face,
> And met thy cruel eye and cloudy brow;
> But thy soul-withering glance I fear not now—
> For dread to prouder feelings doth give place,
> Of deep abhorrence! Scorning the disgrace
> Of slavish knees that at thy footstool bow,
>
> I also kneel—but with far other vow
> Do hail thee and thy herd of hirelings base:—
> I swear, while life-blood warms my throbbing veins,
> Still to oppose and thwart, with heart and hand,
> Thy brutalizing sway—till Afric's chains
> Are burst, and Freedom rules the rescued land,
> Trampling Oppression and his iron rod:
> Such is the vow I take—so help me, God!"[1]

This event might be said to mark the beginning of militant abolitionism, which, under the leadership of Garrison, had a steady growth for a period of thirty years, reaching its climax in 1861 with the outbreak of hostilities.

Before 1831, as already noted, anti-slavery sentiment had been expressed in all sections of the country. Some of the most bitter utterances against slavery had come from the South. After 1831, however, this sentiment was confined principally to the Middle and Northern States. In 1827 Benjamin Lundy estimated that there were in the United States one hundred and thirty anti-slavery societies, of which one hundred and six were in slaveholding states.[2] In 1837, according to the same authority, there was not one such

---

[1] Garrison, the *Liberator*, January 1, 1831.
[2] *Life, Travels and Opinions of Benjamin Lundy*, p. 218.

society existing in a slaveholding state.[3]   Among the many
reasons given for this sudden change of sentiment in the
South were the following: the rapid growth of the cotton industry, which resulted in an increased demand for slave-
labor; the Nat Turner insurrection in 1831; the debates in
the Virginia Legislature of 1831 and 1832, in which were offered plans for partial or total abolition of slavery; the rise
of the new abolition movement in the North under the leadership of Garrison; and the growing opposition to the colonization plan, which many Southerners had been active in promoting.   The reaction in the South following upon these
events was responsible for the almost complete absence of
anti-slavery sentiment in the literature of the South after
about 1831.   In the North, on the other hand, under the influence of Garrison and his followers, sentiment against
slavery increased in extent and in severity throughout the
period.   Here the production of anti-slavery literature was
actively encouraged by the rapid increase in the number of
anti-slavery societies.   The New England Anti-Slavery Society was organized at Boston in 1832, and the American
Anti-Slavery Society at Philadelphia in 1833.   These were
followed immediately by others, so that by October, 1835,
there were in the North three hundred anti-slavery societies
with one hundred thousand members.[4]

I.   MORAL AND RELIGIOUS ARGUMENTS

In this period, as in the two periods already discussed, the
moral and religious arguments against slavery played an
important part in molding public sentiment.   They fell into
two groups: (1) those which showed opposition to slavery
on the ground that it had a detrimental influence upon the
morals and religion of the master and the slave, but which
were not written to create prejudice against the master, and
(2) those which not only represented slavery as a moral and

[3] *Ibid.*, p. 296.   On the other hand, A. E. Grimke, in *Letters to Catherine E.
Beecher* (1838), pp. 58-93, gave an interesting account of the prevalence of the
abolition spirit in certain sections of the South between 1834 and 1837.

[4] Edward Channing, *A History of the United States*, V, 148.

religious detriment to the slaveholder and the slave, but which also revealed a great deal of hostility toward Southerners and their Northern sympathizers and anticipated the bitter sectional prejudice which characterized so much of the anti-slavery literature during the years immediately preceding the Civil War.

Those arguments which were concerned primarily with the effect of slavery upon the master revealed the fact that slavery nourished in him the passion for power and its kindred vices. It gave him license to practice cruelty and lawlessness and destroyed his domestic affections and joys.[5] It also caused him to be indolent and extravagant and in general to dissipate his energies.[6] Emerson said that the planter was the "spoiled child of his unnatural habits," and had contracted in his indolent and luxurious climate the need of excitement by irritating and tormenting his slave."[7] In the British West Indies before slavery was abolished the planters, he said, were full of vices, and their children were "lumps of pride, sloth, sensuality and rottenness."[8] The civility of no race, he continued, could be perfect while another race was degraded:

"It is a doctrine alike of the oldest, and the newest philosophy, that man is one, and that you cannot injure any member, without a sympathetic injury to all the members. America is not civil, whilst Africa is barbarous."[9]

Even persons of the North, it was said, were imitating Southerners and a fondness for show, ornament, and extravagance was to be noticed in all classes of society throughout the country.[10]

[5] William E. Channing, *Slavery* (1835), pp. 90-91; James Fenimore Cooper, "On American Slavery" (1828), in *The American Democrat*, pp. 173-174; William A. Carruthers, *The Kentuckian in New York*, I, 119.

[6] *The Fanatic, or the Perils of Peter Pliant, the Poor Pedagogue* (1846), pp. 21, 45, 55.

[7] Emerson, "Emancipation in the British West Indies" (1844), in *Works*, II, 515.

[8] *Ibid.*, 519.

[9] *Ibid.*, 533.

[10] Elizabeth M. Chandler, *Essays, Philanthropic and Moral* (ed. 1836), pp. 116-117.

The detrimental effect of slavery upon the morals and religion of the slave was also freely discussed. He was lazy, indifferent, and revengeful because he worked without hope of reward.[11] He was also given to stealing, lying, intemperance, and in general to sensual excess,[12] and was "the veriest outcast on the face of God's beautiful creation."[13] One of the most effective of these arguments was that used by Herman Melville in *Mardi* (1849). Several of the characters here—Taji, Yoomy, Babbalanja, King Media, and Mohi—visited the South of Vivenza (or America) in search of Yillah, who was the spirit of ideal happiness. Here they observed slavery in its worst form. They were told by an overseer that the slaves had no souls; that they were brutes; but that since they were fed, clothed, and cared for, they were happy. Babbalanja was greatly moved by the condition of the slaves and spoke with one of them:

"What art thou? . . . . Dost ever feel in thee a sense of right and wrong? Art ever glad or sad?—They tell us thou art not a man:—speak, then, for thyself; say, whether thou beliest thy Maker."

The serf replied:

"Speak not of my Maker to me. Under the lash, I believe my masters, and account myself a brute; but in my dreams, bethink myself an angel. But I am bond; and my little ones;—their mother's milk is gall."[14]

Yoomy interposed:

"Just Oro! do not thunders roll,—no lightnings flash in this accursed land! . . . . Oh fettered sons of fettered mothers, conceived and born in manacles, ... oh, beings as ourselves, how my stiff arm shivers to avenge you! 'Twere absolution for the matricide, to strike one rivet from your chains. My heart outswells its home."[14]

He hoped that there might be some way to loose their bonds

[11] W. E. Channing, *Slavery* (1835), pp. 70-72; R. M. Bird, *Sheppard Lee* (1836), p. 171; Elizabeth Ricord, *Zamba: or the Insurrection* (1842), p. 53.

[12] James Freeman Clarke, *Slavery in the United States* (1842), p. 8; "Slavery in the United States," in the anonymous *Hints and Sketches* (1839), p. 138; "The True Character of Slavery," in the *Pennsylvania Freeman*, April 12, 1838.

[13] Chandler, *op. cit.*, p. 7.

[14] Melville, *Mardi* (ed. 1922), II, 248.

without one drop of blood, but felt that it was right to fight for freedom, whoever might be the thrall.[15] Mohi predicted that there would yet be war.[16] He said that slavery was

"... a blot, foul as the crater pool of hell; it puts out the sun at noon; it parches all fertility; and, conscience or no conscience— ere he die—let every master who wrenches bond-babe from mother, that the nipple tear; unwreathes the arms of sisters; or cuts the holy unity in twain; till apart fall man and wife, like one bleeding body cleft:—let that master thrice shrive his soul; take every sacrament; on his bended knees give up the ghost;—yet shall he die despairing; and live again, to die forever damned.'"[17]

He thought that time would do much by way of solving the problem:

"The future is all hieroglyphics. Who may read? But, methinks the great laggard Time must now march up apace, and somehow befriend these thralls. It cannot be, that misery is perpetually entailed. . . . . . Yes: Time—all-healing Time—Time, great Philanthropist!—Time must befriend these thralls.'"[17]

The moral and religious arguments of the second group were more numerous than those just discussed. These, for the most part, were written to create prejudice against slaveholders and their Northern sympathizers, and must have played an important part during this period in making the South solidly pro-slavery. Most of these attacks were prompted by the growing tendency on the part of many Northerners, during the period, of co-operating with slaveholders by returning fugitive slaves to their owners.[18] One of the earliest novels in American literature to be devoted wholly to the anti-slavery cause was written to condemn this practice. In 1834 Richard Hildreth, the historian, went to the South for his health and remained there nearly two years on a slave plantation. The outcome of this experience was a strong anti-slavery novel published in 1836 under the title of *The Slave: or, Memoirs of Archy Moore*. In his account of the difficulties he experienced in getting his book before

---

[15] *Ibid.*, 249.

[16] *Ibid.*, 250.

[17] *Ibid.*, 252.

[18] For an account of the cases growing out of this practice and other cases resulting from kidnapping, see Channing, *A History of the United States*, VI, 88-118.

the public the author revealed an important phase of Northern sentiment at that time with respect to slavery. He said that the book was written before the spring of 1836 and was carried to New York for publication, but no one dared to publish it. It met with the same timidity in Boston, and was finally printed without any publisher's name on the title-page. With much difficulty a bookseller was found and the first edition was disposed of in four or five months. "But," said he, "no review or magazine, or hardly a newspaper, took any notice of it—a silence caused quite as much by not knowing what to say, as by any indifference to the subject or contents of the book, both of which were certainly, in some respects, well calculated to elicit criticism.'"[19]

In this story the author related the experiences of Archy Moore, whose mother was a slave and whose father, Colonel Moore, was a planter of eastern Virginia. During the time that he was a companion of his half-brother James, Archy was taught to read and write. He was so apt in his studies that he became his half-brother's tutor and dearest friend. On James's death Archy chose labor in the fields in preference to being in the service of another half-brother, who was reputed to be a cruel master. But he found life in the fields under an almost inhuman overseer so unbearable that he welcomed a summons to return to the house where his services had become necessary. Here he fell in love with Cassy, the maid, and later eloped with her when he realized the danger of allowing her to be near the Colonel. They were overtaken and brought back to an even more miserable life than that from which they had escaped. Then after a series of distressing experiences leading to their final separation, Archy escaped to the North and thence to France. He became a pirate, acquired wealth, and sent an agent to America to seek out his wife and child; but on learning that they had not been found, he resolved to revisit America and make the search himself, determined that in the event he should be captured he would be prepared to frustrate his enemies:

[19] Hildreth, *The Slave: or, Memoirs of Archy Moore* (ed. 1840), I, 3.

"Should I be recognized and seized, ... I know a way to disappoint the tyrants; the guilt be on their heads! I cannot be a slave a second time."[20]

The author based most of his opposition to slavery upon moral and religious grounds. He said that slavery embittered the feelings and hardened the heart:

"He who finds himself plundered from his birth, of his liberty and his labor—his only inheritance—becomes selfish, reckless, and regardless of everything save the immediate gratification of the present moment. Plundered of everything himself, he is ready to plunder in his turn, even his brothers in misfortune."[21]

The orthodox doctrine, he said, which slaveholders preached to their slaves, the slaves received with an outward submission, to which their hearts gave the lie:

"Alas Christianity! What does it avail,—thy concern for the poor,—thy tenderness for the oppressed,—thy system of fraternal love and affection. . . . . The tyrants of every age and country, have succeeded in prostituting Christianity into an instrument of their crimes, a terror to their victims, and an apology for their oppressions."[22]

The author also made a severe arraignment of Northern States for delivering into the hands of the slaveholder every miserable fugitive who took refuge within their territory. The slaves in this story, unlike those in most anti-slavery novels—*Uncle Tom's Cabin* not excepted—did not hesitate to resist actively ill-treatment at the hands of persons placed over them. This was best illustrated in the case of Thomas, a slave who promptly interfered when his wife was whipped without cause by an overseer. He later murdered the overseer because he was convinced that her death was due to his cruelty.

Probably no single incident during this period provoked more bitter resentment from the abolitionists than the effort made in 1842 to return to the South a fugitive slave named George Latimer. Latimer was seized in Boston at the request of James B. Grey, of Norfolk, Virginia, who claimed

[20] *Ibid.*, II, 115.
[21] *Ibid.*, I, 68.
[22] *Ibid.*, 114.

him as his property. The incident caused great excitement
in the North and the South. Through the efforts of the abolitionists Grey was forced to surrender his rights to Latimer
for four hundred dollars in cash, and Latimer was given free
papers. It was this incident which called forth Whittier's
well known poem entitled *Massachusetts to Virginia*,
written in December, 1842.[23] In 1843 there was published
in Boston a poem entitled *The Virginia Philosopher*, the
author of which styled himself "Mr. Latimer's Brother."
His purpose was to censure the persons and their abettors who were engaged in the business of re-enslaving
George Latimer after he had obtained freedom for himself and family by a successful flight.[24] The greater part
of the poem the author wrote in the form of a conversation,
between himself and a phantom, in which the pro-slavery
statesmen and clergymen were the chief objects of attack.
He bemoaned the fact that the blaze of his country's glory
in the days gone by had become "quench'd, debased, degraded," but was confident that slavery would be abolished:

"The good and wise of every land
    Are leaguing in resistless band,
    And God himself hath given command,
    And devils must comply."[25]

It was very probably this same incident which led Theodore Parker in 1843 to make a more severe attack upon
Northern sympathizers with slaveholders who attempted to
remand fugitives to slavery, in a satirical work called "Socrates in Boston: A Dialogue between the Philosopher and
a Yankee." Here Socrates returned to earth and conversed
with Jonathan, a Yankee, who sympathized with the slaveholders. The anger of Socrates was aroused by the presence
in Boston of a planter in search of his fugitive slave. Socrates apologized for being a heathen who knew nothing of
religion and righteousness, and asked Jonathan to teach him
the improvements of the last two thousand years. In reply

[23] See below, p. 66.
[24] *The Virginia Philosopher*, p. 3.
[25] *Ibid.*, p. 3.

he was told that right law was the opinion of men able to enforce their opinions; that it was synonymous with justice; and that Christianity consisted in *doctrines* more than in actions. The most important of these doctrines were: read the Bible, observe the Sabbath, attend church, and love the Lord. Socrates forced Jonathan to admit that Christianity also bade one to repent of what was wrong, and taught love of man; but that slavery neither made men wiser nor protected the honor of women and the self-respect of men. "Now," said Socrates, "if the Christian slave love God for his goodness, I see not but he must hate his master for his badness. And since, as you say, 'all men are born free and equal,' slavery is no ordinance of God's goodness, but of man's badness, and therefore avoidable. So the slave has just the same *Christian* right to butcher his master, that your brave fathers had to butcher their tyrants. Still more —to command a man to be a slave is contrary to love of man, and not a Christian command, and therefore is not to be obeyed."[26] Jonathan was made to admit also that masters took no pains to teach their slaves either wisdom or goodness, and still less Christianity; that they degraded the slave in all the qualities of a man, and promoted in him those of a beast; that they were not themselves improved in morals or religion, but were benefited only in the acquirement of wealth. The sketch was closed with the following soliloquy by Socrates:

"Have two thousand years and more gone by, since my time? I heard of Christianity when Paul came to Mars Hill, and blessed his manly heart—as I lay in my grave. This cannot be real. Slavery in a free land; defended in a Christian land; by men that do not *own* slaves! This must be all a dream! Let me pray my old prayer. Oh, thou great One! give me a Mind to see the Truth; a Conscience to discern the Right; a Heart full of Love; A Soul of Faith, and a blameless Life."[27]

The two most bitter anti-slavery plays of the period, *The Branded Hand* (1845), by Mrs. Sophia L. Little, and *Warren: A Tragedy* (1850), attributed to Daniel S. Whitney,

[26] Parker, "Socrates in Boston," in the *Liberty Bell* (ed. 1843), pp. 136-137.
[27] *Ibid.*, p. 144.

were also called forth by the Latimer case and other cases
similar to it.

In *The Branded Hand*, Philander, the hero, was a de-
voutly religious man who was placed in the pillory and
branded in the right hand for assisting slaves to escape to
freedom. At the prison, before the time appointed for his
punishment, he saw in a vision a crown suspended from the
cross and heard a voice urging him to wear the crown. He
promised to remain firm in his faith in God. At the scene
of the pillory a bystander made a remark concerning the
indebtedness of the slaveholder to the church and clergy
for the stand they had taken for slavery, holding them responsible for the suffering of the victim in the pillory. Inquiring of another bystander, of pro-slavery sympathies,
whether this affair would create much excitement in the
North, he received the following reply:

"No. The North does not care, so we help fill her purse, how
many of her sons we imprison and brand. All the North wants is
riches and luxury. There's a great deal of talk there, but it means
nothing."[28]

After the branding the victim was conveyed back to prison
where the vision reappeared to him, informing him that he
had won the crown. The play was closed with the following
speech by the slaveholder, who saw before him the branded
hand, and who was given to understand that he would be tormented forever unless he repented:

"Then will headlong rush
From pleasure on to pleasure madly on:
I cannot yield this will of mine: 'tis strong
And up in arms against Omnipotence.
Stay, I may be deluded by a dream,
Do not God's ministers for slavery plead,
And prove it holy from the sacred text?
Sleep then, Oh, foolish conscience, sleep again!
The anthems of a thousand churches lull thee."[29]

In *Warren: A Tragedy*, Joseph Warren, a free Negro citizen
of Charlestown, Massachusetts, and the grandson of Warren

---

[28] Little, *The Branded Hand*, p. 40.
[29] *Ibid.*, pp. 45-46.

who fell at Bunker Hill, arrived in Charleston, South Carolina, on business just after a law had been enacted there, of which he was ignorant, "designed to rid the state of all free persons of African descent." He was accordingly seized and imprisoned by some of the prominent citizens of Charleston and told that if he could find any responsible white man to give bonds in a sufficient sum to take him out of the state immediately and pay the expense of his imprisonment, he would be discharged. Warren wrote to William Lloyd Garrison and John Quincy Adams for aid, but the letters were intercepted by the persons who imprisoned him, and he was sold at auction for $150 to a deacon of the church. Later he was committed to the charge of the Reverend Dr. Smythe, who was instructed to use whatever means necessary to insure Warren's obedience. Smythe, discovering Warren's independence of spirit, ordered that he be given fifty lashes, and proceeded with administering the sacrament of the Lord's Supper. Warren took the punishment without flinching, at the same time praying for his deliverance and for his enemies. After the communion service, Smythe, impatient with Warren's attitude, ordered such cruel torture that Warren died shortly afterwards. Then after giving orders for his burial, Dr. Smythe proceeded with evening prayers. The author's satire was directed against the religion of Dr. Smythe, whose favorite argument in support of slavery was the one frequently found in the works of pro-slavery writers: namely, that the descendants of Ham were condemned by God to perpetual servitude. Slaves, said Dr. Smythe, "are dependent upon their more enlightened brethren for care and those directions needful to supply their wants; and, of course, the pittance of service which they are able to render ought freely to be rendered, seeing it is impossible for them to discharge a tithe of the obligation that they are under to their masters and mistresses for their care and attention." When asked by one of the slaves at a Christmas service to explain the biblical passage "Whatsoever ye would that men should do to you, do ye even so to them," Dr.

Smythe replied: "Well, Sampsey, I am sorry that anybody should read to servants those portions of the Word of God that are above their comprehension; but as you have heard it, and it troubles your weak mind, I will do what I can to set your mind at rest on the subject. If it had pleased God, Sampsey, to make you a white man, and give you black slaves, why, you would wish them to be obedient and industrious, and honest, would you not, Sampsey?" To Sampsey's reply in the affirmative, Dr. Smythe continued: "Well, then, Sampsey, as it has pleased God to make you a black slave, he expects you to be faithful to your master, industrious, honest and contented." Sampsey, however, seemed to have little faith in Dr. Smythe's interpretation of the Scriptures, for after the services, in a conversation with his chum Billy, he told Billy to "tink of freedom as sure in heaven, and. . . . if you get a chance, old Billy, take it on earth, and be sure that God will one day make de lying preacher smart in his own brimstone, for de false reading ob his holy word."[30]

One other work belonging to this group demands special attention not only because of the strength of its appeal as a religious argument against slavery, but also because its author, Harriet Beecher Stowe, revealed here the same spirit which a little later was to characterize her *Uncle Tom's Cabin*, the most powerful anti-slavery book in American literature. On August 1, 1850, Mrs. Stowe published in the *National Era* a sketch entitled "The Freedman's Dream: A Parable," in which she opposed slavery on religious principles. It was written shortly before the Fugitive Slave Act of 1850 became a law; at a time when, as already noted, the right of slaveholders to remand to slavery fugitives seized in the free states was being vigorously contested by many persons of the North. In this sketch a planter refused to give protection to a fugitive slave and his family and allowed them to be seized by their pursuers. In the planter's dream the sky grew dark and the heavens flashed with light. He was borne

[30] *Warren: A Tragedy*, p. 46.

aloft and driven before the bar of the mighty Judge. The
author said:

"Then an awful voice pierced his soul, saying—'Depart from me
ye accursed! for I was an hungered, and ye gave me no meat; I was
thirsty, and ye gave me no drink; I was a stranger, and ye took me
not in.' And, terrified and subdued, the man made answer, 'Lord,
where?' And immediately rose before him these poor fugitive slaves,
whom he had spurned from his door; and the Judge made answer—
'Inasmuch as ye did it not to one of the least of these my brethren,
ye did it not to me.' And with that, terrified and affrighted, the
man awoke."[31]

The author then drew her moral:

"Of late, there have seemed to be many in this nation, who seem
to think that there is no standard of right and wrong higher than an
act of Congress, or an interpretation of the United States Constitution. It is humiliating to think that there should be in the
church of Christ men and ministers who should need to be reminded
that the laws of their Master are above human laws which come in
conflict with them; and that though heaven and earth pass away,
His word shall not pass away."[31]

II. SOCIAL AND ECONOMIC ARGUMENTS

Many writers of this period, considering slavery in its
relation to the practical problem of earning a livelihood, concluded that its abolition was a social and economic necessity. Arguments based upon these grounds dealt, for the
most part, with the effect of slavery upon the growth of
population and industry and upon living conditions generally.

The slow rate at which the white population of the South
increased, as compared with the rapid growth of the slave
population, made it necessary that slavery should be abolished. Theodore Parker called attention to the fact that
in New England, New York, New Jersey, and Pennsylvania
between 1790 and 1840 the increase in the number of people
was 243 per cent; whereas in Delaware, Maryland, Virginia,
North Carolina, South Carolina, Georgia, and Kentucky,

[31] Stowe, "The Freedman's Dream: A Parable," in the *National Era*,
August 1, 1850.

during the same period, the increase was only 179 per cent.[32] This condition he attributed to slavery. Whittier did likewise and pointed with pride to the fact that the entire population of the North with few exceptions, were working men and women.[33]

It was also argued that industry did not thrive in the slave states, and statistics were furnished to show the extent to which the North had surpassed the South in the number of inventions, tonnage of shipping, and annual earnings. In 1846 there was granted by the national office for inventions made in the slave states one patent for each 96,505 persons; whereas in the same year in the free states there was granted one patent for every 17,249 persons.[34] In 1846 the single port of New York had 70,939 more tons of shipping than all the Southern States combined, and in 1839 the annual earnings of the state of New York were more than $4,000,000 greater than those of six slave states.[35]

The impoverished condition of the poor whites of the South was also attributed to slavery. The vast amount of money necessary for supplying a plantation with slaves had a tendency to place the agriculture of a slaveholding community in the hands of the wealthy, thus working a hardship upon the non-slaveholders.[36] While traveling through the South in 1849, William Cullen Bryant noticed the wretched condition in which the poor white people lived—a condition due to their having no manual occupation provided for them from which they did not "shrink as disgraceful, on account of its being the occupation of slaves"; and he noticed in

---

[32] Parker, *A Letter to the People of the United States Touching the Matter of Slavery* (1848), p. 58.

[33] Whittier, "The Abolitionists; Their Sentiments and Objects" (1833), in *Prose Works*, III, 68-69.

[34] Parker, *op. cit.*, p. 43.

[35] *Ibid.*, pp. 51, 52, 56. The six slave states were North Carolina, South Carolina, Georgia, Alabama, Mississippi, and Louisiana.

[36] Whittier, "Justice and Expediency" (1838), in *Prose Works*, III, 44; Walt Whitman, "American Workingmen Versus Slavery" (1847), in *The Uncollected Poetry and Prose of Walt Whitman*, ed. Holloway, I, 171-172.

some of their faces "that look of mingled distrust and de-
jection which often accompanies the condition of extreme,
hopeless poverty."[37]

III. SENTIMENTAL ARGUMENTS

A great deal of anti-slavery feeling in the literature of
this period was based upon sentimental grounds. This form
of opposition to slavery, ranging from the mildest expressions of sympathy for the slave to very bitter invectives
against slaveholders and their abettors, served to re-enforce
the more intellectual types of argument and to make more
numerous the converts to the cause of abolition. Like the
moral and religious arguments of this period, these appeals
were of two classes: (1) those written solely to oppose slavery, without any effort to create prejudice against Southerners,[38] and (2) those which showed clearly a spirit of
defiance toward slaveholders and their Northern sympathizers and expressed frequently a willingness on the part

[37] Bryant, *Letters of a Traveller; or, Notes of Things Seen in Europe and
America* (ed. 1851), pp. 346-347.

[38] Among the many poems in this group that cannot be given more than the
briefest mention here are the following: "To Earth" (1848), by J. Bayard Taylor, in the *Liberty Bell* (1848), pp. 51-53; "Ode," by N. P. Willis, in the *Pennsylvania Freeman*, August 22, 1839; "The Fugitives' Hymn," by T. Wentworth Higginson, in the *Liberty Bell* (1848), pp. 94-96; "An Appeal for the
Slave," in the *Genius of Universal Emancipation*, II, 3rd Ser., 198, May, 1832;
"Letter from an Infant Slave to the Child of its Mistress" and "The White
Infant's Reply to the Little Slave," in the *Abolitionist, or Record of the New
England Anti-Slavery Society*, I, No. II, 32, 48, February-March, 1833; *An Ad-
dress* (1835), by Daniel G. Colesworthy; "Prayer for the Slave" (1842), by
John Pierpont, in *Anti-Slavery Poems* (ed. 1843), pp. 58-59; "The Mother's
Prayer" (1843), by Thomas Hill, in *Christmas, and Poems on Slavery for
Christmas, 1843*, pp. 5-7; "The Slave's Musings" (1847), in *Poems, Original
and Selected*, ed. D. M. Bennison, pp. 84-85; "Prayer for the Oppressed" and
"Liberty Song" by George Thompson, in the *Prison Bard, or Poems on Various Subjects* (1848), pp. 63, 83, 85; *Niagara* (1848), by C. H. A. Bulkley; and
the following poems in the *Poetical Works of Elizabeth Margaret Chandler*
(1836): "The Afric's Dream," pp. 50-51; "The Kneeling Slave," p. 59; "What
is a Slave Mother?" pp. 70-71; "The Enfranchised Slaves to their Benefac-
tress," p. 73; "The Sold," pp. 99-100; "An Appeal for the Oppressed," pp.
114-115; "The Slave Mother's Farewell," pp. 122-123; and "The Slave
Ship," p. 136.

of their authors to resort to violence, if necessary, in order to insure the destruction of slavery.

James Russell Lowell's opposition to slavery during this period found expression chiefly through sentimental appeals of the first group. As early as 1838 he was sufficiently interested in the subject of slavery to devote several lines to it in his *Class Poem*, but his attitude at that time was quite different from what it was a few years later. In this poem he referred to the abolitionists as "canting fanatics" who exaggerated the tortures of the slave and made war on the North for the ills the South had made.[39] He made a plea for the Indian and asked why the abolitionists had overlooked his wants. By 1843, however, his views had changed considerably. He himself said that his abolitionism began in 1840, the year of his engagement to Miss Maria White, whom he married in 1844. Miss White's pronounced sympathy for the slave very probably had much to do with Lowell's increased interest in the cause of abolition. In 1843 he wrote a poem to be sung at the Anti-Slavery Picnic in Dedham, on the anniversary of West Indian Emancipation. Here he maintained that no man was free who would not strive to free the slave:

> "Men! whose boast it is that ye
> Come of fathers brave and free,
> If there breathe on earth a slave
> Are ye truly free and brave?
> If ye do not feel the chain,
> When it works a brother's pain,
> Are ye not base slaves indeed,
> Slaves unworthy to be freed?
> .   .   .   .
>
> "They are slaves who fear to speak
> For the fallen and the weak;
> They are slaves who will not choose
> Hatred, scoffing, and abuse,
> Rather than in silence shrink
> From the truth they needs must think;
> They are slaves who dare not be
> In the right with two or three."[40]

[39] Lowell, *Class Poem*, p. 22.
[40] Lowell, "Stanzas on Freedom," in *Poetical Works*, p. 56.

From this time on Lowell played an increasingly active part in the abolition movement. Early in 1845 he became a regular contributor to the *Pennsylvania Freeman* and in 1848 corresponding editor of the *National Anti-Slavery Standard*. In both of these papers appeared many of his anti-slavery writings. In the *Standard* he published the last four numbers of *The Biglow Papers,* the first five having already appeared in the *Boston Courier* between June, 1846, and May, 1848. In *The Biglow Papers* he protested vigorously against the Mexican War, which he believed was a war of false pretences that would enlarge the boundaries and prolong the life of slavery.[41] Contending that it was begun and prosecuted in the interest of Southern slaveholders, he utilized every opportunity to satirize the slaveholders and their Northern sympathizers:

> "They jest want this Californy
> So's to lug new slave-states in
> To abuse ye, an' to scorn ye,
> An' to plunder ye like sin.
>
> .   .   .   .
>
> " 'Taint by turnin' out to hack folks
> You're agoin' to git your right,
> Nor by lookin' down on black folks
> Coz you're put upon by wite;
> Slavery aint o' nary color,
> 'Taint the hide thet makes it wus,
> All it keers fer in a feller
> 'S jest to make him fill its pus.
>
> .   .   .   .
>
> "Massachusetts, God forgive her,
> She's akneelin' with the rest,
> She, thet ough' to he' clung forever
> In her grand old eagle-nest;
> She thet ough' to stand so fearless
> Wile the wracks are round her hurled,
> Holdin' up a beacon peerless
> To the oppressed of all the world!"[42]

[41] In December, 1844, when efforts were being made to annex Texas to the Union, a movement generally regarded as aiming at the enlarging of slave territory, Lowell had written "The Present Crisis," another well known anti-slavery poem.

[42] Lowell, "The Biglow Papers." 1st Ser., No. I, in *Poetical Works*, p. 174

The Biglow Papers were an immediate success[43] and helped greatly in unifying public opinion in the North. They "turned the tables," said Lowell's biographer, "and put Anti-slavery, which had been fighting sturdily on foot with pikes, into the saddle, and gave it a flashing sabre."[44] Lowell was so greatly concerned over the attitude of America toward the question of slavery that in 1845 he gave warning of the calamity that would inevitably accompany emancipation unless this attitude changed fundamentally:

> "Out of the land of bondage 'tis decreed our slaves shall go,
> And signs to us are offered, as erst to Pharaoh;
> If we are blind, their exodus, like Israel's of yore,
> Through a Red Sea is doomed to be, whose surges are of gore."[45]

This same fear had been expressed shortly before by both Longfellow and Garrison. In "The Warning" (1842) Longfellow, relating the story of the death of Samson, who,

> "Destroyed himself, and with him those who made
> A cruel mockery of his sightless woe,

compared Samson to the African slave, of whom he urged his countrymen to beware:

> "There is a poor, blind Samson in this land,
> Shorn of his strength and bound in bonds of steel,
> Who may, in some grim revel, raise his hand,
> And shake the pillars of this Common-weal,
> Till the vast Temple of our liberties
> A shapeless mass of wreck and rubbish lies."[46]

Garrison also was convinced that the day of the slave's deliverance was not far distant and that it would be accompanied by great distress:

> "Wo if it come with storm, and blood, and fire,
> When midnight darkness veils the earth and sky!
> Wo to the innocent babe—the guilty sire—
> Mother and daughter—friends of kindred tie!

[43] The first edition of fifteen hundred copies was sold in one week after the publication of the poem in book form.

[44] H. E. Scudder, *James Russell Lowell*, I, 265.

[45] Lowell, "On the Capture of Fugitive Slaves Near Washington," in *Poetical Works*, p. 83.

[46] Longfellow "Poems on Slavery," in *Poetical Works*, p. 45.

> Stranger and citizen alike shall die!
> Red-handed Slaughter his revenge shall feed,
> And Havoc yell his ominous death-cry,
> And wild Despair in vain for mercy plead—
> While Hell itself shall shrink, and sicken at the deed!''[47]

Of the sentimental appeals of the second group—those intended primarily to arouse sectional feeling—W. H. Burleigh's poem entitled ''A Word to the South'' and Whittier's ''Massachusetts to Virginia'' were the best examples.[48] Burleigh's poem was written in October, 1835, at a time when pro-slavery meetings in the North were frequent and when hostility towards the abolitionists was growing rapidly. It was originally published in the *Liberator* shortly after a mob in Boston had dispersed a meeting of the Female Anti-Slavery Society and attacked Garrison with such violence that the city authorities could protect him only within the walls of a jail.[49] The following stanzas were taken from the poem:

> ''Let the storm come! A cry for blood hath gone
> Out on the winds of heaven! The *chivalrous* South
> Calls on the North to render up her sons—
> To sacrifice her worthiest, and appease
> The *holy* wrath of those who rob their God;
> And the pale North hath bowed, and kissed the foot
> Of her imperious master!
>
> '' 'Ho!—the chain!
> Fetter the press! put out the light of truth!
> Hang the disseverers of our sacred bond!'
> Go, mocker! chain the unfettered winds, which sweep
> Over your fervid plains, freighted with groans
> From the down-trodden . . . .
> Fetter the swelling ocean, that its waves
> Shall slumber, hushed and tranquil; with a nod
> Turn the sun backward from his path of light;

[47] Garrison, ''Universal Emancipation,'' in *Sonnets and Other Poems* (ed. 1843), pp. 9-11.

[48] Another poem belonging to this group, though less defiant than Burleigh's and Whittier's, was Elizabeth Margaret Chandler's ''The Recaptured Slave,'' found in her *Poetical Works* (1836), pp. 93-95, in which the slave, having for a short time enjoyed freedom, vowed never again to ''wear the chains of bondage.''

[49] Burleigh, *Poems*, p. 86.

Quench the rejoicing stars, and blot the moon
From the fair page of heaven; *then* turn and throw
Your manacles on mind—and fetter speech,
And thought, and action; and with dreadless hand
Hurl the Eternal from his throne, and seize
The sceptre of the Universe! and then,
When God is God no longer, *we* will fear,
And, cringing, do your bidding. *Not till then.*

"Let the storm come! It beat with fiercer rage
When cried the multitude, with maniac shout,
'Let Him be crucified!' Ye war with God!
Impious and unbelieving! He hath bared
His right arm for the battle, and hath thrown
His buckler over us—and every wound,
And every outrage which we suffer now,
In the hot conflict for the Right, shall be
A token and a pledge of victory!"[50]

Whittier's "Massachusetts to Virginia" (1842) was occasioned by the attempt on the part of James B. Grey, of Norfolk, to re-enslave George Latimer. The poet began by disavowing any intention of inciting warfare between the two sections, yet Massachusetts, he said, did not fear Virginia's threats. He reminded Virginia of the days when she with Massachusetts strove for and achieved liberty; but informed her that on the question of slavery she need not look for sympathy from Massachusetts:

"We hunt your bondmen flying from slavery's hateful hell;
Our voices, at your bidding, take up the bloodhound's yell;
We gather, at your summons, above our fathers' graves,
From Freedom's holy altar-horns to tear your wretched slaves!

"We wage no war, we lift no arm, we fling no torch within
The fire-damps of the quaking mine beneath your soil of sin;
We leave ye with your bondmen, to wrestle, while ye can,
With the strong upward tendencies and Godlike soul of man!

"But for us and for our children, the vow which we have given
For freedom and humanity is registered in heaven;
No slave-hunt in our borders,—no pirate on our strand!
No fetters in the Bay State,—no slave upon our land!"[51]

---

[50] *Ibid.,* pp. 87-88.
[51] Whittier, *Poetical Works,* III, 86.

IV. PLANS FOR THE EMANCIPATION OF THE SLAVE

Here, as in the preceding periods, there were advocates of both gradual and immediate emancipation. Even though converts to the latter increased throughout the period with startling rapidity, chiefly because of the work of Garrison and his followers, gradual abolition, nevertheless, still retained prominent advocates. Their attitude was due largely to the belief that sudden emancipation would work too great a hardship upon both the master and the slave. By some, emancipation was considered not a question of constitutional right, but rather one of expediency. James Fenimore Cooper said that slavery could be legally abolished by amending the Constitution; but that it would be madness for Congress to propose such an amendment, because it would "infallibly fail, thereby raising an irritating question without object."[52] To the citizen of the non-slaveholding state, slavery he said, offered little more than a question of abstract principles; whereas to the Southerner it offered a question of the "highest practical importance, and one that, mis-managed, might entirely subvert the order of his social organization."[53] W. E. Channing also advocated gradual emancipation. He contended that sudden emancipation would be cruelty, not kindness, to the slave, because he was unprepared to understand or to enjoy it. He thought that the state should first furnish him a guardian, not an owner, to supply the lack of that discretion which he had not attained. He also suggested, as another means of raising the slave and fitting him to act from higher motives than compulsion, the introduction of a system of bounties and rewards.[54] He said that the plan of the Colonization Society to remove slavery by "draining" it off to another country was about as "reasonable as that of draining the Atlantic."[55]

The advocates of immediate emancipation during this

---

[52] Cooper, "On American Slavery," in the *American Democrat* (1838), pp. 175-176.

[53] Cooper, "On Slavery in the District of Columbia," in *ibid.*, p. 178.

[54] Channing, "Slavery" (1835), in *Works*, p. 727.

[55] Channing, "Remarks on the Slavery Question," in *ibid.*, p. 784.

period suggested a variety of methods whereby the slaves might be freed. The poet Whittier, in 1833, criticized severely the Colonization Society, calling attention to the fact that during the period of its existence nearly one million human beings had died in slavery, and the number of slaves had increased more than a half a million.[56] He advocated immediate abolition as the only practicable scheme of emancipation and wished that it might be attained "not with the weapons of violence and blood, but with those of reason and truth, prayer to God, and entreaty to man."[57] He would begin with the District of Columbia and with what were at that time (1833) the territories of Florida and Arkansas, all of which came under the direct jurisdiction of the general government. He believed that if the government did not take the initiative in this matter, the slave sooner or later would become conscious of his "brute strength, his physical superiority," and cause serious trouble.[58] Contending that immediate abolition was a safe, just, and peaceful remedy for the evils of the slave system,[59] he showed that in no instance in the past had immediate emancipation been attended with violence and disorder on the part of the emancipated.[60] James Freeman Clarke urged that only those slaves able to care for themselves—and he thought that these were in the majority—be emancipated immediately; but he offered no definite plan whereby this might be done.[61]

Two authors writing anonymously in the *National Era* during this period were more specific than Clarke. They favored the method that Great Britain had employed in emancipating her slaves. The first suggested that the federal government, with the consent of the slaveholding states, pay the owners $500,000,000 for the three million slaves. To

[56] Whittier, "Justice and Expediency," in *Prose Works*, III, 15.

[57] *Ibid.*, 26.

[58] *Ibid.*, 33.

[59] This argument was used also in an anonymous dramatic sketch entitled "Duty and Safety of Emancipation" (1842), in the *Monthly Offering* (ed. John A. Collins), pp. 106-110.

[60] Whittier, *op. cit.*, 35.

[61] Clarke, *Slavery in the United States* (1843), p. 24.

meet the expenses of such a plan he suggested that there be maintained such a rate of duties upon importations as would produce the greatest possible revenue.[62] The plan of the second writer provided that owners of slaves should receive from the state an equivalent of half the value of the slaves. Payments could be made by the creation of state stock to be made over to the owners of the slaves and to be paid in five instalments. He said that since the value of real and personal property would be increased by emancipation, the expenses of such a plan could be met by a proportionate increase in the taxes on such property.[63]

This period from 1831 to 1850 might, therefore, be termed the first stage in the growth of the new abolition movement which had been initiated by Garrison and which was to reach its maturity in 1861 with the outbreak of hostilities. In the South anti-slavery sentiment rapidly declined during this period; whereas in the North, confined to narrower limits than formerly, it enjoyed a steady growth, despite the opposition which came not only from the South, which was fast becoming solidly pro-slavery, but also from the pro-slavery North. Indeed, most of the anti-slavery literature of the period was written with a view to converting the North to the cause of abolition. The breach between the abolitionists and the slaveholders was being further widened by the efforts of the abolitionists to aid fugitive slaves in escaping from their owners. The chief anti-slavery arguments appearing in the literature of the period were based upon moral, religious, social, economic, and sentimental grounds, and found utterance in all of the popular literary forms of the time. Advocates of colonization and gradual emancipation were still to be found, but they were less conspicuous than those of immediatism.

[62] ''A Plan for the Abolition of Slavery,'' by a North Carolinian, in the *National Era*, April 27, 1847.

[63] See the *National Era*, May 10, 1849.

CHAPTER IV

THE SECOND PERIOD OF MILITANT ABOLITIONISM
(1850-1861)

The second stage of militant abolitionism extended from 1850 to 1861. Opposition to slavery as revealed in the literature of America during this period was greater and more effective than ever before in the history of the abolition movement. It found expression in all the literary forms of the period, and became a powerful means of converting thousands of people of the North to the cause of abolition; while it also served to intensify the feeling of the South against abolition, and thus to make all the more difficult any peaceable solution of the problem. The passage of the Fugitive Slave Act on September 18, 1850, and the subsequent attempts to enforce it revealed slavery in one of its worst forms and called forth most of the anti-slavery productions of the period. The real effect of this Act upon the anti-slavery movement in America, said Mr. Edward Channing, "was not so much the increase or diminution of running away from the Slave States or the increase of the free negro colony in Canada, or the spectacular events that are associated with fugitive slave cases; it was that these things put together converted hundreds of thousands of people of the North from a position of indifference or of hostility to abolition to a position of hostility towards the slave power. It induced hundreds of thousands of voters, who cared very little whether the negro was a slave or a free man, to use all means at their disposal to stop the further extension of slavery and put an end to it whenever they could, constitutionally."[1] Of the many arguments used against slavery at this time, those based upon moral, religious, and sentimental grounds were the most numerous, and, by the very nature of their appeal, were capable of influencing the greatest number of people; yet strong pleas for the abolition

[1] Channing, *A History of the United States*, VI, 103.

of slavery as a social, economic, and political necessity were not wanting.

I. MORAL AND RELIGIOUS ARGUMENTS

The extraordinary growth of the moral and religious movement against slavery between 1850 and 1861 must be attributed largely to the passage of and the attempt to put into execution the Fugitive Slave Act of 1850. The abolitionists instantly resented this law and supported most of their arguments by references to its injustice. One of the first to do this was the poet Whittier. In a poem entitled "A Sabbath Scene" (1850), he attacked Northern clergymen who were urging the prompt execution of the law as a Christian duty. After describing vividly a female fugitive seeking refuge in a church, the pastor of which assisted her pursuer in binding her hands and feet, the poet wrote:

> "My brain took fire: 'Is this,' I cried,
> 'The end of prayer and preaching?
> Then down with pulpit, down with priest,
> And give us Nature's teaching!
>
> " 'For shame and scorn be on ye all
> Who turn the good to evil,
> And steal the Bible from the Lord,
> To give it to the Devil!' "[2]

The first really significant reaction to this law, however, was Harriet Beecher Stowe's *Uncle Tom's Cabin,* which first appeared in the *National Era,* Washington, D.C., between June 5, 1851, and April 1, 1852, and which became the most popular and effective of the anti-slavery literary productions. The author said that for many years of her life she had avoided all reading upon or allusion to the subject of slavery, "considering it as too painful to be inquired into, and one which advancing light and civilization would certainly live down"; but when she heard, "with perfect surprise and consternation, Christian and humane people actually recommending the remanding escaped fugitives into slavery, as a duty binding on good citizens," she realized the

---

[2] Whittier, *Poetical Works,* III, 162.

necessity of exhibiting slavery in its true light, of showing it "fairly, in its best and its worst phases."[3] In *Uncle Tom's Cabin* she not only brought together in a most effective way all of the important arguments against slavery which had appeared in the literature before her time, but by her skilful employment of numerous narrative devices for making her story convincing, she supplied her successors in the anti-slavery novel with the best methods of attacking slavery. Whether she was describing the comforts and pleasures of slave life, such as were made possible by the generosity of a Mrs. Shelby and a St. Clare, or the worst side of that life, as exemplified in Haley, Legree, and the other villainous characters, her argument never lost its forcefulness. Slavery in no form, she contended, was justifiable. There were ten chances of a slave's finding an abusive and tyrannical master, to one of his finding a considerate and kind one;[4] and even when he chanced to be sold to a kind master, either the loss of the master's fortune, as in the case of Mr. Shelby, or his death, as in that of St. Clare, usually rendered the slave's condition even more wretched than it could have been had he never enjoyed kindly treatment. The action of the Shelbys in disposing of Tom was intended to show that the most humane and generous slaveholders were powerless to protect their favorite slave when economic pressure was brought upon them.

Numerous instances were cited in this novel of the detrimental effect of slavery from a moral and religious point of view. When Mr. Shelby reported that Tom and Eliza's boy were to be sold,

"Mrs. Shelby stood like one stricken. Finally, turning to her toilet, she rested her face in her hands, and gave a sort of groan.
" 'This is God's curse on slavery—a bitter, bitter, most accursed thing—a curse to the master and a curse to the slave! I was a fool to think I could make anything good out of such a deadly evil. It is a sin to hold a slave under laws like ours—I always thought so when I was a girl—I thought so still more after I joined the church; but I thought I could gild it over—I thought by kindness, and care,

[3] Stowe, *Uncle Tom's Cabin* (ed. 1852), II, 314.
[4] *Ibid.*, 144.

and instruction, I could make the condition of mine better than freedom—fool that I was!' "[5]

In a conversation with Miss Ophelia, St. Clare contended that slavery was more detrimental morally to the master than to the slave:

"It takes no spectacles to see that a great class of vicious, improvident, degraded people among us, are an evil to us, as well as to themselves. . . . . They are in our houses, they are the associates of our children, and they form their minds faster than we can; for they are a race that children always will cling to and assimilate with. If Eva, now, was not more angel than ordinary, she would be ruined. We might as well allow the small-pox to run among them, and think our children would not take it, as to let them be uninstructed and vicious, and think our children will not be affected by that."[6]

Topsy, before she came into direct contact with Eva; Cassy, before she freed herself from the demoralizing influence of Legree; and Legree himself were but a few of the many products of the slave system. After the death of Eva, St. Clare reflected upon the sin of slavery more seriously than ever before:

"My view of Christianity is such that I think no man can consistently profess it without throwing the whole weight of his being against this monstrous system of injustice that lies at the foundation of all our society, and, if need be, sacrificing himself in the battle. That is, I mean that *I* could not be a Christian otherwise, though I have certainly had intercourse with a great many enlightened and Christian people who did no such thing; and I confess that the apathy of religious people on this subject, their want of perception of wrong that filled me with horror, have engendered in me more skepticism than any other thing."[7]

When published in book form *Uncle Tom's Cabin* was an immediate popular success.[8] On the day of its publication three thousand copies were sold, and, within one year, more than three hundred thousand were sold in this country alone.

[5] *Ibid.*, I, 57-58.

[6] *Ibid.*, II, 24.

[7] *Ibid.*, 137.

[8] For an account of the popularity of the work in this country and abroad see James Ford Rhodes, *History of the United States*, I, 278-285, and Florine Thayer McCray, *The Life-Work of the Author of Uncle Tom's Cabin*, pp. 105-123.

In commenting upon the influence of this novel, Mr. Edward Channing said:

"*Uncle Tom's Cabin* did more than any other one thing to arouse the fears of the Southerners and impel them to fight for independence. On the other hand, the Northern boys who read it in the fifties were among those who voted for Abraham Lincoln in 1860 and followed the flag of the Union from Bull Run to Appomattox. Its influence on the plain people of France and Great Britain was so tremendous that no man possessed of political instinct in either of those countries,—no matter what were his wishes and those of his class,—no ruler of Great Britain or of France could have recognized a Confederacy whose corner-stone rested on the mutilated body of 'Uncle Tom'."[9]

In 1852, the same year in which *Uncle Tom's Cabin* appeared in book form, G. C. Howard, manager of the Museum at Troy, New York, desirous of seeing his daughter Cordelia take the part of Eva, requested George L. Aiken to dramatize the story. Aiken complied and the play was at once a great popular success. There were several other adaptations of Mrs. Stowe's novel, including one by Mrs. Stowe herself, called *The Christian Slave* (1855), but the Aiken version was the most popular one.[10] When one considers the unprecedented popularity of the novel itself and the suitability of much of the material of the story for dramatic representation, it is not difficult to account for the great popularity of the play. Apart from the necessary changes incident to its passing from novel to play, the work, which covered six acts, was a close following of the original and exhibited practically the same anti-slavery features. The desperate struggles of Eliza and George Harris for their freedom, the cruelties of Loker, Marks, and Legree, the tragic death of Uncle Tom, as well as the more pleasant side of slavery as described at the Shelby and St. Clare homes—all were included, with the addition, for theatrical effectiveness, of a final scene in which, amid gorgeous clouds, little Eva was borne to heaven, while St. Clare and Uncle Tom looked anxiously up to her.

[9] Channing, *A History of the United States*, VI, 114-115.

[10] Among other persons who dramatized the novel shortly after its appearance were the following: Charles W. Taylor, Clifton W. Tayleure, Mrs. Anna Marble, Mark Lemon and Tom Taylor, H. J. Conway, and Henry E. Stevens.

Mrs. Stowe's own dramatic version of the story, which she published in 1855 and called *The Christian Slave,* was based upon only a portion of the novel. Although George Harris, Loker, and Marks did not appear here at all; and although the auction mart, which formed the first scene of the fifth act in the Aiken version, was omitted, nevertheless the general spirit of the original story and many other of its anti-slavery features were retained. It was written in three acts, the first two of which contained descriptions of the Shelby and St. Clare homes, and the last a description of Legree's cruelty to his slaves.

Remarkable as *Uncle Tom's Cabin* undoubtedly was, it did not complete the labors of its author for the slave; for in two other novels, *Dred* (1856) and *The Minister's Wooing* (1859), she continued her fight for his emancipation. The scene of *Dred* was laid in North Carolina, in the vicinity of the Great Dismal Swamp. Nina Gordon, the mistress of her deceased father's estate, allowed Harry, a mulatto half-brother, whose judgment and business tact qualified him admirably as her adviser and protector, to transact her business. Having discouraged two of her suitors to whom she had thoughtlessly allowed herself to become engaged, Nina discovered that Edward Clayton was the man whom she really loved, and she looked forward with delight to becoming his wife. She did not live to realize her hopes, however, for of the many who subsequently succumbed to the ravages of the cholera, she was among the first. At her death the entire property, including the slaves, passed into the hands of her brother, Tom Gordon, a villain of the worst type. Tom's cruelty forced Harry and his wife, Lisette, to seek refuge in the Great Dismal Swamp, where they were protected by Dred, a mysterious Negro and a religious fanatic who dwelt there. Tom pursued them, and during the encounter which ensued Dred was killed. The minor plot dealt with the activities of John Cripps, a worthless trader, whose neglect of his wife and children was responsible for his wife's death. The cruelty of Cripps and his second wife compelled

Old Tiff, their Negro servant and the only person to whom the children might look for protection, to flee with the children into the Swamp. Here they joined the other fugitives. Clayton furnished the fugitives with money and sent them to the North. Later he bought a large tract of land in Canada, moved thither his servants, and formed a township there. Through Edward Clayton the author exposed many of the injustices of slavery, particularly as they affected the slave. This was done, for example, in Clayton's defense of Milly, who had been beaten badly and shot by a man to whom she had been hired as a servant. Clayton subsequently refused to remain in the practice of law in a state in which no protection was offered the slave. Mrs. Stowe's account of the activities of Tom Gordon, John Cripps, and the other villainous characters revealed much regarding the demoralizing influence of slavery upon both the upper and the lower classes of Southern society. Her attitude toward the religion of the slaveholders and their Northern abettors was probably best expressed by Father Dickson. Addressing a group of Presbyterian ministers, for the most part from the North, he said:

"The church is becoming corrupted. Ministers are drawn into connivance with deadly sin. Children and youth are being ruined by habits of early tyranny. Our land is full of slave-prisons; and the poor trader—no man careth for his soul! Our poor whites are given up to ignorance and licentiousness; and our ministers, like our brother Bonnie, here, begin to defend this evil from the Bible. Brother Calker, here, talks of the Presbyterian Church. Alas! in her skirts is found the blood of poor innocents, and she is willing, for the sake of union, to destroy them for whom Christ died. Brethren, you know not what you do. You enjoy the blessings of living in a land uncursed by any such evils. Your churches, your schools, and all your industrial institutions, are going forward, while ours are going backward; and you do not feel it, because you do not live among us. But take care! One part of the country cannot become demoralized, without, at last, affecting the other. The sin you cherish and strengthen by your indifference, may at last come back in judgments that may visit even you. I pray God to avert it! But, as God is just, I tremble for you and for us!"[11]

[11] Stowe, *Dred*, II, 198. For another effective religious argument made during this period, see Henry Ward Beecher's "American Slavery," an address de-

Shortly after this utterance Father Dickson, by the direction of Tom Gordon, was suspended from a tree in the presence of his wife and children and whipped severely until rescued by Edward Clayton.

In John Brougham's dramatic version of *Dred*[12] (1856), even though the love story of Nina and Clayton received greater proportionate attention than it did in the novel, most of the anti-slavery features of the original story were retained. Nina and Clayton were among the fugitives who sought safety in the Swamp; and Tom Gordon, who pursued them, was killed by Dred. Mrs. Stowe's camp meeting scene, in which Dred figured so significantly and which gave her an opportunity of attacking the evils of slavery through the clergy, was mentioned in the play; but Milly, one of the best drawn of her female Negro characters, and the father and the sister of Clayton did not appear at all. Local color, however, remained, and some few characters were well drawn, notably Old Tiff, who lost none of his pride and honesty.

Mrs. Stowe did not write *The Minister's Wooing* solely to attack slavery; yet through her leading character, Dr. Hopkins, she expressed very strong sentiment against it on religious grounds. Dr. Hopkins became convinced as he reflected upon the evils of the slave system, that he ought to express publicly his condemnation of slavery. In a conversa-

---

livered in New York on May 6, 1851, before the American and Foreign Anti-Slavery Society. Here he answered the familiar argument of pro-slavery writers that the Bible sanctioned slavery, by showing that slavery among the Hebrews was very different from American slavery. The bond-slaves of the Hebrews could be made only among the heathen; no one could be made a slave from among them until he had been introduced into the privileges of the church; and the master was obliged to give them a religious education. Then there were only five books; and in these every slave had to be educated. If the same regulation should be carried out in America, it would require the Southern slave-owner to send his slave to the academy and then to college. Again, among the Hebrews, if a slave was wronged or abused, he could go into a court and get speedy and sure redress. "Ah!" said he, "if you will only bring American slavery on the platform of Hebrew slavery—if you will give the slave the Bible, and send him to school, and open the doors of the court to him, then we will let it alone—it will take care of itself." See Beecher, *Patriotic Addresses*, p. 184.

[12] C. W. Taylor and H. J. Conway also wrote dramatic versions of this story.

tion with Mrs. Scudder he remarked that the enslaving of
Africans was a disgrace to the Protestant religion, and that
he could not look upon slaves without feeling as if they were
asking him what he, a Christian minister, was doing that he
did not come to their aid.[13]   In speaking upon the subject of
slavery with Simeon Brown, a wealthy slaveholder and a
member of his congregation who refused to be converted to
the cause of abolition, he made the following query:

"Did it ever occur to you, my friend, that the enslaving of the
African race is a clear violation of the great law which commands
us to love our neighbor as ourselves,—and a dishonor upon the
Christian religion, more particularly in us Americans, whom the
Lord hath so marvelously protected in our recent struggle for our
own liberty?"[14]

These sentiments were even more vigorously expressed
shortly after in a sermon before his congregation. Simeon
Brown severed his connection with the Doctor's church, but
the Doctor to the end of his life, said the author, "was the
same steady, undiscouraged worker, the same calm witness
against popular sins and proclaimer of unpopular truths,
ever saying and doing what he saw to be eternally right, without the slightest consultation with worldly expediency or
earthly gain."[15]

These novels by Harriet Beecher Stowe, particularly
Uncle Tom's Cabin, exerted a tremendous influence upon the
minor anti-slavery writers of the period, most of whose
novels were built upon the same general plan as hers and contained almost the same subject-matter. The separation of
husbands from their wives and parents from their children,
sometimes because of the financial ruin of the master, but
more often for less justifiable reasons; the cruelties of overseers; the hair-breadth escapes of fugitives from their
wicked pursuers; the insincerity of pro-slavery clergymen;
the demoralizing influence of the slave system as a whole
upon the white people of the South, and so forth, were all

[13] Stowe, *The Minister's Wooing,* p. 144.
[14] *Ibid.,* pp. 158-159.
[15] *Ibid.,* p. 570.

repeated in these imitations.[16] In *Cousin Franck's House-hold* (1853), Emily Clemens Pearson, like the author of *Uncle Tom's Cabin,* condemned the practice among masters of selling certain members of a slave family and retaining others, and emphasized the immoral effect of slavery upon the master and the slave. Because Mrs. Hartley could not endure in her home the presence of certain of her slaves of whom her husband was the father, she compelled Mr. Hartley to dispose of them. "His beautiful wife," said the author, "could not endure the sight of them, because . . . . they so much resembled him; and she was always begging him to sell them, or send them off to his Alabama plantation.["][17] Although these slaves, through their own ingenuity, eventually secured their freedom, Mr. Hartley's selling them resulted in the tragic death, through grief and insanity, of their slave mother. The whole of Virginia society, the author contended, was degenerating because of slavery. "Virginians," said one of the characters, "have genius enough perhaps, but they are too lazy to exercise it." "If there is no motive for exertion," said another, "what can result but mental barrenness and moral sterility; in a word, social retrograde?"[18] William Wells Brown, a Negro author, published

[16] Two novels by minor writers of the period, *Jamie Parker, the Fugitive* (1851), by Emily Catherine Pierson, and *Thrice Through the Furnace* (1852), by Sophia Louise Little, contained incidents resembling certain ones in *Uncle Tom's Cabin,* but probably were not influenced by it. *Jamie Parker* had been published several months before *Uncle Tom's Cabin* was completed; and although *Thrice Through the Furnace* was published after *Uncle Tom's Cabin,* the author in her preface said that it was written before Mrs. Stowe's novel was seen by her or was published. Like *Uncle Tom's Cabin,* both of these novels were written to oppose the enforcement of the Fugitive Slave Act. In *Jamie Parker* the suffering and death of Jamie's mother through grief over her son's being falsely accused of theft and sold at auction, the death of Old Scipio, with Jamie at his side reading Scipio's favorite passage from the Scriptures, and Jamie's escape to Canada during the excitement which arose on the plantation when one of the slaves murdered the overseer, were very effectively described. *Thrice Through the Furnace* described the three crises through which three fugitives passed in their flight to Canada. They finally reached their destination through the assistance of a Quaker.

[17] Pearson, *Cousin Franck's Household*, p. 107.

[18] *Ibid.*, p. 84.

in London in 1853 an anti-slavery novel entitled *Clotel; or The President's Daughter,* in which he made considerable use of the religious argument. Here a female slave, Currer, had two daughters—Clotel and Althesa—of whom Thomas Jefferson was reported to be the father. At a slave auction the mother and daughters were separated, each being sold to different persons residing in different cities. Concerning the sale of Clotel the feeling of the author was expressed in the following lines:

> " 'O God! my every heart-string cries,
> Dost thou these scenes behold
> In this our boasted Christian land,
> And must the truth be told?
>
> " 'Blush, Christian, blush! for e'en the dark,
> Untutored heathen see
> Thy inconsistency; and lo!
> They scorn thy God, and thee!' ' "[19]

Clotel was bought by Horatio Green, of Richmond, Virginia, who became the father of her daughter Mary, but who later married a white girl and went out of Clotel's life. After serving as the slave of several different masters, Clotel, disguised as a slaveholder, escaped to Cincinnati with another slave and thence to Richmond to secure her daughter, who had become the servant of the Greens; but here she was arrested, taken to Washington, and imprisoned with a view to being sent to New Orleans. She escaped, however, and when hotly pursued committed suicide by leaping into the Potomac River. The religious argument here was presented largely through a series of attacks upon the pro-slavery sermons of a missionary, employed on the farm where Currer was a slave, to insure the obedience of the slaves. "You are servants," said he; "do, therefore, as you would wish to be done by, and you will be both good servants to your masters and good servants to God."[20] He informed them that if they should happen to receive punishment which they did not deserve, they should bear it patiently and be thankful that God was

[19] Brown, *Clotel; or The President's Daughter*, p. 64.
[20] *Ibid.*, p. 94.

punishing them in this world rather than in the next. Furthermore, they may have done something bad which was never discovered, and God, who saw everything, would not allow them to escape without punishment.[21] In a novel called *The Curse Entailed* (1857), by Harriet H. Bigelow, the financial ruin of the master was responsible for the separation of the slaves and would have led to the enslavement of two white children, Edward and Emily LeRux, whose mother had been stolen from her parents when she was a girl and sold as a slave to a planter of Louisiana, had not evidence been produced showing that the mother was white. Just before his death the father of the children described to his son the effect that slavery had had upon the morals of the nation and urged him never to submit to the lash as a slave:

"God will yet have a reckoning with this guilty nation, and right the wrongs of its millions of down-trodden victims. By the passage of the Fugitive Bill to a law, this nation has *sealed* her doom. She has administered to her own vitals the fatal poison of despotism, which now rages through all her system; and the day is not distant when American republican liberty will sleep in the grave of oblivion, or this nation be dissolved to its original individual elements. . . . .

"O Edward! I adjure thee, hate American slavery, fight it to your last breath; let not her murderous, overwhelming power strike you with fear; give her no quarter; die if you must, like a freeman, but never submit to the lash as a slave! Slavery has destroyed your father and mother; and, when I am gone, she will struggle to hold you and my noble Emily in her loathsome embrace. But there comes a soothing whisper to my soul, saying, that, as you have not partaken in her sins, God will deliver you from her plagues.''[22]

There was also in this novel a bitter attack upon pro-slavery clergymen.[23] Another novel containing scenes and incidents

[21] *Ibid.*, p. 96. Two later editions of this novel, less rare than the first or London edition, were published in Boston—one in 1864, entitled *Clotelle: A Tale of the Southern States*, and the other in 1867, entitled *Clotelle; or, The Colored Heroine*. These differed in many respects from the first edition. There was no reference in them to Thomas Jefferson; Currer became Agnes, and her daughters were Isabella and Marion. Clotelle, the heroine, was the daughter of Isabella. For the most part, Isabella's experiences were those of Clotel in the first edition and the experiences of Clotelle resembled those of Mary in the first edition. The last four chapters of the edition of 1867, dealing with the Civil War, did not appear in the first and second editions.

[22] Bigelow, *The Curse Entailed*, pp. 348-349.

[23] See pp. 271-272.

resembling certain ones in *Uncle Tom's Cabin* was *Liberty or Death; or, Heaven's Infraction of the Fugitive Slave Law* (1859), by Hattia M'Keehan.[24] It dealt with a female slave's attempt to escape across the Ohio River with her children and other fugitives. When overtaken she murdered one of her children and would have murdered the others, but was prevented from doing so by her pursuers. Guilty of two charges—violation of the Fugitive Slave Law and the murder of her daughter—she was remanded to slavery in Kentucky on the first charge; and when the Ohio authorities ordered her to be brought there to answer to the second, she was sold by her mistress, Mrs. Nero, into the far South, Louisiana. The author was very severe on pro-slavery clergymen. One of the characters, Mr. Nero, said:

"I scorn the servility of slavery pulpits, the impiety and duplicity of the clergy, who libel heaven and dishonor the God that made them by maintaining that slavery's a divine institution! .... Whenever pro-slavery divines make out their case, and show that the Bible sanctions the institution, then my reverence for the Supreme Being will prompt me to kick out of door that venerable book."[25]

Omitting many of the incidents commonly found in the anti-slavery novels of the period, Elizabeth D. Livermore, in *Zoë; or the Quadroon's Triumph* (1855), made effective use of the moral and religious argument by showing the harmful effect of race prejudice upon a highly sensitive but well-meaning character. Zoë, the heroine of the story and the daughter of a former slave of Santa Cruz, was sent to Denmark to be educated, but was unable to thrive under the environment she found there because of the unsympathetic and prejudiced attitude of her teacher. The attitude of the whites toward her when she returned to Santa Cruz, particularly that of the parents of her dearest friend and classmate,

[24] The same story was published at Harrisburg in 1862 and entitled *Liberty or Death! or, The Mother's Sacrifice*, by Mrs. J. P. Hardwick. This later edition, which is exceedingly rare, is in the Library of Congress. The edition of 1859, published at Cincinnati, and equally rare, is in the Harvard College Library.

[25] M'Keehan, *Liberty or Death; or, Heaven's Infraction of the Fugitive Slave Law*, p. 31.

Hilda, had an equally disastrous effect upon her sensitive mind. During her leisure moments Zoë had written her views on Negro slavery. These at her death she gave to Hilda to publish and to distribute among her oppressed people. Zoë believed that the slaveholders were in reality less fortunate than the slaves. In a conversation with Hilda she said:

"You cannot think that the unjust are ever happier than the injured, if innocent. If the slaves act as well as their circumstances will allow them, they are very near to 'Our Father,' which of itself is happiness; while the injurer, by his very injustice, shuts out God's presence from his soul, and what misery can be so great as that?"[26]

When Zoë expressed surprise that Hilda's parents should object to their being friends, Hilda replied,

"I thought you knew, dear, that there is no bottom to the iniquities and absurdities which the system of slavery has entailed upon white people of this island. One is, it has eaten up their souls, leaving them with just about as much capacity of perceiving rightly the eternal truth of things, as my great century doll with Mr. Andersen's spectacles on. . . . . I have come to the conclusion, that if some of the other races don't rise to their position and sway among the nations, the world will shrivel all up like an old, dry piece of parchment and blow away into the sea in the next hurricane."[27]

In commenting upon a conversation between Zoë's mother, Sophia, and an adulteress, the author touched upon the immoral effect of slavery upon slave women:

"Sophia's heart sank within her at the thought of the easy virtue of the women of her people, whom the taint of slavery still infected in the holiest sanctuary of married life, and blasted the hopes with which the truth of loving hearts was plighted."[28]

In two of the plays of the period, *The Escape; or, A Leap for Freedom* (1858), by William Wells Brown, who had lived in the South for eighteen years, and *Neighbor Jackwood* (1857), by J. T. Trowbridge, the same method as that used by the novelists was evident. The author of *The Escape* humorously satirized the religion and morals of certain slaveholders whom he had had an opportunity of observing while liv-

[26] Livermore, *Zoë; or The Quadroon's Triumph*, p. 69.
[27] *Ibid.*, p. 244.
[28] *Ibid.*, p. 16.

ing in the South. The play described the struggles of three slaves, Glen, his wife Melinda, and Cato, for their freedom, which they finally secured by defeating their pursuers and escaping to Canada. The author also condemned a practice which he had observed among these slaveholders of separating a slave woman from her husband and marrying her to another slave, and described a marriage ceremony, known as "jumping the broomstick," which he said had been adopted in many rural districts of the South by certain slaveholders for their slaves. According to this method a marriage between two slaves was completed when both had jumped over a broomstick and joined hands. Cato had been married in this way to the wife of another slave. The author also satirized the religion of pro-slavery clergymen whom he had known by having the Reverend Mr. Pinchen describe the manner in which he had converted a slave-trader:

"Before he got religion, he was one of the worst men to his niggers I ever saw; his heart was as hard as stone. But religion has made his heart as soft as a piece of cotton. Before I converted him, he would sell husbands from their wives, and seem to take delight in it; but now he won't sell a man from his wife, if he can get any one to buy both of them together. I tell you, sir, religion has done a wonderful work for him."[29]

Next to the dramatic versions of Harriet Beecher Stowe's novels, *Neighbor Jackwood*, a dramatic version of Trowbridge's own novel of that name, was probably the most effective criticism of the attitude of slaveholders and their Northern sympathizers toward fugitive slaves that appeared on the American stage during this period. It described the kind of treatment Neighbor Jackwood, an industrious farmer of Vermont, showed the fugitive slave Camille. When pursued by slave-hunters, Camille hid in Jackwood's haystack during a fierce storm, and was thought drowned. She was rescued by Jackwood and restored to consciousness at the home of the Rukelys, only to be caught again when Enos Crumlett, the conventional Yankee rascal so common in the American drama, reported her whereabouts to the slave-

---

[29] Brown, *The Escape; or, A Leap for Freedom*, pp. 19-20.

hunter. When she was brought to court and her identity was being sworn to by her pursuers, Hector Dunbury, a white man of Vermont whom she had met in the South and grown to love, rushed into the room and rescued her, aided by Jackwood and others, including Enos Crumlett, who had then become one of her staunchest friends. Dunbury, who had gone to New York and found her owner, secured her freedom and then became her husband. The scenes taking place in the home of the Jackwoods, together with those in which Enos Crumlett and Grandmother Rigglesty took part, were quite vividly portrayed. The Fugitive Slave Law was satirized and the evils of slavery in general were emphasized through the experiences of Camille. Unlike most slaves appearing in the American drama, Camille was represented as an intelligent, virtuous girl who would sooner die a slave than win freedom by yielding to one whom she could not love. Through Neighbor Jackwood the author satirized the religion of Mr. Rukely who, rather than oppose the Fugitive Slave Law, allowed Camille to be taken:

"I tell ye what! I respect the laws, and I don't think I'm a bad citizen, gen'ly speakin'. But, come case in hand, a human critter's of more account than all the laws in Christendom. When He was on 'arth, ... He never stopped to ax whether it was lawful to do a good deed, but went and done it."[30]

Rukely soon admitted that Jackwood was right, for said he:

"I find there is a difference between writing from the head and acting from the heart. . . . . How have we talked, and written, and fallen asleep, with our cold dead theories, like the thoughtless world around us! But there is a living soul in that room! We are responsible for her to our Divine Master! We will save her."[31]

Hector Dunbury shared Jackwood's views on the subject. In rescuing Camille he said:

"I call upon all to do the duty of men! Dogs! bloodhounds! You mocker of justice, in the form of a judge! hear me. . . . . Under an inhuman law [referring to the Fugitive Slave Law], you have hunted down a human soul! It is recorded! . . . . As ye have done it unto one of these, ye have done it unto Him!"[32]

[30] Trowbridge, *Neighbor Jackwood*, p. 53.

[31] *Ibid.*, p. 53.

[32] *Ibid.*, p. 71.

As anti-slavery propaganda this play was very significant. When first produced in March, 1857, it ran for three weeks and for several years after was popular on the Boston stage.

II. SOCIAL AND ECONOMIC ARGUMENTS

To even the casual observer during this period a striking contrast was evident between the growing industrial prosperity in the North, where a large variety of industries had been flourishing under a system of free labor, and the opposite state of affairs in the South, where undue emphasis upon the cotton industry had resulted in almost total dependence upon slave labor. By the impartial observer slave labor was considered far more expensive than free labor. Frederick Law Olmsted, whose publications based upon his extended journeys throughout the South were said to constitute "in their own way an indictment against slavery quite as forcible as that of *Uncle Tom's Cabin*,"[33] attributed to slavery the great difference between the value of property and all commercial and industrial prosperity in Virginia and in the neighboring free states. He said that a man forced to labor under the slave system was driven to "indolence, carelessness, and indifference to the results of skill, heedlessness, inconstancy of purpose, improvidence, and extravagance"; whereas precisely the opposite qualities were encouraged and inevitably developed in a man who had to make his living by his labor voluntarily directed.[34] Hinton Rowan Helper, a native of North Carolina, in 1857 cited copious statistical facts showing the extent to which the North had surpassed the South in commerce, agriculture, manufactures, arts, sciences, and literature, and contended that this great difference in prosperity was to be attributed solely to slavery.[35] On June 4, 1860, in a speech delivered in the United States Senate on the bill for the admission of Kansas to the Union

[33] Jesse Macy, *The Anti-Slavery Crusade* (ed. 1921), p. 137. These publications were *A Journey in the Seaboard Slave States* (1856), *A Journey Through Texas* (1857), and *A Journey in the Back Country* (1861).

[34] Olmsted, *A Journey in the Seaboard Slave States* (1856), pp. 147-148.

[35] Helper, *The Impending Crisis of the South: How to Meet It*.

as a free state, Senator Charles Sumner used a forceful economic argument against slavery by showing that even though the South had the advantage over the North in size, happiness of climate, natural highways, exhaustless motive power distributed throughout its space, and in navigable rivers, nevertheless, because of slavery, it was far inferior to the North in agriculture, manufactures, commerce, growth of population, value of property, and in educational establishments.[36] Another writer contended that the amount of cotton produced by slave labor was less than one-third of what it would have been under a system of free labor, and that with the latter there would no longer be such "thriftlessness, desolation, and debasement" as then existed in the South; but that the colored man would be of increased value to the country; the poor whites of the South would have an incentive to work without their energies being paralyzed by laws framed exclusively for the benefit of the slaveholder; and a large portion of the white population of the North would migrate to the South to add to the general improvement.[37]

With these social and economic disadvantages of slavery there were frequently combined political disadvantages. Attention was called to the alarming extent to which the small slaveholding minority controlled almost every means offered the large non-slaveholding class in the South of earning a livelihood and of enjoying certain other rights.[38] It was estimated that out of nine million Southern white people in 1860, a body of not more than ten thousand families constituted the ruling South in economic, social, and political life.[39] The inevitable tendency of slavery, said James Russell Lowell, was to concentrate in the hands of a few the soil, the capital, and the power of that section of the country where it

[36] Sumner, *The Barbarism of Slavery* (ed. 1863), pp. 20-32.

[37] John S. C. Abbott, *South and North; or, Impressions Received During a Trip to Cuba and the South* (1860), pp. 329-330.

[38] For an excellent account of the cotton-planter as a power in the social, economic, and political life of the South during this period, see William E. Dodd, *The Cotton Kingdom*.

[39] A. B. Hart, *Slavery and Abolition*, p. 68.

existed, and "to reduce the non-slaveholding class to a continually lower and lower level of property, intelligence, and enterprise," with the result that their increase in numbers added much to the economical hardship of their position and nothing to their political weight in the community.[40] It mattered not how enormous the wealth might be which was centered in the hands of a few, it had no longer the conservative force or the beneficent influence which it exerted when equally distributed, but lost more of both where a system of absenteeism prevailed as largely as in the South.[40] Hinton Rowan Helper saw in slavery alone the source of all these evils:

"In our opinion, an opinion which has been formed from data obtained by assiduous researches and comparisons, ... the causes which have sunk a large majority of our people in galling poverty and ignorance, rendered a small minority conceited and tyrannical, and driven the rest away from their homes; entailed upon us a humiliating dependence on the Free States; disgraced us in the recesses of our own souls, and brought us under reproach in the eyes of all civilized and enlightened nations—may all be traced to one common source, and there find solution in the most hateful and horrible word, that was ever incorporated into the vocabulary of human economy—*Slavery!*[41]

It is impossible to estimate the far-reaching effect which arguments of this kind had upon the anti-slavery movement preceding the Civil War. Helper's book aroused considerable interest in the North and in the South. In 1857, the year in which it was published, thirteen thousand copies were put upon the market.[42] In 1860, when it was adopted by the Republicans and distributed as propaganda, it met with instant and bitter opposition from the Southerners, who were then more prosperous than they were ten years before when the statistics upon which Helper had based his argument were compiled.

[40] Lowell, "The Election in November," in *Political Essays*, pp. 32-33.

[41] Helper, *The Impending Crisis of the South: How to Meet It*, p. 25. For Helper's suggestions for a remedy see below, pp. 100-101.

[42] Edward Channing, *A History of the United States*, VI, 206.

III.   SENTIMENTAL ARGUMENTS

Between the passage of the Fugitive Slave Act of 1850 and the election of Lincoln in 1860, followed a few months later by the firing upon Fort Sumter, an enormous amount of anti-slavery literature was produced.   The moral, religious, social, and economic movement against slavery during this period was sufficient to convince thousands of Northern people, hitherto hostile or indifferent to abolition, of the injustice of slavery.   But something more was needed than mere conviction of its injustice.   The people had to be moved to action.   The sentimental arguments attempted to accomplish this result.   These were of two classes, each differing from the other in the intensity of its feeling against slaveholding.

The best examples of the first group were furnished by Walt Whitman and Dion Boucicault.   These writers showed no hostility to the slaveholder,[43] but allowed the strength of their opposition to slavery to be determined by the depth of their sympathy for the slave.   In "Walt Whitman" (1855), a poem which in 1881 appeared under the title of "Song of Myself," the poet Whitman expressed keen sympathy for the fugitive slave without attacking directly the master or suggesting any other remedy for the slave's condition than that of assisting him to escape his pursuers:

"The runaway slave came to my house and stopped outside,
I heard his motions crackling the twigs of the woodpile,
Through the swung half-door of the kitchen I saw him limpsy and weak,
And went where he sat on a log, and led him in and assured him,
And brought water, and filled a tub for his sweated body and bruised feet,

[43] In his anti-slavery poems Whitman was more severe upon Northern sympathizers with slavery than upon the slaveholders themselves.   See in his *Complete Prose Works* (ed. 1892) the following early poems: "Dough-Face Song," pp. 339-340; "Blood-Money," pp. 372-373; "Wounded in the House of Friends," pp. 373-374; and in *Leaves of Grass*, ed. Holloway, "A Boston Ballad, 1854," pp. 225-227.   See also Henry B. Binns, *A Life of Walt Whitman*, pp. 39-40.

And gave him a room that entered from my own, and gave him
　　some coarse clean clothes,
And remember perfectly well his revolving eyes and his awk-
　　wardness,
And remember putting plasters on the galls of his neck and
　　ankles;
He staid with me a week before he was recuperated and passed
　　north,
I had him sit next me at table—my fire-lock leaned in the
　　corner."[44]

Boucicault's sympathy for the slave was shown in *The Octoroon* (1859), a play based upon a novel by the British writer, Mayne Reid, called *The Quadroon; or A Lover's Adventures in Louisiana* (1856). In the novel Edward Ruth-erford, an Englishman, while being nursed back to health at the home of the Creole, Miss Eugenie Besançon, whose life he had saved in a steamboat disaster off the Louisiana coast, fell in love with Miss Besançon's quadroon slave, Aurore. Before plans could be perfected for his securing Aurore, Gayarre, the unprincipled manager of the Besançon estate, had the estate and slaves sold for debt so that he might pur-chase Aurore for himself. Rutherford and a mysterious youth named Eugene lost their last dollar at a gambling house in New Orleans, on the night before the sale, in their endeavor to win sufficient money with which to buy Aurore. Just before Aurore was sold the youth brought Rutherford three thousand dollars with which to buy her, but this was not enough, for the agent of Gayarre was able to bid higher and Aurore became the property of Gayarre. Rutherford, assisted by Eugene, stole Aurore during the night, but was pursued and caught by the friends of Gayarre. He was about to be hanged when the sheriff rescued him. At the trial Eugene produced documents, taken by Aurore from Gay-arre's desk, which showed that Aurore was free and that fifty thousand dollars in bank stock had been bequeathed to Miss Besançon by her father, to be paid to her upon the day on which she should be of age. Gayarre had stolen this from

[44] Whitman, *Leaves of Grass*, ed. Holloway, pp. 31-32. For other lines in this poem written in the same spirit, see *ibid.*, p. 56.

her. Accordingly, he was imprisoned, and Rutherford and Aurore were free to marry. The youth, Eugene, turned out to be Miss Besançon, who, from the time that she first met Rutherford, had been in love with him, and had later disguised herself as a youth to assist him in winning Aurore, in spite of her own unrequited love for him. Boucicault made several changes in this story to meet the tastes of the American theater-going public just before the Civil War. He changed the title from *The Quadroon* to *The Octoroon,* giving his heroine one-eighth instead of one-fourth of Negro blood. He gave to his hero, George Peyton, many of the characteristics of Edward Rutherford; to Jacob M'Closky many of those of Gayarre; to Zoë many of those of Aurore; and to Dora Sunnyside only a few of those of Eugenie Besançon. The other important characters of the play, such as Pete, Salem Scudder, Mrs. Peyton, Paul, and Wahnotee, the Indian, had no prototypes in the novel. Such scenes in the play as the photographing of M'Closky while he was murdering Paul, Zoë's taking poison, the burning steamer from which M'Closky escaped, and the death of Zoë did not appear in Reid's novel. M'Closky received no punishment, although his deeds were almost similar to those of Gayarre, who, in the novel, was sent to prison. When M'Closky was last seen, he was fighting with the enemy. Boucicault felt that to have the hero, a white man, and the heroine, a girl with Negro blood in her veins, marry, as they did in the novel and in his English version of the play, would have affected seriously the popularity of the play; and so, in the American version he had Zoë take poison and die unmarried. He did, however, retain many of the anti-slavery features of the original story. For instance, he gave suggestions of the general setting of the novel. The scene of both was laid in Louisiana with scenes on the Mississippi in the background; the auction scene appeared in both the novel and the play; and in both there was opposition to lynching just before the villain was exposed. The following speeches uttered by George Peyton in the second act also savored of anti-slavery sentiment:

"Zoe, listen to me, then. I shall see this estate pass from me without a sigh, for it possesses no charm for me; the wealth I covet is the love of those around me—eyes that are rich in fond looks, lips that breathe endearing words; the only estate I value is the heart of one true woman, and the slaves I'd have are her thoughts. . . . .

"Your birth—I know it. Has not my dear aunt forgotten it— she who had the most right to remember it? You are illegitimate, but love knows no prejudice."[45]

This play was an immediate popular success and for several years was favorably received in many places in the United States and abroad.

Many minor writers of this group deserve mention. In a novel entitled *The Garies and Their Friends* (1857), by Frank J. Webb, the sympathy of the reader was evoked by the hardships which the Garies experienced because of race prejudice. Mr. Garie, a white man, lived on his Georgia plantation with one of his slaves by whom he had children. They would have married, but the laws of the state forbade such a union. Mr. Garie was persuaded, however, to move to the North where his children could be educated. Here he was murdered when a pro-slavery mob attacked his house, and his wife—they were married after reaching the North —died as a result of the shock. The remainder of the story dealt with the experiences of the Garie children, together with the successes of the Negroes in the North in spite of difficulties they experienced in securing an education and employment. In Mattie Griffith's *Madge Vertner,* a novel which appeared serially in the *National Anti-Slavery Standard* between July 30, 1859, and May 5, 1860, the heroine urged many slaves to escape and at her death secured the promise of Colonel Vertner, her father, to liberate his slaves; but like many other well-meaning slaveholders, he could not command the courage to do so. Before her death Madge Vertner discovered that she was the daughter of the Colonel by a quadroon. Among the other minor writers of this group were Elizur Wright, the author of a poem entitled "The Fugitive Slave to the Christian" (1853), in which he elicited

[45] Boucicault, "The Octoroon," in *Representative American Plays,* ed. A. H. Quinn, p. 443.

sympathy for the slave by having him plead to the Christian for assistance in escaping his pursuers; J. M. Whitfield, a Negro of Buffalo, New York, whose *America and Other Poems* (1853), contained many fervent appeals in behalf of the slave;[46] Maria Lowell, whose poem entitled "The Slave Mother" (published posthumously in 1855) touchingly described a slave mother holding her child upon her knee and praying that it might not live to experience the hardships of slavery; and J. C. Swayze, the author of *Ossawattomie Brown; or, The Insurrection at Harper's Ferry* (1859), a play showing sympathy for the slave indirectly through the author's treatment of John Brown.

The authors of the second group of sentimental arguments were more vehement in their attack upon slavery than those already discussed. Their object was to expose the cruelties of masters and overseers and to emphasize any other evils incident to the system by so cleverly playing upon the emotions of the reader as to create the greatest amount of sentiment possible against slavery. Their utterances, most of which were prompted by the attempt on the part of many Northerners to enforce the Fugitive Slave Act, must have gone far toward preparing the conscience of the North for the rupture which came in 1861.

The best examples of this kind of appeal were furnished by Harriet Beecher Stowe. The slaves in *Uncle Tom's Cabin* and *Dred* passed through numerous crises in the handling of which she utilized every opportunity to secure the desired emotional effect. Two quotations from *Uncle Tom's Cabin* will be sufficient to illustrate her method. While Tom was spending his last few moments with his grieved family before Haley came to take him away, Mrs. Shelby came in to speak with him:

" 'Tom,' she said, 'I come to——' and stopping suddenly, and regarding the silent group, she sat down in the chair, and, covering her face with her handkerchief, began to sob.

[46] See, for example, his "America," "How Long," "Stanzas for the First of August," and "Prayer of the Oppressed."

" 'Lor, now, missis, don't—don't!' said Aunt Chloe, bursting out in her turn; and for a few moments they all wept in company. And in those tears they all shed together, the high and the lowly, melted away all the heart-burnings and anger of the oppressed. O, ye who visit the distressed, do ye know that everything your money can buy given with a cold, averted face, is not worth one honest tear shed in real sympathy?''[47]

A more pathetic scene occurred on the boat which bore Tom and other slaves to the South. Among Haley's slaves on this journey were a woman and her child whom Haley had bought with a view to selling on some plantation in the far South. The woman was made to believe, however, that she was to be hired out as a cook in Louisville, where she would be with her husband. Before the boat reached Louisville Haley sold the child for forty-five dollars and later stole it from its mother as she was surveying the crowd on the wharf at Louisville, hoping to see her husband. When she returned to her seat where a moment before she had left the child, the child was gone. "Her slack hands," said the author, "fell lifeless by her side. Her eyes looked straight forward, but she saw nothing. All the noise and hum of the boat, the groaning of the machinery, mingled dreamily to her bewildered ear; and the poor, dumb-stricken heart had neither cry nor tear to show for its utter misery.''[48] Tom, who saw the entire transaction, tried to console the mother:

"Honestly, and with tears running down his own cheeks, he spoke of a heart of love in the skies, of a pitying Jesus, and an eternal home; but the ear was deaf with anguish, and the palsied heart could not feel.

"Night came on—night, calm, unmoved, and glorious, shining down with her innumerable and solemn angel eyes, twinkling, beautiful, but silent. There was no speech nor language, no pitying voice or helping hand, from that distant sky. One after another, the voices of business or pleasure died away; all on the boat were sleeping, and the ripples at the prow were plainly heard. Tom stretched himself out on a box, and there, as he lay, he heard, ever and anon, a smothered sob or cry from the prostrate creature—'O! what shall I do? O, Lord, O, good Lord, do help me!' and so ever and anon, until the murmur died away in silence.

[47] Stowe, *Uncle Tom's Cabin*, I, 145-146.
[48] *Ibid.*, 190.

the river rippled and dimpled just as brightly as if it had not closed
above it.

"Patience! patience! ye whose hearts swell indignant at wrongs
like these. Not one throb of anguish, not one tear of the oppressed,
is forgotten by the Man of Sorrows, the Lord of Glory. In his
patient, generous bosom he bears the anguish of a world. Bear
thou, like him, in patience, and labor in love; for sure as he is
God, 'the year of his redeemed *shall* come.' "[49]

As already noted, the most significant utterances against
slavery during this period were prompted by the effort of
many Northerners to enforce the Fugitive Slave Act. Two
specific instances of this should be given because of the bitter
opposition that was provoked from the abolitionists. In
April, 1851, Thomas Sims, a colored man, was found in Boston, arrested on a false charge of theft, then claimed as a
fugitive slave, and carried back to Georgia. On April 9, 1852,
religious exercises were held in Boston for the purpose of
protesting against such events. Theodore Parker delivered
one of the addresses and composed an ode for the occasion.
Here he called the attention of his hearers to the "Southern
chains" that surrounded their home, and urged them, if they
did not wish to wear those chains, to protect the slave:

"Sons of men who dared be free
    For truth and right, who cross'd the sea,
Hide the trembling poor that flee
    From the land of slaves!

.   .   .   .   .   .

"By yon sea that freely waves,
By your fathers' honored graves,
Swear you never will be slaves,
    Nor steal your fellow man!

"By the heaven whose breath you draw,
By the God whose higher law
Fills the heaven of heavens with awe;
    Swear for freedom now!

---

[49] *Ibid.*, 191-192.

"Men whose hearts with pity move,
Men that trust in God above,
Who stoutly follow Christ in love,
Save your brother men!"[50]

Three days later Wendell Phillips, in an address entitled "Sims Anniversary," advised the slave to flee if he got a chance; and if it should be impossible to do this, to "arm himself, and by resistance secure in the Free States a trial for homicide,"—trusting that no jury would be able "so far to crush the instincts of humanity as not to hold him justified."[51] In the same address he expressed the belief that force only would be adequate to accomplish the downfall of slavery; and that if he lived until the day of the conflict, he would say to every slave, "Strike now for Freedom";[52] for he believed that no civil war was "any more sickening than the thought of a hundred and fifty years of slavery."[53] Then with increased warmth of feeling he elaborated upon this idea. He asked where was there a battlefield, however ghastly, that was not as "white as an angel's wing" compared with that darkness which had brooded over the South for two hundred years:

"Weigh out the fifty thousand hearts that have beaten their last pulse amid agonies of thought and suffering fancy faints to think of, and the fifty thousand mothers who, with sickening senses, watch for footsteps that are not wont to tarry long in their coming, and soon find themselves left to tread the pathway of life alone,—add all the horrors of cities sacked and lands laid waste,—that is war,—weigh it now against some young, trembling girl sent to the auction-block, some man like that taken from our court-house and carried back to Georgia; multiply this individual agony into three millions; multiply that into centuries; and that into all the relations of father and child, husband and wife; heap on all the deep moral degradation both of the oppressor and the oppressed,—and tell me if Waterloo or Thermopylae can claim one tear from the eye even of the tenderest spirit of mercy, compared with this daily system of hell amid the most civilized and Christian people on the face of the earth."[54]

[50] John Weiss, *Life and Correspondence of Theodore Parker*, II, 109.
[51] Phillips, *Speeches, Lectures, and Letters*, pp. 77-78.
[52] *Ibid.*, p. 85.
[53] *Ibid.*, p. 86.
[54] *Ibid.*, p. 86.

Frederick Douglass very probably had in mind the Sims case when, in an address delivered July 4, 1852, on the anniversary of the signing of the Declaration of Independence, he told his audience that if he had the ability and could reach the nation's ear, he would "pour out a fiery stream of biting ridicule, blasting reproach, withering sarcasm, and stern rebuke"; for it was not light that was needed, but fire. He asked his hearers if they meant to mock him by inviting him to speak on such an occasion, and informed them that to him the Fourth of July was not a day for rejoicing, but for mourning:

"What to the American slave, is your Fourth of July? I answer; a day that reveals to him, more than all other days in the year, the gross injustice and cruelty to which he is the constant victim. To him your celebration is a sham; your boasted liberty, an unholy license; your national greatness, swelling vanity; your sounds of rejoicing are empty and heartless; your denunciations of tyrants, brass-fronted impudence; your shouts of liberty and equality, hollow mockery; your prayers and hymns, your sermons and thanksgivings, with all your religious parade, and solemnity, are, to him, mere bombast, fraud, deception, impiety, and hypocrisy—a thin veil to cover up crimes which would disgrace a nation of savages. There is not a nation on the earth guilty of practices, more shocking and bloody, than are the people of these United States, at this very hour."[55]

The other case was that of Anthony Burns, a fugitive slave, who in 1854 was arrested in Boston and remanded to slavery. The event aroused so much resentment in Massachusetts that no other fugitive from labor was ever arrested on her soil.[56] Thomas Wentworth Higginson was one of the few men who, on May 26, 1854, made an attack on the Court House at Boston with the hope of rescuing Burns and received a cut on his chin which left a permanent scar.[57] Two days later he wrote from Worcester, Massachusetts, to the Reverend Samuel May, Jr.:

"I hear rumors of my arrest, but hardly expect it. If true, I

[55] Douglass, *Oration Delivered in Corinthian Hall, Rochester*, p. 20.
[56] Edward Channing, *A History of the United States*, VI, 111.
[57] M. T. Higginson, *Thomas Wentworth Higginson*, p. 144.

hope no United States Officer will be sent up, for I cannot answer for his life in the streets of Worcester.''[58]

Shortly afterwards he was arrested, but the indictment was ultimately quashed.[59]   This event also was the occasion of Walt Whitman's satire against pro-slavery Bostonians entitled ''A Boston Ballad, 1854,'' first published in 1855.[60] Henry D. Thoreau was so incensed over the treatment accorded Burns in Massachusetts that on June 16, 1854, he wrote in his Journal:

"For my part, my old and worthiest pursuits have lost I cannot say how much of their attraction, and I feel that my investment in life is worth many per cent. less since Massachusetts .... deliberately and forcibly restored an innocent man, Anthony Burns, to slavery. I dwelt before in the illusion that my life passed somewhere only between heaven and hell, but now I cannot persuade myself that I do not dwell wholly within hell.   The sight of that political organization called Massachusetts is to me morally covered with scoriae and volcanic cinders, such as Milton imagined.   If there is any hell more unprincipled than our rulers and our people, I feel curious to visit it. . . . . It is time we had done referring to our ancestors.   It is not an era of repose.   If we would save our lives, we must fight for them.''[61]

Thoreau was equally defiant in his ''Slavery in Massachusetts,'' an address delivered at the anti-slavery celebration at Framingham, July 4, 1854. Here he uttered publicly the same kind of sentiment, expressing contempt for the courts and refusing Massachusetts his allegiance. It was on this day also that William Lloyd Garrison burned before the audience, among other documents, a copy of the Fugitive Slave Law and the Constitution of the United States, which he called ''a covenant with death and an agreement with hell.''[62]

This spirit of defiance characterized also the works of

[58] *Ibid.*, p. 145.
[59] Higginson, *Cheerful Yesterdays*, p. 162.
[60] See *Leaves of Grass*, ed. Holloway, pp. 225-227.
[61] Thoreau, *Journal*, VI, 355-357. Five years later, following John Brown's capture at Harper's Ferry, Thoreau was equally severe in his criticism of certain citizens of Massachusetts because of their attitude toward Brown. See *Journal*, XII, 400 ff.
[62] W. P. and F. J. Garrison, *William Lloyd Garrison*, III, 412.

many minor sentimentalists of this group. E. P. Rogers said that if ever the slave catcher crossed his threshold, his "bleeding form" should "welter there";[63] and William Denton made a vow that no sun should pass over his head without his doing some act

> "To break the proud oppressor's yoke
> .   .   .   .   .   .
> And send Oppression to its grave."[64]

The majority of the minor writers of this group, however, achieved their effects largely through their descriptions of the cruelties suffered by the slave at the hands of unprincipled overseers and slave catchers. In some instances the slave was successful in escaping to the North,[65] but most often he met death through suicide,[66] or at the hands of his pursuers[67] or even of a parent. In a novel entitled *Chattanooga* (1858), by John Jolliffe, a beautiful slave woman, Huldah, was assisted in escaping from a cruel master by an Indian. The Indian afterwards married her and took her to Europe, where they remained four years. On their return to America they were sought by Huldah's former master. In the conflict that ensued Huldah murdered her child to prevent his being sold into slavery, and allowed herself to be seized, bound, and sold to a trader in Louisiana. Her husband and father were both killed in their effort to protect her. In Louisiana Huldah toiled incessantly, and, when very old, died in the field under the lash of the slave driver. Many scenes in the book were effective from an emotional point of view. Huldah's separation from her family early in the story when she was sold to a slave trader in Louisiana, and the scene in which she drew a dagger from her bosom, plunged it into the heart of her child, and threw upon his

[63] Rogers, *A Poem on the Fugitive Slave Law* (1855), p. 10.

[64] Denton, "On Being Asked to Take the Oath of Allegiance" (1859), in *Poems for Reformers*, p. 57.

[65] See H. L. Hosmer, *Adela, the Octoroon* (1860).

[66] See Thomas B. Thorpe, *The Master's House* (1854).

[67] See M. Roland Markham, *Alcar, the Captive Creole* (1857). In *The Yankee Slave Driver; or, The Black and White Rivals* (1860), by William W. Smith, a young master's cruelty was responsible for the death of three of his slaves.

bleeding wound the flag of her country were especially strong in the emotional element. An equally forceful description of the horrors of slavery appeared in a poem entitled ''Bury Me in a Free Land'' (1858), by Frances Ellen Watkins, a Negro poet:

> ''You may make my grave wherever you will,
> In a lowly vale or a lofty hill;
> You may make it among earth's humblest graves,
> But not in a land where men are slaves.
>
> .   .   .   .
>
> ''I could not rest if I heard the tread
> Of a coffle-gang to the shambles led,
> And the mother's shriek of wild despair
> Rise like a curse on the trembling air.
>
> ''I could not rest if I heard the lash
> Drinking her blood at each fearful gash,
> And I saw her babes torn from her breast,
> Like trembling doves from their parent nest.
>
> ''I'd shudder and start, if I heard the bay
> Of the bloodhounds seizing their human prey;
> If I heard the captive plead in vain
> As they tightened afresh his galling chain.
>
> ''If I saw young girls, from their mothers' arms
> Bartered and sold for their youthful charms,
> My eye would flash with a mournful flame,
> My death-paled cheek grow red with shame.
>
> ''I would sleep, dear friends, where bloated Might
> Can rob no man of his dearest right;
> My rest shall be calm in any grave,
> Where none calls his brother a slave.
>
> ''I ask no monument proud and high,
> To arrest the gaze of passers by;
> All that my spirit yearning craves,
> Is—bury me not in the land of slaves.''[68]

IV.   PLANS FOR THE EMANCIPATION OF THE SLAVE

During this period the majority of the advocates of both gradual and immediate emancipation favored colonizing the Negro in Africa or elsewhere. A rather elaborate plan of gradual emancipation was offered by Hinton Rowan Helper.

[68] Watkins, ''Bury Me in a Free Land,'' in the *National Anti-Slavery Standard*, December 4, 1858.

He urged that a general convention of non-slaveholders of the South be called with a view to perfecting this plan, which provided, among other things: (1) that the non-slaveholding whites of the South organize to combat slavery; (2) that they refuse to co-operate with slaveholders in politics, religion, business, and social life generally; (3) that they give no recognition to pro-slavery men except as ruffians, outlaws, and criminals; (4) that they hire no more slaves, but give the greatest possible encouragement to free white labor; (5) that a tax of sixty dollars be levied on every slaveholder for every Negro in his possession at that time [1857] or at any inter-mediate time between 1857 and July 4, 1863—such money to be used for transporting the Negroes to Africa, to Central or South America, or to a comfortable settlement within the boundaries of the United States; (6) that an additional tax of forty dollars a year be levied on every slaveholder for every Negro found in his possession after July 4, 1863; and (7) that if slavery should not be totally abolished by the year 1869, the annual tax be increased to one hundred dollars or sufficiently above that amount to prove an infallible death-blow to slavery on or before July 4, 1876.[69]

Sarah J. Hale also favored abolition, but was convinced that the condition of the slave was not such as to fit him for immediate emancipation. In *Northwood; or Life North and South* [70] (1852), her hero, Sidney Romilly, retained and edu-cated his slaves so that they might be prepared when emanci-pation should come. Romilly believed that a great future awaited the Negro in Africa:

[69] Helper, *The Impending Crisis of the South: How to Meet It*, pp. 155, 156, 178.

[70] This novel was a revision of an earlier story entitled *Northwood; A Tale of New England* (1827) in which the only reference to slavery was made by the hero, who expressed the desire that the time might come when the slaves could be emancipated without danger to themselves or to the country, but at that time he did not see how masters could do better by their slaves than treat them humanely. See *Northwood; A Tale of New England*, I, 157-158. The success of this early edition of *Northwood*, said the author, led to her being made editor of the *Ladies' Magazine*, "the first literary work exclusively devoted to women ever published in America."—S. J. Hale, *Northwood; or Life North and South*

"I am intending to help colonize Liberia. What a glorious prospect is there opened before the freed slaves from America? . . . . Millions on millions of his black brothers will bless him. And if there is a country on earth where some future hero, greater even than our Washington, may arise, it is Africa.'"[71]

Likewise in *Liberia; or Mr. Peyton's Experiment* (1853), by the same author, the hero, Charles Peyton, who had profound sympathy for the African, would not free his slaves until he was able to send them to Liberia. After long and patient observation he had become convinced that nowhere else than in Africa was the African able to attain to his fullest development. Here, unhampered by race prejudice, his former slaves began life anew and became worthy and respectful citizens. A more detailed plan of gradual abolition was presented by Elizabeth A. Roe in *Aunt Leanna, or, Early Scenes in Kentucky* (1855). She related the experiences of a New England family, the Lyons, who moved from Vermont to Kentucky and made many self-sacrificing efforts for the emancipation and improvement of the slaves. Their participation in slaveholding took the form of buying Negroes who were inhumanely treated by their masters, of later emancipating them, and of fitting them for independent living in the free states. The author herself was the youngest member of the Lyon family; and so, wrote her story not as fiction, but as a record of real events in which she herself played an important part. The cruelty of the neighboring slaveholders toward their slaves was contrasted vividly with the kindliness of the Lyons toward theirs, and considerable attention was given to a discussion of the colonization of the Negroes in Africa. The expense of sending Negroes to Africa, the author contended, was far less than that of a national war, which she said was inevitable unless some plan of colonization could be effected. Her plan called for the organization of family, neighborhood, county, state, and national colonization societies—all working together harmoniously. By such

---

(ed. 1852), p. iii. In the edition of 1852 Chapters XIV and XXXIV contained anti-slavery material which did not appear in the earlier edition.

[71] Hale, *Northwood; or Life North and South*, p. 405.

a scheme she was confident that in thirty years every Negro could be in Africa or in some other suitable place far from the whites. She thought that by moral suasion the South could be induced to cooperate with this movement, especially if compensation should be made to those Southerners who would suffer great losses by emancipation.

As would be expected, between 1850 and 1861, a great many abolitionists, influenced largely by the work of William Lloyd Garrison, continued without abatement their advocacy of immediatism. Ralph Waldo Emerson, impressed by the method that Great Britain had employed with regard to her slaves, urged, in an address at Concord on May 3, 1851, that the slaves be freed immediately and that the owners of them be compensated by the government.[72] Most of the advocates of immediate emancipation, however, so far as American literature is concerned, favored colonization after the Negroes should be freed and educated. Harriet Beecher Stowe belonged to this group. She believed that the Negro race could attain to its fullest development only in Africa. After George Harris had received a thorough education at a French university, he moved with his family to Liberia:

" 'I go to *Liberia*,' he said, 'not as to an Elysium of romance, but as to a *field of work*. I expect to work with both hands—to work *hard;* to work against all sorts of difficulties and discouragements; and to work till I die. This is what I go for; and in this I am quite sure I shall not be disappointed.' "[73]

Even Topsy later became a missionary to one of the stations in Africa, and Cassy's son, having been educated by Northern friends of the Negro, was making plans to follow with his family. Mrs. Stowe did not favor, however, an immediate

---

[72] Emerson, "The Fugitive Slave Law (1851), in *Complete Works,* XI, 208 ff. Harriet H. Bigelow, in her novel entitled *The Curse Entailed* (1857), likewise favored immediate emancipation, but she opposed the idea that the North should compromise with the South by buying its slaves and emancipating them; for to do so, she said, would serve to "fasten slavery tighter upon the nation. . . . . It would soon become an extra stimulus for them [the Southerners] to kidnap our children, that they might sell them back to us as slaves." See *The Curse Entailed*, p. 465.

[73] Stowe, *Uncle Tom's Cabin,* II, 303.

exodus of the freedmen to Africa. She thought that they should first be educated by the Americans in order to be prepared for the work awaiting them in their native land:

"To fill up Liberia with an ignorant, inexperienced, half-barbarized race, just escaped from the chains of slavery, would be only to prolong, for ages, the period of struggle and conflict which attend the inception of new enterprises. Let the church of the north receive these poor sufferers in the spirit of Christ; receive them to the educating advantages of Christian republican society and schools, until they have attained to somewhat of a moral and intellectual maturity, and then assist them in their passage to these shores, where they may put in practice the lessons they have learned in America."[74]

Henry Ward Beecher likewise favored colonizing the Negroes after they should be freed and educated:

"I am for colonization. If any one wishes to go to Africa I would give him the means of going, and for the sake of the continent of Africa, colonization is the true scheme; but if colonization is advocated for our sake, I say, Get thee behind me, Satan, thou savorest not of the things that be of God, but those that be of men. Do your duty first to the colored people here, educate them, Christianize them, and *then* colonize them."[75]

A brief survey of the material discussed in this chapter will reveal the fact that between 1850 and 1861 the abolition movement had a rapid, uninterrupted growth which must be attributed largely to the passage of the Fugitive Slave Act of 1850 and to the many attempts to enforce it. The first significant reaction to this Act came with the publication in 1851-1852 of *Uncle Tom's Cabin*. This remarkable book, which combined most of the arguments and methods of the anti-slavery writers who came before 1851-1852, and anticipated most of those of the writers who followed, presented the program of the anti-slavery movement more effectively and demanded its acceptance more powerfully than any other

[74] *Ibid.,* 318.

[75] Beecher, "American Slavery" (1851), in *Patriotic Addresses*, p. 186. For similar views, see Sidney A. Story, *Story of Republican Equality* (1856), p. 503, and H. L. Hosmer, *Adela, The Octoroon* (1860), pp. 383-386. For an opposing view, see William Wells Brown, *Clotel; or The President's Daughter,* p. 158.

single production of the period.   The spirit of defiance, which at this time characterized the actions and utterances of a large number of people, also found expression in much of the anti-slavery literature of the period and gave strong intimations of the coming conflict.   There was strong advocacy of gradual and immediate emancipation and of colonization—colonization, however, not of the free Negro, but of the *freed* Negro, who should be first educated in America and afterwards sent to Africa.

CHAPTER V

THE CIVIL WAR PERIOD (1861-1865)

During the period of the Civil War, when the problem of greatest concern to the North was that of preserving the Union, an enormous amount of patriotic literature was produced, much of which, though anti-Southern in sentiment, may not properly be termed anti-slavery. To the authors of such literature the welfare of the slave was of little concern when the very life of the nation was so dangerously near extinction. On the other hand, it must not be inferred that there was any loss of interest in the welfare of the slave on the part of the abolitionists. Throughout this period their opposition to slavery upon moral, religious, social, economic, and political grounds found fullest and most effective expression in the novel; whereas their sentimental arguments were confined chiefly to poetry.

I.   MORAL AND RELIGIOUS ARGUMENTS

The moral and religious arguments against slavery, so far as the American literature of this period is concerned, with few exceptions dealt with the effect of slavery upon the white people of the South.[1]

The morals of these people were said to be on a lower level than those of the slave.[2] Especially was this true of the poor whites, who were said to be "indolent, shiftless, and thieving," and given to "whisky-drinking, snuff-dipping, clay-eating," and many other vices. Brothers, it was said, intermarried with sisters, fathers cohabited with daughters, and husbands sold or bartered away their wives as freely as

[1] One of these exceptions was the argument in *Among the Pines* (1862), by J. R. Gilmore ("Edmund Kirke"), in which it was held that the detrimental effect of slavery upon the morals and intellect of the slave constituted the strongest argument against slavery. See *Among the Pines*, pp. 27, 32, 33.

[2] See J. T. Trowbridge, *Cudgo's Cave* (1863), p. 20, a novel in which were described some of the conflicts in East Tennessee between the secessionists and those who remained loyal to the Union.

they would their dogs, or as the planter would his slaves.[3]
Slavery had become the non-slaveholders' curse and infatua-
tion, "for it fascinated while it crushed them; and drugged
and stupified while it robbed and degraded them.'"[4] A concrete
illustration of the ill effect of slavery upon the morals of a
slave-trader was given by Stephen C. Bulfinch in *Honor; or,
The Slave-Dealer's Daughter* (1864). Here a Northern boy
intending to marry the daughter of a slave-trader, barely
escaped with his life when pro-slavery rioters gathered to
murder him because they suspected he was an abolitionist.
The slave-trader himself attempted to murder his prospec-
tive son-in-law when the latter refused a dowry of twenty
thousand dollars accompanying the girl because it had been
made by slave-trading. The author of the story expressed
the belief that slavery was consummating its work of evil by
the crimes and horrors of the Civil War, and hoped that it
would find therein its own destruction.[5] The moral evils
due to the indiscriminate mingling of the two races in the
South, it was said, would be stopped if slavery should be
abolished. Since the black man, who was inferior to the
white, did not seek the white, but the white the black, slavery,
by making possible a continual infusion of fresh white blood
into the black man's veins, kept him alive; but if the slaves
were free and no longer under the absolute control of their
masters, such immorality would no longer exist, for indiscriminate mingling between the races would cease and the
Negroes, thus unmixed, isolated, and inferior, would soon
die.[6]

Considerable emphasis was placed also upon the detrimental effect of slavery upon the religion of Southern white
people. It was said that some of them had never heard of a

[3] Edmund Kirke, *Down in Tennessee* (1864), p. 184. See also John H.
Aughey, *The Iron Furnace; or, Slavery and Secession* (1863), pp. 212-216.
This work was written after its author's temporary residence in the South, particularly in Mississippi, where, at the outbreak of the Civil War, he was engaged
in evangelistic work.

[4] Epes Sargent, *Peculiar: A Tale of the Great Transition* (1864), p. 99.

[5] Bulfinch, *Honor; or, The Slave-Dealer's Daughter*, p. 3.

[6] Edmund Kirke, *op. cit.*, p. 27.

Bible; consequently, they had very crude notions of God and religious duty. In fact, they had no religion.[7] In a novel by M. B. Smith, entitled *My Uncle's Family; or, Ten Months at the South* (1863), a New England girl, Bernice, on the death of her parents went to South Carolina to live with her uncle, Mr. Delano, who owned slaves. During her ten months' residence there she was able to reform his slaves and, with the aid of a minister from her home, to convert her uncle and his wife, causing them to liberate their slaves and to move to the North, where they employed them as servants. While in the South Mr. Delano seldom attended church because he discovered that the minister was a hypocrite. He said to Bernice:

"I can't swallow such preaching as we have here. . . . . You have been used to hearing the Gospel preached at home, but here you will meet with a lame attempt to bring up the old Jewish law and remodel it to suit our state of society. It is too hypocritical for me. When ministers become apologists for wrong, deliver me from them, I say. I am bad enough, God knows, but I have been too well brought up to listen to such doctrines with any degree of patience."[8]

The hero of Epes Sargent's *Peculiar: A Tale of the Great Transition* (1864), probably the most effective anti-slavery novel of the Civil War period, had heard preachers "stand up in their pulpits and . . . . blaspheme God by calling slavery a Divine institution. . . . . The Northern clergymen he encountered held usually South-side views of the subject, and so his prejudice against the cloth grew to be somewhat too sweeping and indiscriminate. Judged of by its relations to slavery, religion seemed to him an audacious system of impositions, raised to fortify a lie and a wrong by claiming a Divine sanction for merely human creeds and inventions.'"[9]

II. SOCIAL AND ECONOMIC ARGUMENTS

The authors of the most significant social and economic arguments against slavery that appeared in the literature of this period contended that slave labor was the chief source

---

[7] *Ibid.*, p. 186.

[8] Smith, *My Uncle's Family*, p. 69.

[9] Sargent, *op. cit.*, p. 31.

of all the social and economic evils in the South. Since the opportunities offered the laboring man were always fewer where slavery existed than elsewhere, educational facilities and living conditions generally were necessarily worse. The direct effect of slavery was not to remove the black man from competition with white labor, as some politicians had tried to persuade the people, but rather was it "to give to slaveholders the monopoly and control of the most desirable kinds of labor, and to enable them to degrade and impoverish the white laboring man."[10] The result was that the masses were living in ignorance and poverty and the rich receiving all the benefits to be derived from labor. Not one in a thousand of the poor people, it was said, could read, and not one in ten thousand could write.[11] In describing the wretched condition of education in the South, due to poverty, the author of *Down in Tennessee* had one of the poor whites say:

"Ye see we hain't no schules round yere; an' ef we hed, pore men karn't pay no fifty dollar a yar ter guv' thar childerings larnin'. Dad an' I, 'fore them dinged Fed'rate rags got so thick in the Kentry' nuver seed five dollar' from un' yar eend ter 'tother.'"[12]

Wretched living conditions generally were due to slave labor. In *Peculiar* during a conversation between two characters, Mr. Vance and Quattles, concerning the effect of slavery upon the economic status of the poor white people, Quattles explained the situation as follows:

"Wall, as I war sayin', one cuss of slavery ar', it drives the poor whites away from honest labor; makes 'em think its meansperretid ter hoe corn an' plant 'taters. An' this feelin', yer see, ar' all ter the profit uv the rich men,—the Hammonds, Rhetts, an' Draytons,— 'cause why? 'cause it leaves ter the rich all the good land, an' drives the poor whites ter pickin' up a mean livin', any way they kin, outside uv hard work! Howsomever, I didn't see this: an' so, like other mis'rable fools, I thowt I war a sort uv a 'ristocrat myself, 'cause I could put on airs afore a nigger. An' this feelin' the slave-owners try to keep in the mean whites; try to make 'em feel proud they're not niggers in a rice-swamp.'"[13]

[10] *Ibid.*, p. 96
[11] Edmund Kirke, *op. cit.*, p. 186.
[12] *Ibid.*, p. 86.
[13] Sargent, *op. cit.*, pp. 240-241.

Seeing in the abolition of slavery a cure for these evils, the author contended, through the mouth of another of his characters, that the loss which the planter would suffer from emancipation had been overestimated; that the planter's land would soon double by the act; and that the freed slaves would remain on the soil with greater incentives to labor than they had had at any time before.[14] What was first needed, however, was victory for the Union Army; and it was suggested that while the Civil War was in progress, Northern soldiers should begin an educational campaign among the Southern women by scattering Union publications broadcast over the conquered districts, and by starting a free press wherever the North should hold a foot of Southern soil; for it was believed that if the women were converted, the country would be saved.[15]

III.   POLITICAL ARGUMENTS

In the novels of this period there was also some opposition to slavery on political grounds. Attention was called to some of the disadvantages from a political point of view that the poor white people and Negroes experienced in the South as a result of slavery. It was said that the slaveholders controlled all legislative action to the detriment of the non-slaveholders, and that the abolition of slavery was necessary in order that the life of the nation might be preserved and a lasting peace insured.[16] One of the characters in Epes Sargent's *Peculiar* lamented the fact that the Negro had for so many years been denied the rights of a citizen, and asked that he be given an opportunity of proving himself worthy of all the civil rights enjoyed by others. When asked if he would also grant the black man social equality, this character replied:

"I would admit him to all the civil rights of the white. There are many men whom I am willing to acknowledge my equals, whose society I may not covet. That does not at all affect the question

[14] *Ibid.*, p. 150.
[15] Edmund Kirke, *op. cit.*, p. 194.
[16] *Ibid.*, p. 227.

of their rights. Let us give the black man a fair field. Let us not begin by declaring his inferiority in capacity, and then anxiously strive to prevent his finding a chance to prove the declaration untrue.''[17]

IV.   SENTIMENTAL ARGUMENTS

The sentimental appeals for the emancipation of the slave as found in the literature of the Civil War period may be divided into two classes: first, those which revealed little or nothing regarding contemporary events, and which might just as well have appeared during any other period of the anti-slavery movement; and second, those which reflected admirably the spirit of the time, and which were intended primarily to be an inspiration to the Union Army, in the success of which the authors of them saw the end of slavery.[18]

Of the productions of the first group, a story by Louisa M. Alcott entitled "M. L." (1863) was the best example.[19] The hero of this story, Paul Frere, was a mulatto slave, the son of a Cuban planter and a quadroon. On the death of his father, he fell into the hands of a cruel master, Maurice Lecroix, whose initials "M. L." were branded on Paul's hand. After many hardships, due in part to his attempts to escape from slavery, Paul was rescued through the aid of his sister Nathalie, who had fallen heir to her father's name and for-

[17] Sargent, op. cit., p. 149.

[18] An enormous amount of Civil War literature was anti-Southern in sentiment, but contained no reference to Negro slavery. In dealing with this literature, except in the case of productions by authors who were known to be opponents of slavery, one can never be certain whether it was prompted by the author's desire for the emancipation of the slave, as well as for the preservation of the Union, or by his desire for the preservation of the Union only. In view of this fact, only those works containing specific reference to Negro slavery, or those by writers concerning whose views on the question there can be no doubt, are included.

[19] See Appendix, p. 126 ff., for a reprint of the entire story. Another example of this group was ''The Lady and Her Slave: A Tale'' (1863), by Martha W. Cook, in which a dying slave woman related to her mistress the details of her being disgraced by her master and asked that her daughter be freed so that a similar fate might not be hers. The mistress was moved by the dying woman's plea, was converted to the cause of abolition, and resolved that all women should be freed and their spotless fame upheld. See the *Continental Monthly*, III, 330-333, March, 1863.

tune. Paul left the island, passing for a Spaniard. After
studying music in Germany, he came to America an accomplished musician; and at the opening of the story was the
teacher of Claudia, a beautiful, wealthy girl. Shortly after
they had become engaged, Paul wrote an account of his past
and brought it to Claudia's home with the intention of giving
it to her. A leaf from this memoir was picked up and read
by Jessie Snowden, Claudia's friend, who also admired
Paul. Jessie instantly made public the secret, hoping to
bring about a separation between Paul and Claudia. Despite
the harsh criticisms of her friends, her temporary ostracism,
and the pleas of Paul that she break the engagement, Claudia
kept her promise. On her face, said the author, "there
came a light more beautiful than any smile; on cheek and
forehead glowed the fervor of her generous blood; in eye and
voice spoke the courage of her steadfast heart, as she flung
down the barrier, saying only 'Mine still, mine forever,
Paul!' and with that tender welcome took the wronged man
to the shelter of her love."[20] When asked by Paul whether
she remembered the price her action might cost her, Claudia
replied:

"I do remember that I cannot pay too much for what is priceless; that when I was loveless and alone, there came a friend who
never will desert me when others fail; that from lowly places poets,
philosophers, and kings have come; and when the world sneers at
the name you give me, I can turn upon it saying with the pride
that stirs me now: 'My husband has achieved a nobler success than
men you honor, has surmounted greater obstacles, has conquered
sterner foes, and risen to be an honest man.' "[20]

In describing the expression on Paul's face after he was assured of Claudia's fidelity to him, the author said:

"As he spoke, Paul looked a happier, more *contented* slave,
than those fabulous captives the South boasts of, but finds it hard
to show."[21]

The sentimental arguments of the second group were inspired by events growing out of the Civil War. Whether
they were written to celebrate such signal victories for the

[20] Alcott, "M.L.," in the Boston *Commonwealth*, February 14, 1863.
[21] *Ibid.*, February 21, 1863.

abolitionists as the emancipation of the slaves in the District of Columbia, the issuing of Lincoln's Emancipation Proclamation, and the passage of the Thirteenth Amendment to the Constitution, or whether they were written merely to lessen the effect of some defeat the North had suffered at the hands of the Southerners, their purpose was always the same—to instill courage into the fighting forces of the North.

Most of the sentimental appeals written during the early part of the war were urgent pleas to the citizens of the North for a united stand against the enemy. After the firing upon Fort Sumter in April, 1861, the time for truce and compromise was felt to be over.

> "Sumter's flames in Southern waters
> Are the first wild beacon light
> And on Northern hills reflected
> Give the signal for the fight."[22]

In July, 1861, William Cullen Bryant inquired whether Americans, "like cravens," would stand aloof when the enemy was aiming a death blow at the heart of their country, the "marvel of the earth." He inquired also whether the founders of their nation bled in vain, or vainly planned to leave their country great and free; and promptly replied that their sleeping ashes sent up from below the "thrilling murmur, No!"[23] Two months later, after summoning men from various occupations and sections of the land and pleading with them to

> "Strike to defend the gentlest sway
> That Time in all his course has seen,"

he concluded his appeal as follows:

> "Few, few were they whose swords of old
> Won the fair land in which we dwell;
> But we are many, we who hold
> The grim resolve to guard it well.
> Strike, for that broad and goodly land,
> Blow after blow, till men shall see

[22] Charles G. Leland, "Out and Fight" (April 27, 1861), in Burton E. Stevenson, *Poems of American History*, pp. 409-410.

[23] Bryant, "Not Yet," in *Thirty Poems*, pp. 101-103.

>   That Might and Right move hand in hand,
>   And glorious must their triumph be.''[24]

James Russell Lowell asked for peace through war;[25] and Richard Henry Stoddard called upon the men of the North and West to fight for their country if they loved freedom better than slavery, for

>   ''They have torn down your banner of stars;
>   They have trampled the laws;
>   They have stifled the freedom they hate
>   For no cause!
>   Do you love it or slavery best?
>   Speak! Men of the North and West.
>
>   .   .   .   .
>
>   ''Not with words; they laugh them to scorn,
>   And tears they despise;
>   But with swords in your hands and death
>   In your eyes!
>   Strike home! leave to God all the rest;
>   Strike! Men of the North and West.''[26]

Following the emancipation of the slaves in the District of Columbia in 1862 a great many anti-slavery poems were written in celebration of the event. The presence of an auction block in the nation's capital, where men and women were sold like so many cattle, had for several years provoked very bitter resentment not only from the abolitionists, but from persons not otherwise noted for their anti-slavery sentiments. Consequently, shortly after the beginning of the war, when this practice was abandoned, there was great rejoicing. Many regarded the war as God's punishment of America for enslaving the Africans and saw in the emancipation of the slaves in the District of Columbia a beginning of the end of slavery.[27] The poet Whittier rejoiced over the

[24] Bryant, ''Our Country's Call,'' in *ibid.*, pp. 104-107.

[25] Lowell, ''The Washers of the Shroud'' (October, 1861), in *Complete Poetical Works*, ed. Scudder, p. 336.

[26] Stoddard, ''Men of the North and West'' (1861), in Burton E. Stevenson, *Poems of American History*, p. 409. See also ''A War Hymn,'' by Theodore Tilton, in *Douglass' Monthly*, November, 1862, in which the poet made a fervent plea to the Supreme Being for a Union victory.

[27] See *A Poem* (1862), by James Madison Bell, a Negro poet, who thanked

victory even though it came by a method other than that
which he had hoped for, but saw in all of it the planning of
a "wiser hand than man's":

> "Not as we hoped; but what are we?
> Above our broken dreams and plans
> God lays, with wiser hand than man's,
> The corner-stones of liberty.

> "I cavil not with Him: the voice
> That freedom's blessed gospel tells
> Is sweet to me as silver bells,
> Rejoicing! yea, I will rejoice!"[28]

The same idea was expressed in an anonymous poem entitled
"Corn is King," published in August, 1862. This poem also
served to inspire the Northern troops by calling their attention to the condition of the Southern cotton industry:[29]

> "Southward rolls the cry of gladness
> On past Washington;
> Where the bond-slave stoops no longer,
> But stands up, a Man!
> O'er battle-fields of 'Ole Virginny,'
> Floats the black man's song:
> 'Brudder, God is takin' vengeance
> For de darkeys' wrong!
> Shout, shout, for God and Freedom!
>   Sing, darkies, sing!
> Ole Massa Cotton's dead foreber;
>   Young Massa Corn am king!'

> .   .   .   .

> "Let the tidings swell o'er ocean
> To another shore,
> Till proud England pales and trembles
> Where she scoffed before!
> Ne'er again shall serpent-friendship

God that the capital of the nation was free; explained the horrors of the Civil
War as God's punishment of America for her treatment of the Africans; and
concluded with a prophecy that a glorious peace would be secured when
"Liberty" should be inscribed upon the banners of the Union.

[28] Whittier, "Astraea at the Capital" (1862), in *Poetical Works*, III, 235.

[29] The Southerners had overestimated the extent to which England was de-
pendent upon their cotton, for in 1860 they believed that it was so necessary to
her well-being that they could rely upon it as a means of bringing about a
recognition from her of the Confederacy as a separate nation. See Channing,
A History of the United States, VI, 337 ff.

Rise to hiss and sting!
Cotton leagues no more with Traitors:
Honest Corn is King!
Jubilate! God and Freedom!
Sing, Americans, sing!
Tyrant Cotton's dead forever!
Honest Corn is King."[30]

Another event that was responsible for a great many anti-slavery poems was Lincoln's issuing of the Emancipation Proclamation of January 1, 1863.[31] The anti-slavery poets rejoiced in this triumph of Freedom in the midst of war, anarchy, discord, slavery, and death, and predicted that rich harvests would be reaped as a result of the event.[32] On the same day Emerson read in Music Hall his "Boston Hymn," and in the following month published it in the *Atlantic Monthly*. In this poem God was represented as addressing the Americans in behalf of the African, and urging the North to give him "beauty for rags" and the South "honor . . . . for his shame."[33] Whittier and Holmes likewise celebrated the event. In "The Proclamation" (1863), Whittier com-

[30] "Corn is King," in the *Continental Monthly*, II, 237, August, 1862.

[31] Lincoln's Preliminary Emancipation Proclamation was issued on September 22, 1862. For an interesting controversy, regarding immediate emancipation, between Horace Greeley and President Lincoln, which preceded Lincoln's Preliminary Proclamation by a little more than a month, see Greeley's "The Prayer of Twenty Millions," in the New York *Tribune*, August 19, 1862, and Lincoln's reply written on August 22 and published in the *Tribune*, August 25, 1862. Greeley urged the necessity of strict enforcement of the emancipating provisions of the new Confiscation Act, contending that "every hour of deference to slavery was an hour of added and deepened peril to the Union." On September 24, two days after Lincoln's Preliminary Proclamation was issued, Greeley wrote in the *Tribune*: "Let the President know that everywhere throughout all the land he is hailed as Wisest and Best, and that by this great deed of enfranchisement to an oppressed people—a deed, the doing whereof was never before vouchsafed to any mortal ruler—he recreates a nation." Then he expressed the hope that the freedmen might use their freedom wisely and that wisdom might enter into the hearts of all the people.

[32] See "National Ode," in the *Continental Monthly*, III, 554-556, May, 1863, and a poem entitled "President Lincoln's Proclamation of Emancipation," in the *Liberator*, January 2, 1863.

[33] Emerson, "Boston Hymn," in *Poems*, ed. Edward W. Emerson, pp. 203-204.

manded the freedman to arise, but to spare his oppressor—
to heap "only on his head the coals of prayer":

> "Go forth like him! like him return again,
> To bless the land whereon in bitter pain
> Ye toiled at first,
> And heal with freedom what your slavery cursed."[34]

In his "Hymn, after the Emancipation Proclamation"
(1865), Holmes expressed joy over the emancipation of the
slave, asked that assistance be given against the enemy, and
that God's healing hand be then laid upon stricken America.[35]

Toward the close of the Civil War period there were
other events which inspired expressions of sympathy for the
slave. Among these were Lincoln's defeat of McClellan for
the Presidency on November 8, 1864,[36] the entrance of the
Union troops into the city of Richmond on April 3, 1865,[37]
the assassination of Lincoln,[38] and the passage of the Thir-

[34] Whittier, *Poetical Works*, p. 194.

[35] Holmes, *Complete Poetical Works*, p. 194. On January 1, 1864, at a celebration of the first anniversary of Lincoln's Emancipation Proclamation, James
Madison Bell delivered a long poem called *A Poem Entitled the Day and the
War*. He lamented the long period of enslavement of his race, but rejoiced that
with the Emancipation Proclamation he saw an end of slavery. He asked
America if she had any excuse to offer for her treatment of the African and
urged her to banish slavery from her realm forever. Next he attacked European
governments for the sympathy and material assistance which they had given
the South. Then after lauding the Negro troops for their bravery in battle, and
relating a vision of the war in which were portrayed in vivid colors the horrors
of a battle-field, he concluded by eulogizing the act of Lincoln in issuing the
Emancipation Proclamation and predicted that when posterity should enumerate
the benefactors of mankind, Lincoln's name would be first.

[36] See Christopher Pearse Cranch's poem entitled "November 8th, 1864,"
in which it was predicted that the North would be victorious in the conflict, but
that there would be no peace until slavery was destroyed.—Cranch, *The Bird
and the Bell, with Other Poems*, pp. 313-317.

[37] Three days after the Union Army entered Richmond the Reverend John
Pierpont, who was then eighty years old, and who for several years had been an
active abolitionist, celebrated the event in a poem in which he expressed gratitude
for the successes of the Union forces and the destruction of slavery, and said
that he was then ready, when called, to "depart in peace."—Pierpont, "Poem,"
in the *Liberator*, November 3, 1865.

[38] Following the death of Lincoln on April 15, 1865, such writers as Bryant,
Whitman, Holmes, Stoddard, H. T. Tuckerman, G. H. Boker, and others wrote

teenth Amendment to the Constiution of the United States. The passage of the Thirteenth Amendment abolishing slavery, the ratification of which by the requisite number of states was announced on December 18, 1865, inspired the poet Whittier's "Laus Deo" (1865). The last three stanzas of this poem may not be inappropriate as a conclusion to the last period of the abolition movement, for in them the poet spoke not only for himself, but for his many fellow-abolitionists who rejoiced with him over such a significant achievement:

"Blotted out!
All within and all about
Shall a fresher life begin;
Freer breathe the universe
As it rolls its heavy curse
On the dead and buried sin!

"It is done!
In the circuit of the sun
Shall the sound thereof go forth.
It shall bid the sad rejoice,
It shall give the dumb a voice,
It shall belt with joy the earth!

"Ring and swing,
Bells of joy! On morning's wing
Send the song of praise abroad!
With a sound of broken chains
Tell the nations that He reigns,
Who alone is Lord and God!"[39]

---

fine tributes in verse to the martyred President, in many of which expressions of sympathy for the slave were found. See Bryant's "Death of Lincoln," written in April, 1865, and published in the *Atlantic Monthly* in January, 1866, and Boker's "Abraham Lincoln," in the *Liberator*, September 22, 1865. See also Henry Ward Beecher's "Sermon on the Death of President Lincoln," delivered in Plymouth Church, Brooklyn, April 23, 1865, and published in *Patriotic Addresses*, pp. 701-712.

[39] Whittier, "Laus Deo," in *Poetical Works*, III, 256.

CHAPTER VI

CONCLUSION

The literature of America showing opposition to slavery has here been divided into five periods, each period representing a definite stage of development in the anti-slavery movement prior to 1865. The first period ended in January, 1808, when the Slave-Trade Act of 1807, which abolished the African slave-trade in theory, if not in practice, became effective; the second, in 1831, when William Lloyd Garrison published the first number of the *Liberator* and became the leading figure in the anti-slavery movement; the third, in 1850, the year of the passage of the Fugitive Slave Law, the effect of which was the conversion of thousands of people to the cause of abolition; the fourth, in 1861, when the Civil War began; and the fifth, in 1865, when it closed.

Prior to 1808 such anti-slavery sentiment as appeared in the literature of America reflected admirably the spirit of the time. It was based chiefly upon moral, religious, social, economic, and sentimental grounds and was expressed in all of the popular literary forms of the period. In the seventeenth and eighteenth centuries, when the literature itself was for the most part didactic and religious, the arguments against slavery were most often moral and religious. The Puritans and Quakers were the best representatives of this kind of opposition, though in the latter part of the period other writers made use of it to great advantage. The Puritans, being concerned primarily with the moral and religious instruction of the slave, theorized regarding his freedom, but took very few definite steps toward universal emancipation. The Quakers, on the other hand, were interested not only in the moral and religious welfare of the slave, but also in his being accorded every privilege of an American citizen; consequently, they liberated their own slaves and urged others to do likewise. From the latter part of the eighteenth century until the abolition of the slave-trade in January, 1808, much of the opposition to slavery was colored by the political philosophy of the time. The doctrine of the natural and inalienable rights of man, which was being proclaimed on every hand, was made to apply also to the slave. Opposition on social, economic, and sentimental grounds appeared also in the literature of this period. Early in the period many writers who may have had no special interest in or sympathy for the African felt that his presence in America would eventually have a detrimental effect upon the social and economic condition of the white people who lived where slavery existed; and so, opposed it. Then there were others who opposed it out of sheer sympathy for the slave and used all of the persuasive powers at their command to win over those who held opposite views. As these writers came more and more under the influence of the sentimentalism of European writers, this kind of opposition to slavery became more prevalent, and between 1770 and 1800 colored much of the anti-slavery literature of America. With the formation of anti-slavery societies in several of the states between 1775 and the close of the century, the efforts of the abolitionists were united and the production of anti-slavery literature was greatly stimulated. Up to about the last decade of the eighteenth century the chief literary forms through which anti-slavery sentiment had been expressed were poetry and the essay. At that time the novel and the drama supplemented these, giving to the abolitionists additional means with which to spread their doctrine. With few exceptions, plans for the emancipation of the slaves prior to 1808 provided for gradual emancipation. Many of these also included suggestions for colonizing free Negroes in Africa, the West Indies, or elsewhere.

In the second or transition period of the abolition movement(1808-1831) opposition to slavery, so far as American literature is concerned, was less extensive and on the whole more mild in tone than that of the first period. It was based upon moral, religious, sentimental, social, and economic grounds and appeared in all of the popular literary forms of the day. During the latter part of the period it increased in severity, reaching its height between 1829 and 1831, when William Lloyd Garrison became the leading figure in the abolition movement. Expressions of anti-slavery sentiment before 1831 were not confined to any one section of the country, but appeared in Southern as well as in Northern literature. At this time the majority of abolitionists still favored colonization and gradual emancipation, though the number of advocates of immediatism was rapidly increasing. The period was one of preparation for the long struggle which began with the publication of the first number of Garrison's *Liberator* on January 1, 1831, and continued with unrelenting severity until slavery was abolished.

The third period (1831-1850) became the first stage in the development of the new abolitionism which was begun by Garrison in 1831 and which reached its height in 1861, when the Civil War began. After 1831 very little sentiment against slavery appeared in the literature of the South. In the North, on the other hand, it steadily grew in extent and in intensity. The rapid increase in the number of anti-slavery societies systematized the work of the abolitionists and inspired the production of an enormous amount of anti-slavery literature. The bitterness already existing between the abolitionists and the slaveholders was intensified by the efforts of the abolitionists to assist fugitive slaves in escaping from their masters. The chief anti-slavery arguments, which appeared in all of the popular literary forms of the period, were moral, religious, social, economic, and sentimental. Throughout the period there were ardent advocates of immediate emancipation and bitter opponents of colonization, in which many saw an attempt on the part of slaveholders and their abettors to facilitate the holding of slaves by ridding the country of the free Negroes.

In the second stage of the new abolitionism (1850-1861), anti-slavery sentiment in the literature of America was greater and more effective than in any other period of the abolition movement. The passage of the Fugitive Slave Act on September 18, 1850, and the subsequent attempts to enforce it revealed slavery in one of its worst forms and gave rise to most of the anti-slavery literary productions of the period. Here, again, the most significant arguments were moral, religious, and sentimental; yet strong pleas for the abolition of slavery as a social and economic necessity were not lacking. Of the various literary forms through which this opposition was expressed, the novel was the most popular. Harriet Beecher Stowe's *Uncle Tom's Cabin* was the first significant reaction in literature to the attempts to enforce the Fugitive Slave Act, and furnished most of the effective methods by which subsequent writers attacked slavery. It presented the evils of slavery more effectively and called for its destruction more urgently than any other single production of the period. As a result, thousands of persons hitherto hostile or indifferent to abolition were converted to the cause. The spirit of defiance which characterized much of the anti-slavery literature of the period suggested strongly the break which was to come in 1861.

The fifth and last period of the abolition movement, as reflected in the literature of America, extended from the beginning to the end of the Civil War. In this period opposition to slavery on moral, religious, social, economic, and political grounds found fullest and most effective expression in the novel; whereas the sentimental appeals for the freedom of the slave appeared for the most part in the poetry of the period. Since most of these productions were inspired by events of the Civil War, they reflected admirably the spirit of the time and gave encouragement to the Union soldiers. Such events as the firing upon Fort Sumter, the abolition of slavery in the District of Columbia, the issuing of the Emancipation Proclamation, the death of Lincoln, and the passage of the Thirteenth Amendment to the Constitution of the United States inspired most of the anti-slavery literature of the period.

APPENDIX

THE CORRESPONDENT, NO. 8[1]

By

JOHN TRUMBULL

(From the *Connecticut Journal and New Haven Post-Boy*,
July 6, 1770)

It is strange that any persons should be so infatuated, as to deny the right of enslaving the black inhabitants of Africa. I cannot look on silently and see this inestimable privilege, which hath been handed down inviolable from our ancestors, wrenched out of our hands, by a few men of squeamish consciences, that will not allow them, or others peaceably to enjoy it. I therefore engage in the dispute and make no doubt of proving to every unprejudiced mind, that we have a natural, moral, and divine right of enslaving the Africans.

I shall pass over the arguments drawn from the gradation of things throughout the universe, and the privilege every creature naturally enjoys, of trampling upon those, who stand below him in the scale of being. For I must confess, however oddly it may sound, that after a long course of observations upon the conduct of mankind, and many nice calculations upon the magnitude and density of human nature in different latitudes, I am much in doubt, whether there be any thing in our boasted original superiority.

It is positively foretold in the scriptures, that the children of Ham, should be servants of servants to their brethren. Now if our adversaries will but allow these two points, that a prophecy concerning any thing that shall be done, may be construed into a permission for the doing of it, and that the Africans are the children of Ham, which is plain from their being servants of servants to their brethren; the controversy is brought to a point, and there needs nothing further to be said upon the subject.

Besides, was not the slave trade carried on exactly in the same manner, by Abraham and several other good patriarchs, whom we read of in ancient history? Those gentlemen will doubtless be al-

---

[1] This essay, now very rare, appeared in the *Connecticut Journal and New Haven Post-Boy* on July 6, 1770. It can be found in the Yale University Library and in the Library of Congress.

lowed to have been perfect patterns and examples. (N.B. I am not now speaking concerning the cases of divorce and polygamy.)

The whole world is the property of the righteous; consequently the Africans, being infidels and heretics, may rightly be considered as lawful plunder.

I come now to the most weighty part of the argument; and that it may be conducted with due decorum, I desire my readers to lay their hands on their hearts, and answer me to this serious question, Is not the enslaving of these people the most charitable act in the world? With no other end in view than to bring those poor creatures to Christian ground, and within hearing of the gospel, we spare no expense of time or money, we send many thousand miles across the dangerous seas, and think all our toil and pains well rewarded. We endure the greatest fatigues of body, and much unavoidable trouble of conscience, in carrying on this pious design; we deprive them of their liberty, we force them from their friends, their country and every thing dear to them in the world; despising the laws of nature, and infringing upon the rules of morality. So much are we filled with disintered [*sic*] benevolence! so far are we carried away with the noble ardor, the generous enthusiasm of Christianizing the heathen! And are they not bound by all the ties of gratitude, to devout [*sic*] their whole lives to our service, as the only reward that can be adequate to our superabundant charity?

I am sensible that some persons may doubt whether so much pains be taken in teaching them the principles of Christianity; but we are able to prove it not only by our constant assertions, that this is our sole motive, but by many instances of learned pious negroes. I myself have heard of no less than three, who know half the letters of the alphabet, and have made considerable advances in the Lord's prayer and catechism. In general, I confess they are scarcely so learned; which deficiency we do not charge to the fault of any one, but have the good nature to attribute it merely to their natural stupidity; and dulness of intellect.

But with regard to morality, I believe we may defy any people in the world to come into competition with them: There is among them no such thing as luxury, idleness, gaming, prodigality, and a thousand such like vices, which are wholly monopolized by their masters. No people are more flagrant examples of patience, for-bearance, justice and a forgiving temper of mind, &c. And none are so liberally endowed with that extensive charity, which the scriptures tell us, endureth all things.

I would just observe that there are many other nations in the world, whom we have equal right to enslave, and who stand in as much need of Christianity, as these poor Africans. Not to mention the Chinese, the Tartars, or the Laplanders, with many others, who would scarcely pay the trouble of Christianizing, I would observe that the Turks and the Papists, are very numerous in the world, and that it would go a great way towards the millennium, if we should transform them to Christians.

I propose at first, and by way of trial, in this laudable scheme, that two vessels be sent, one to Rome, and the other to Constantinople, to fetch off the Pope and the Grand Signior; I make no doubt but the public, convinced of the legality of the thing, and filled to the brim, with the charitable design of enslaving infidels, will readily engage in such an enterprise. For my part, would my circumstances permit, I would be ready to lead in the adventure and should promise myself certain success, with the assistance of a select company, of seamen concerned in the African trade. But at present, I can only shew my zeal, by promising when the affair is concluded, and the captives brought ashore, to set apart several hours in every day, when their masters can spare them, for instructing the Pope in his creed, and teaching the Grand Signior, to say his catechism.

"M. L."[1]

BY

Louisa M. Alcott

(From the Boston *Commonwealth*, January 24-February 21, 1863)

CHAPTER I

> "The sun set—but not his hope:
> Stars rose—his face was earlier up:
> He spoke, and words more soft than rain
> Brought back the Age of Gold again:
> His action won such reverence sweet,
> As hid all measure of the feat."

"Hush! let me listen."

Mrs. Snowden ceased her lively gossip, obedient to the command, and leaning her head upon her hand, Claudia sat silent.

Like a breath of purer air, the music floated through the room, bringing an exquisite delight to the gifted few, and stirring the dullest nature with a sense of something nobler than it knew. Frivolous women listened mutely, pleasure-seeking men confessed its charm, world-worn spirits lived again the better moments of their lives, and wounded hearts found in it a brief solace for the griefs so jealously concealed. At its magic touch the masks fell from many faces and a momentary softness made them fair, eye met eye with rare sincerity, false smiles faded, vapid conversation died abashed, and for a little space, Music, the divine enchantress, asserted her supremacy, wooing tenderly as any woman, ruling royally as any queen.

Like water in a desert place, Claudia's thirsty spirit drank in the silver sounds that fed her ear, and through the hush they came to her like a remembered strain. Their varying power swayed her like a wizard's wand, its subtle softness wrapped her senses in a blissful calm, its passion thrilled along her nerves like south winds full of an aroma fiery and sweet, its energy stirred her blood like

---

[1] This story was published serially in the Boston *Commonwealth* between January 24 and February 21, 1863. The numbers of the *Commonwealth* in which it appeared are in the Boston Athenaeum Library and are exceedingly rare. Miss Alcott had endeavored to have the story published as early as 1860, for in February of that year she wrote in her Journal: "Mr. —— won't have 'M.L.,' as it is antislavery and the dear South must not be offended."—
In Ednah D. Cheney, *Louisa May Alcott: Her Life, Letters and Journals*, p. 98.

martial music or heroic speech,—for this mellow voice seemed to bring her the low sigh of pines, the ardent breath of human lips, the grand anthem of the sea. It held her fast, and lifting her above the narrow bounds of time and place, blessed her with a loftier mood than she had ever known before, for midsummer night and warmth seemed born of it, and her solitary nature yearned to greet the genial influence as frost-bound grasses spring to meet the sun.

What the song was, she never heard, she never cared to know; to other ears it might be love-lay, barcarole, or miserere for the dead,—to her it was a melody devout and sweet as saintliest hymn, for it had touched the chords of that diviner self whose aspirations are the flowers of life, it had soothed the secret pain of a proud spirit, it had stirred the waters of a lonely heart, and from their depths a new born patience rose with healing on its wings.

Silent she sat, one hand above her eyes, the other lying in her lap, unmoved since with her last words it rose and fell. The singer had been forgotten in the song, but as the music with triumphant swell soared upward and grew still, the spell was broken, the tide of conversation flowed again, and with an impatient sigh, Claudia looked up and saw her happy dream depart.

"Who is this man? you told me but I did not hear."

With the eagerness of a born gossip, Mrs. Snowden whispered the tale a second time in her friend's ear.

"This man (as you would never call him had you seen him) is a Spaniard, and of noble family, I'm sure, though he denies it. He is poor, of course,—these interesting exiles always are,—he teaches music, and though an accomplished gentleman and as proud as if the 'blue blood' of all the grandees of Spain flowed in his veins, he will not own to any rank, but steadily asserts that he is 'plain Paul Frere, trying honestly to earn his bread, and nothing more.' Ah, you like that, and the very thing that disappoints me most, will make the man a hero in your eyes."

"Honesty is an heroic virtue, and I honor it wherever it is found. What further, Jessie?" and Claudia looked a shade more interested than when the chat began.

"Only that in addition to his charming voice, he is a handsome soul, beside whom our pale-faced gentlemen look boyish and insipid to a mortifying degree. Endless romances are in progress, of which he may be the hero if he will, but unfortunately for his fair pupils the fine eyes of their master seem blind to any 'tremolo movements' but those set down in the book; and he hears them warble '*O mio Fernando*' in the tenderest of spoken languages as tranquilly as if it were a nursery song He leads a solitary life, devoted to his books and art, and rarely mixes in the society of which *I* think him a great ornament. This is all I know concerning him, and if you ever care to descend from your Mont Blanc of cool indifference, I fancy this minstrel will pay you for the effort. Look! that is he, the dark man with the melancholy eyes; deign to give me your opinion of my modern 'Thaddeus.' ''

Claudia looked well, and, as she did so, vividly before her mind's eye rose a picture she had often pondered over when a child.

A painting of a tropical island, beautiful with the bloom and verdure of the South. An ardent sky, flushed with sunrise canopied the scene, palm trees lifted their crowned heads far into the fervid air, orange groves dropped dark shadows on the sward where flowers in rank luxuriance glowed like spires of flame, or shone like stars among the green. Bright-hued birds swung on vine and bough, dainty gazelles lifted their human eyes to greet the sun, and a summer sea seemed to flow low—singing to the bloomy shore. The first blush and dewiness of dawn lay over the still spot, but looking nearer, the eye saw that the palm's green crowns were rent, the vines hung torn as if by ruthless gusts, and the orange boughs were robbed of half their wealth, for fruit and flowers lay thick upon the sodden earth. Far on the horizon's edge, a thunderous cloud seemed rolling westward, and on the waves an ominous wreck swayed with the swaying of the treacherous sea.

Claudia saw a face that satisfied her eye as the voice had done her ear, and yet its comeliness was not its charm. Black locks streaked an ample forehead, black brows arched finely over southern eyes as full of softness as of fire. No color marred the pale bronze of the cheek, no beard hid the firm contour of the lips, no unmeaning smile destroyed the dignity of a thoughtful countenance, on which nature's hand had set the seal wherewith she stamps the manhood that no art can counterfeit.

But as she searched it deeper, Claudia saw upon the forehead lines that seldom come to men of thirty, in the eye the shadow of some past despair, and about the closely folded lips traces of an impetuous nature tamed by suffering and taught by time. Here, as in the picture, the tempest seemed to have gone by, but though a gracious day had come, the cloud had left a shade behind. Sweet winds came wooingly from off the shore, and the sea serenely smiled above the wreck, but a vague unrest still stirred the air, and an undertone of human woe still whispered through the surges' song.

"So Dante might have looked before his genius changed the crown of thorns into a crown of roses for the woman he loved," thought Claudia, then said aloud in answer to her friend's last words,

"Yes, I like that face, less for its beauty than its strength. I like that austere simplicity of dress, that fine unconsciousness of self, and more than all I like the courtesy with which he listens to the poorest, plainest, least attractive woman in the room. Laugh, if you will, Jessie, I respect him more for his kindness to neglected Mary Low, than if for a fairer woman he had fought as many battles as Saint George. This is true courtesy, and it is the want of this reverence for womanhood in itself, which makes many of our so-called gentlemen what they are, and robs them of one attribute of real manliness."

"Heaven defend us! here is an Alpine avalanche of praise from our Diana! Come, be made known to this Endymion before you can congeal again," cried Jessie; for Claudia's words were full of energy, and in her eye shone an interest that softened its cold brilliancy and gave her countenance the warmth which was the charm it needed most. Claudia went, and soon found herself enjoying the delights of conversation in the finer sense of that word. Paul Frere did not offer her the stale compliments men usually think it proper to bestow upon a woman, as if her mind were like a dainty purse too limited for any small coin of any worth, nor did he offer her the witty gossips current in society, which, like crisp bank bills, rustle pleasantly, and are accepted as a "counterfeit presentiment," of that silver speech, which should marry sound to sense. He gave her sterling gold, that rang true to the ear, and bore the stamp of genuine belief, for unconsciously he put himself into his words, and made them what they should be,—the interpreters of one frank nature to another.

He took the few pale phantoms custom has condemned to serve as subjects of discourse between a man and a woman in a place like that, and giving them vitality and color, they became the actors of his thought, and made a living drama of that little hour. Yet he was no scholar erudite and polished by long study or generous culture. Adversity had been his college, experience his tutor, and life the book whose lessons stern and salutary he had learned with patient pain. Real wrong and suffering and want had given him a knowledge no philosopher could teach, real danger and desolation had lifted him above the petty fears that take the heroism out of daily life, and a fiery baptism had consecrated heart and mind and soul to one great aim, beside which other men's ambitions seemed most poor. This was the secret charm he owned, this gave the simplicity that dignified his manner, the sincerity that won in his address; this proved the supremacy of character over culture, opulence and rank, and made him what he was—a man to command respect and confidence and love.

Dimly Claudia saw, and vaguely felt all this in that brief interview; but when it ended, she wished it were to come again, and felt as if she had left the glare and glitter of the stage whereon she played her part, for a moment had put off her mask to sit down in the ruddy circle of a household fire where little shadows danced upon the walls, and tender tones made common speech divine.

"It will be gone tomorrow, this pleasure beautiful and brief, and I shall fall back into my old disappointment again, as I have always done before"; she sighed within herself. Yet when she sat alone in her own home, it seemed no longer solitary, and like a happy child she lulled herself to sleep with fitful snatches of a song she had never heard but once.

CHAPTER II

Claudia stood alone in the world, a woman of strong character and independent will, gifted with beauty, opulence and position, possessing the admiration and esteem of many, the affection of a few whose love was worth desiring. All these good gifts were hers, and yet she was not satisfied. Home ties she had never known, mother-love had only blessed her long enough to make its loss most keenly felt, the sweet confidence of sisterhood had never warmed her with its innocent delights, "father" and "brother" were unknown words upon her lips, for she had never known the beauty and the strength of man's most sincere affection.

Many hands had knocked at the closed door, but knocked in vain, for the master had not come, and true to her finer instincts, Claudia would not make a worldly marriage or try to cheat her hunger into a painted feast. She would have all or nothing, and when friends urged or lovers pleaded, she answered steadily:

"I cannot act a lie, and receive where I have nothing to bestow. If I am to know the blessedness of love, it will come to me, and I can wait."

Love repaid her loyalty at last. Through the close-scented air of the conservatory where she had lived a solitary plant, there came a new influence, like a breath of ocean air, both strengthening and sweet. Then the past ceased to be a mournful memory; for over her lost hopes, the morning glories that had early died,—over her eager desires, the roses that had never bloomed—over broken friendships, the nests whence all the birds were flown—a pleasant twilight seemed to fall, and across the sombre present came the ruddy herald of a future dawn. It brought the magic moment when the flower could bloom, the master's hand whose touch unbarred the door, the charmed voice that woke the sleeping princess, and sang to her of
"That new world, which is the old".

In "plain Paul Frere," Claudia found her hero, recognized her king, although like Bruce he came in minstrel guise and accepted royally the alms bestowed.

Slowly, by rare interviews, the swift language of the eye, and music's many wiles, Paul caught deeper glimpses into Claudia's solitary life, and felt the charm of an earnest nature shining through the maidenly reserve that veiled it from his search. He sang to her, and singing, watched the still fire that kindled in her eye, the content that touched her lips with something softer than a smile, the warmth that stole so beautifully to her face, melting the pride that chilled it, banishing the weariness that saddened it, and filling it with light, and hope, and bloom, as if at his command the woman's sorrows fell away and left a happy girl again. It was a dangerous power to wield, but with the consciousness of its possession came a sentiment that curbed a strong man's love of power, and left the subject to a just man's love of right.

He denied himself the happiness of ministering to Claudia the frequent feasts she loved, for it was offering her a wine more subtle than she knew, a wine whose potency her friend already felt. He seldom sang to her alone, but conversation was a rich reward for this renunciation, for in those hours, beautiful and brief, he found an interest that "grew by what it fed on," and soon felt that it was fast becoming sweeter to receive than to bestow.

Claudia was a student of like dangerous lore, for she too scanned her new friend warily and well; often with keen perceptions divining what she dared not seek, with swift instincts feeling what she could not see. Her first judgments had been just, her first impressions never changed. For each month of increasing friendship, was one of increasing honor and esteem.

This man who earned his bread, and asked no favors where he might have demanded many, who would accept no fictitious rank, listen to no flattering romance, who bore the traces of a fateful past, yet showed no bitterness of spirit, but went his way steadfastly, living to some high end unseen by human eyes, yet all-sustaining in itself,—this man seemed to Claudia the friend she had desired, for here she found a character built up by suffering and time, an eager intellect aspiring for the true, and valiant spirit looking straight and strong into the world.

To her ear the music of his life became more beautiful than any lay he sang, and on his shield her heart inscribed the fine old lines,

"Lord of himself, though not of lands,
And having nothing, yet hath all."

CHAPTER III

One balmy night, when early flowers were blossoming in Claudia's garden, and the west wind was the almoner of their sweet charities, she sat looking with thoughtful eyes into the shadowy stillness of the hour.

Miss Blank, the mild nonentity who played propriety in Claudia's house, had been absorbed into the darkness of an inner room, where sleep might descend upon her weary eyelids without an open breach of that decorum which was the good soul's staff of life.

Paul Frere, leaning in the shadow, looked down upon the bent head whereon the May moon dropped a shining benediction; and as he looked, his countenance grew young again with hope, and fervent with a strong desire. Silence had fallen on them, for watching *her,* Paul forgot to speak, and Claudia was plucking leaf after leaf from a flower that had strayed from among the knot that graced her breast. One by one the crimson petals fluttered to the ground, and as she saw them fall a melancholy shadow swept across her face.

"What has the rose done that its life should be so short?" her friend asked as the last leaf left her hand.

As if the words recalled her to the present, Claudia looked at the dismantled stem, saying regretfully, "I forgot the flower, and now I have destroyed it with no skill to make it live again." She paused a moment, then added smiling as if at her own fancies, though the regretful cadence lingered in her voice, "This is my birth-night, and thinking of my past, the rose ceased to be a rose to me, and became a little symbol of my life. Each leaf I gathered seemed a year, and as it fell I thought how fast, how vainly, they had gone. They should have been fairer in aspirations, fuller of duties, richer in good deeds, happier in those hopes that make existence sweet, but now it is too late. Poor rose! Poor life!" and from the smiling lips there fell a sigh.

Paul took the relic of the rose, and with a gesture soft as a caress, broke from the stem a little bud just springing from its mossy sheath, saying with a glance as full of cheer as hers had been of despondency, "My friend, it never is too late. Out of the loneliest life may bloom a higher beauty than the lost rose knew. Let the first sanguine petals fall, their perfume will remain a pleasant memory when they are dead; but cherish the fairer flower that comes so late, nurture it with sunshine, baptise it with dew, and though the garden never knows it more, it may make summer in some shady spot and bless a household with its breath and bloom. I have no gift wherewith to celebrate this night, but let me give you back a happier emblem of the life to be, and with it a prophecy that when another six and twenty years are gone, no sigh will mar your smile as you look back and say, 'Fair rose! Fair life!' "

Claudia looked up with traitorous eyes, and answered softly—"I accept the prophecy, and will fulfil it, if the black frost does not fall." Then with a wistful glance and all persuasive tone, she added, "You have forgotten one gift always in your power to bestow. Give it to me to-night, and usher in my happier years with music."

There was no denial to a request like that, and with a keen sense of delight Paul obeyed, singing as he had never sung before, for heart and soul were in the act, and all benignant influences lent their aid to beautify his gift. The silence of the night received the melody, and sent it whispering back like ripples breaking on the shore; the moonbeams danced like elves upon the keys, as if endowing human touch with their magnetic power; the west wind tuned its leafy orchestra to an airy symphony, and every odorous shrub and flower paid tribute to the happy hour.

With drooping lids and lips apart, Claudia listened, till on the

surges of sweet sound her spirit floated far away into that blissful
realm where human aspirations are fulfilled, where human hearts
find their ideals, and renew again the innocent beliefs that made
their childhood green.

Silence fell suddenly, startling Claudia from her dream. For
a moment the radiance of the room grew dark before her eyes, then
a swift light dawned, and in it she beheld the countenance of her
friend transfigured by the power of that great passion which heaven
has gifted with eternal youth. For a long moment nothing stirred,
and across the little space that parted them the two regarded one
another with wordless lips, but eyes whose finer language made all
speech impertinent.

Paul bent on the woman whom he loved a look more tender than
the most impassioned prayer, more potent than the subtlest appeal,
more eloquent than the most fervent vow. He saw the maiden color
flush and fade, saw the breath quicken and the lips grow tremulous,
but the steadfast eyes never wavered, never fell, and through those
windows of the soul, her woman's heart looked out and answered
him.

There was no longer any doubt or fear or power to part them
now, and with a gesture full of something nobler than Pride, Paul
stretched his hand to Claudia, and she took it fast in both her own.

To a believer in metempsychosis it would have been an easy task
to decide the last shape Mrs. Snowden had endowed with life,
for the old fable of the "cat transformed into a woman," might
have been again suggested to a modern Aesop.

Soft of manner, smooth of tongue, stealthy of eye, this feline
lady followed out the instincts of her nature with the fidelity of
any veritable puss. With demure aspect and pleasant purrings she
secured the admiration of innocents who forgot that velvet paws
could scratch, and the friendship of comfortable souls who love
to pet and be amused. Daintily picking her way through the
troubles of this life, she slipped into cosy corners where rugs
were softest and fires warmest, gambolling delightfully while the
cream was plentiful, and the caresses graciously bestowed. Gossips
and scandal were the rats and mice she feasted on, the prey she
paraded with ill-disguised exultation when her prowlings and
pouncings had brought them to light. Many a smart robin had
been fascinated by her power, or escaping left his plumes behind;
many a meek mouse had implored mercy for its indiscretion but

found none, and many a blithe cricket's music ended when she glided through the grass. Dark holes and corners were hunted by her keen eye, the dust of forgotten rumors was disturbed by her covert tread, and secrets were hunted out with most untiring patience.

She had her enemies, what puss has not? Sundry honest mastiffs growled when she entered their domains, but scorned to molest a weaker foe; sundry pugs barked valiantly till she turned on them and with un-sheathed claws administered a swift quietus to their wrath; sundry jovial squirrels cracked their jokes and flourished defiance, but skipped nimbly from her way, and chattered on a bow she could not climb. More than one friend had found the pantry pillaged, and the milk of human kindness lapped dry by an indefatigable tongue; and yet no meeker countenance lifted its pensive eyes in church, no voice more indignantly rebuked the shortcomings of her race, and no greater martyr bewailed ingratitude when doors were shut upon her, and stern housewives shouted "scat!"

Wifehood and widowhood had only increased her love of freedom and confirmed her love of power. Claudia pitied her, and when others blamed, defended or excused, for her generous nature had no knowledge of duplicity or littleness of soul. Jessie seemed all candor, and though superficial, was full of winning ways and tender confidences that seemed sincere, and very pleasant to the other's lonely heart. So Jessie haunted her friend's house, rode triumphantly in her carriage, made a shield of her regard, and disported herself at her expense, till a stronger force appeared, and the widow's reign abruptly ended.

The May moon had shown on Claudia's betrothal, and the harvest moon would shine upon her marriage. The months passed like a happy dream, and the midsummer of her life was in its prime. The stir and tattle that went on about her was like an idle wind, for she had gone out of the common world and believed that she cared little for its censure or its praise. What mattered it that Paul was poor—was she not rich? What mattered it that she knew little of his past—had she not all the present and the future for her own? What cared she for the tongues that called him "fortune-hunter", and herself romantic? he possessed a better fortune than any she could give, and she was blessed with a romance that taught her wiser lessons than reality had ever done. So they went their way, undisturbed by any wind that blew. Paul still gave her lessons, still retained his humble home as if no change had befallen him, and Claudia with all her energies alert, bestirred herself to "set her house in order, and make ready for the bridegroom's coming." But as each night fell, patient Teacher, busy Housewife vanished, and two lovers met. The sun set on all their cares, and twilight shed a peace upon them softer than the dew, for Joy was the musician now, and Love the fairy hostess of the guests who made high festival of that still hour.

The months had dwindled to a week, and in the gloaming of a sultry day, Paul came early to his tryst. Claudia was detained by lingering guests, and with a frown at their delay, her lover paced the room until she should come. Pausing suddenly in his restless march, Paul drew a letter from his breast and read it slowly as if his thoughts had been busy with its contents. It was a letter of many pages, written in decided characters, worn as if with frequent reading, and as he turned it his face wore a look it had never shown to Claudia's eyes. With a sudden impulse he raised his right hand to the light, and scanned it with a strange scrutiny. Across the palm stretched a wide purple scar, the relic of some wound healed long ago, but not effaced by time. Claudia had once asked as she caressed it what blow had left so deep a trace, and he had answered with a sudden clenching of the hand, a sudden fire in the eye, "Claudia, it is the memorial of a victory I won ten years ago; it was a righteous battle, but its memory is bitter. Let it sleep; and believe me, it is an honest hand, or I could never look in your true face and give it you again.

She had been content, and never touched the sad past by a word, for she wholly trusted where she wholly loved.

As Paul looked thoughtfully at that right hand of his, the left dropped at his side, and from among the loosely held papers, a single sheet escaped, and fluttered noiselessly among the white folds of the draperies, that swept the floor. The stir of departing feet aroused him from his reverie; with a quick gesture he crushed the letter, and lit it at the Roman lamp that always burned for him. Slowly the fateful pages shrivelled and grew black; silently he watched them burn, and when the last flame flickered and went out, he gathered up the ashes and gave them to the keeping of the wind. Then all the shadows faded from his face, and left the old composure there.

Claudia's voice called from below, and with the ardor of a boy he sprang down to meet the welcome he was hungering for.

As the door closed behind him, from the gloom of that inner room Jessie Snowden stole out and seized her prize. Listening with sharpened sense for any coming step, she swept the page with her keen eye, gathering its meaning before a dozen lines were read. The paper rustled with the tremor of her hand, and for a moment the room spun dizzily before her as she dropped into a seat, and sat staring straight into the air with a countenance where exultation and bewilderment were strangely blended. "Poor Claudia," was the first thought that took shape in her mind, but a harder one usurped its place, an ominous glitter shone in her black eyes, as she muttered with a wicked smile, "I owe him this, and he shall have it."

An hour later Paul and Claudia sat in that same spot together, not yet content, for opposite still lounged Jessie Snowden, showing no symptoms of departure. Her cheek burned with a brilliant color, her black eyes glittered with repressed excitement and in gesture, look and tone there was a peculiar sharpness as if every sense were unwontedly alert, every nerve unwontedly high strung. She was not loquacious, but seemed waiting till speech would take effect; for all her feline instincts were awake, and she must torture a little before she dealt the blow. She knew the lovers wished her gone, yet still sat watchful and wary, till the auspicious moment came.

Paul was restless, for his southern temperament, more keenly alive to subtle influences than colder natures, vaguely warned him of the coming blow, unwillingly yielded to the baleful power it could not comprehend, unconsciously betrayed that Jessie's presence brought disquiet, and so doing placed a weapon in her hand, which she did not fail to use. Her eye was on him constantly, with a glance that stirred him like an insult, while it held him like a spell. His courtesy was sorely tried, for whether he spoke or was mute, moved about the room or sat with averted face, he felt that eye still on him, with a look of mingled hatred, pity and contempt. He confronted it and bore it down; but when he turned, it rose again and haunted him with its aggressive shine. He fixed his regard on Claudia, and so forgot for a time, but it was always there and proved itself no fancy of a tired brain.

Claudia was weary and grudged the quiet hour which always left her refreshed, when no unwelcome presence marred its charm. She was unutterably tired of Jessie, and if a wish could have secured her absence, she would have vanished with the speed of a stage sprite at the wizard's will.

"Is't the old pain, Paul? Let me play Desdemona, and bind my handkerchief about your forehead as I have done before," and Claudia's voice soothed the ear with unspoken love.

Paul had leaned his head upon his hand, but as she spoke he lifted it and answered cheerfully, "I have no pain, but something in the atmosphere oppresses me. I fancy there is thunder in the air".

"There is"—and Jessie laughed a laugh that had no mirth in it, as she sat erect with sudden interest in her voice.

Paul swept aside the curtain, and looked out; the sky was cloudless and the evening star hung luminous and large on the horizon's edge.

"Ah, you think I am a false prophet, but wait an hour then look again. *I* see a fierce storm rolling up, though the cloud is 'no bigger than a man's hand' now".

As she spoke Jessie's eye glanced across the hand Paul had extended for the fan which Claudia was offering; he did not see the look, but unfurling the daintily carved toy, answered calmly as the stirred air cooled the fever of his cheek: "I cannot doubt you, Mrs. Snowden, for you look truly sibylline tonight; but if you read the future with such a gifted eye, can you not find us a fairer future than your storm foretells?"

"Did you ever know before that there was gipsy blood in my veins, and that I possessed the gipsy's power of second sight? Shall I use it, and tell your fortune like a veritable witch? May I, Claudia?"

Jessie's friend looked at her with a touch of wonder; for the flush was deepening on her cheek, the fire kindling in her eyes, and her whole aspect seemed to stir and brighten like a snake's before it springs.

"If Paul pleases I should like to hear your 'rede,' and we will cross your palm with silver by and by. Indeed I think the inspired phrenzy is descending upon you, Jessie, for you look like an electric battery fully charged, and I dare not touch you lest I should receive a shock," Claudia answered, smiling at the sudden change.

"I *am* a battery to-night, and you *may* have your shock whenever you please. Come, Mr. Frere, your sovereign consents, come and let me try my power—if you dare."

A slight frown contracted Paul's brows, and a disdainful smile flitted across his lips; but Claudia waited and he silently obeyed.

"Not this hand, fate lies only in the *right.*"

"Jessie, take mine instead, our fortunes henceforth will be the same!" cried Claudia, with eager voice remembering the mark Paul never showed.

But Jessie only laughed the metallic laugh again, clear and sharp as the jangle of a bell; and with a gesture of something like defiance Paul stretched his right hand to her, while the disdainful smile still sat upon his lips. Jessie did not touch it, but bent and scanned it eagerly, though nothing could be seen but the wide scar across the shapely palm.

A dead silence fell upon the three. Paul stood composed and motionless, Jessie paled visibly, and the quick throb of her heart grew audible, but Claudia felt the pain of that rude scrutiny, and leaning toward them asked impatiently, "Sibyl, what do you read?"

Jessie swayed slowly backward, and looking up at the defiant face above her, answered in a whisper that cut the silence like a knife.

"I see two letters,—M. L."

Paul did not start, his countenance did not change, but the fan dropped shattered from his grasp—the only sign that he had heard. Claudia's eyes were on them, but she could not speak, and the sibilant whisper came again.

"I know it all, for *this* remained to tell the secret, and *I* am the master now. See here!" and with a peal of laughter Jessie threw the paper at his feet.

CHAPTER IV

Paul gave one glance at the crumpled sheet, then turned on her with a look that sent her trembling to the door, as a gust would sweep a thistle down before it. It was the look of a hunted creature, driven to bay; wrath, abhorrence, and despair stirred the strong man's frame, looked out at his desperate eye, strengthened his uplifted arm, and had not his opponent been a woman some swift retribution would have fallen on her, for there was murder in his fiery blood.

Claudia sprang to his side, and at the touch of those restraining hands a stern pallor settled on his countenance, a hard-won self-control quenched his passion, a bitter truth confronted his despair, and left him desolate but not degraded. His eye fixed on Jessie, and its hopelessness was more eloquent than a torrent of entreaties, its contempt more keen than the sharpest reproach.

"Go," he said with a strange hush in his voice, "I ask nothing of you, for I know you would be merciless to me; but if there be any compassion, any touch of nobleness in your nature you will spare your friend, remembering what she has been to you. Go, and mar my hard-won reputation as you will, the world's condemnation I will not accept, my judge is *here*."

"There will be no need of silence a week hence when the marriage day comes around and there is no bridegroom for the bride. I foretold the storm, and it has come; heaven help you through it, Claudia. Good night, pleasant dreams, and a fair tomorrow!"

Jessie Snowden tried to look exultant, but her white lips would not smile, and though the victory was hers she crept away like one who has suffered defeat.

Paul locked the door behind her, and turning, looked at Claudia with a world of anguish in his altered face. She moved as if to go to him, but a gesture arrested her, and uttering a broken exclamation Paul struck his scarred hand on the chimney piece with a force that left it bruised and bleeding, and dropping his hot forehead on the marble stood silent, struggling with a grief that had no solace.

Claudia paused a moment, mute and pale, watching the bowed figure and the red drops as they fell, then she went to him, and holding the wounded palm as if it were a suffering child, she laid her cheek to his, whispering tenderly: "Paul, you said this was an honest hand and I believe it still. There should not be a grain of dust between us two,—deal frankly with me now, and let me comfort you."

Paul lifted up his face wan with the tearless sorrow of a man, and gathering the beloved comforter close to his sore heart looked long into the countenance whose loving confidence had no reproach for him as yet. He held her fast for a little space, kissed her lips and forehead lingeringly, as if he took a mute farewell, then gently put her from him saying, as she sank into a seat—

"Claudia, I never meant to burden you with my unhappy past, believing that I did no wrong in burying it deep from human sight, and walking through the world as if it had never been. I see my error now, and bitterly I repent it. Put pity, prejudice, and pride away, and see me as I am. Hear and judge me, and by your judgment I will abide."

He paused, silently gathering calmness from his strength, and courage from his love; then, as if each word were wrung from him by a sharper pang than he had ever known before, he said slowly: "Claudia, those letters were once branded on my hand, they are the initials of a name—'Maurice Lecroix.' Ten years ago he was my master, I his slave."

If Paul had raised his strong right arm and struck her, the act would not have daunted her with such a pale dismay, or shocked the power more rudely from her limbs. For an instant the tall shape wavered mistily before her and her heart stood still; then she girded up her energies, for with her own suffering came the memory of his, and, true woman through it all, she only covered up her face and cried: "Go on, I can hear it, Paul!"

Solemnly and steadily, as if it were his dying shrift, Paul stood before the woman he loved and told the story of his life.

"My father—God forgive him—was a Cuban planter, my mother a beautiful Quadroon, mercifully taken early out of slavery to an eternal freedom. I never knew her but she bequeathed to me my father's love, and I possessed it till he died. For fifteen years I was a happy child, and forgot that I was a slave—light tasks, kind treatment, and slight restraints so blinded me to the real hardships of my lot. I had a sister, heiress of my father's name and fortune, and she was my playmate all those years, sharing her pleasures and her pains with me, her small store of knowledge, her girlish accomplishments as she acquired them, and—more than all—the blessing of an artless love. I was her proud protector, her willing servitor, and in those childish days we were what heaven made us, brother and sister fond and free.

I was fifteen when my father died, and the black blight fell upon me in a single night. He had often promised me my freedom—strange gift from a father to a son!—but like other duties it had been neglected till too late. Death came suddenly, and I was left a sadder orphan than poor Nathalie, for my heritage was a curse that cancelled all past love by robbing me of liberty.

"Nathalie and I were separated—she went to her guardian's protection, I to the auction block. Her last words were, 'Be kind to Paul.' They promised; but when she was gone they sold me far away from my old home, and then I learned what it was to be a slave. Ah, Claudia, you shudder when I say those words; give your abhorrence to the man who dared to love you, but bestow a little pity

on the desolate boy you never knew. I had a hard master, he a re-
bellious spirit to subdue; for I could not learn subjection, and my
young blood burned within me at an insult or a blow. My father's
kindness proved the direst misfortune that could have befallen me,
for I had been lifted up into humanity and now I was cast back
among the brutes; I had been born with a high heart and an eager
spirit, they had been cherished fifteen years, now they were to be
crushed and broken by inevitable fate.

"Year after year I struggled on, growing more desperate, and
tugging more fiercely at my chain as each went by, bringing manhood but not the right to enjoy or make it mine. I tried to escape,
but in vain, and each failure added to my despair. I tried to hear of
Nathalie, but she had learned to look on me in another light, and had
forgotten the sweet tie that bound us once. I tried to become a chattel
and be content, but my father had given me his own free instincts,
aspirations, and desires, and I could not change my nature though
I were to be a slave forever.

"Five miserable years dragged by—so short to tell of, such an
eternity to live! I was twenty, and no young man ever looked into
the world more eager to be up and doing, no young man ever saw so
black a future as that which appalled me with its doom. I would not
accept it, but made a last resolve to try once more for liberty, and if I
failed, to end the life I could no longer bear. Watchfully I waited,
warily I planned, desperately I staked my last hope—and lost it.
I was betrayed and hunted down as ruthlessly as any wolf; but I
tried to keep my vow; for as my pursuers clutched me I struck the
blow that should have ended all, and the happiest moment of my life
was that swift pang when the world passed from me with the
exultant thought, 'I am free at last!' "

Paul paused, spent and breathless with rapid speech and strong
emotion, and in the silence heard Claudia murmuring through a rain
of tears: "Oh, my love! my love! was there no friend but death?"

That low cry was a stronger cordial to Paul's spirit than the rar-
est wine grape that ever grew. He looked yearningly across the narrow space that parted them, but though his eye blessed her for her
pity, he did not pass the invisible barrier he had set up between them
till her hand should throw it down or fix it there forever.

"These are bitter things for you to hear, dear heart. God knows
they were bitter things to bear, but I am stronger for them now and
you the calmer for your tears. A little more and happier times are

coming. I could not lie, but came out of that 'valley of the shadow' a meeker soul; for though branded, buffeted, and bruised, I clung to life, blindly believing help must come, and it did. One day a shape passed before my eyes that seemed the angel of deliverance—it was Nathalie, and she was my master's guest. I gathered covertly that she was a gentle-woman, that she was mistress of her fortune now, and soon to be a happy wife; and hearing these things I determined to make one appeal to her in my great need.

"I watched her, and one blessed night, defying every penalty, and waiting till the house was still, and her light burned alone as I had seen it many times before, I climbed the balcony and stood before her saying, 'I am Paul, help me in our father's name.' She did not recognize the blithe boy in the desperate man, but I told my misery, implored compassion and relief, I looked at her with her father's face, and nature pleaded better than my prayers, for she stretched her hands to me, saying, with tears as beautiful as those now shining on your cheek, 'Who should help you if not I? Be comforted and I will atone for this great neglect and wrong. Paul, have faith in me; I shall not fail.'

"Claudia, you loved me first for my great reverence for woman-kind; this is the secret of the virtue you commend, for when I was most desolate a woman succored me. Since then, in every little maid, I see the child who loved me when a boy, in every blooming girl, the Nathalie who saved me when a man, in every woman, high or low, the semblance of my truest friend, and do them honor in my sister's name."

"Heaven crown her with a happy life!" prayed Claudia, with fervent heart, and still more steadily her lover's voice went on.

"She kept her word, and did a just deed generously, for money flowed like water till I was free, then giving me a little store for present needs, she sent me out the richest man that walked the world. I left the island and went to and fro seeking for my place upon the earth. I never told my story, never betrayed my past, I have no sign of my despised race but my Spanish hue, and taking my father's native country for my own I found no bar in swarthy skin, or the only name I had a right to bear. I seared away all traces of a master's claim, and smiled as the flame tortured me, for liberty had set her seal upon my forehead, and my flesh and blood were *mine*.

"Then I took the rights and duties of a man upon me, feeling their weight and worth, looking proudly on them as a sacred trust won by much suffering, to be used worthily and restored to their bestower richer for my stewardship. I looked about me for some work to do, for now I labored for myself, and industry was sweet. I was a stranger in a strange land, friendless and poor; but I had energy and hope, two angels walking with me night and day.

"Music had always been my passion; now I chose it as my staff of life. In hospitable Germany I made true friends who aided me, and doing any honest work by day, I gave my nights to study, trying to repair the loss of years.

"Southern trees grow rapidly, for their sap is stirred by whirlwinds and fed with ardent heats. Fast I struggled up, groping for the light that dawned more fairly as I climbed; and when ten years were gone I seemed to have been born anew. Paul the slave was dead and his grave grown green; Paul the man had no part in him beyond the mournful memory of the youth that pined and died too soon. The world had done me a great wrong, yet I asked no atonement but the liberty to prove myself a man; no favor but the right to bury my dead past and make my future what I would. Other men's ambitions were not mine, for twenty years had been taken from me and I had no time to fight for any but the highest prize. I was grateful for the boon heaven sent me, and felt that my work was to build up an honest life, to till the nature given me, and sow therein a late harvest, that my sheaf might yet be worthy the Great Reaper's hand. If there be any power in sincere desire, any solace in devout belief,— that strength, that consolation will be mine. Man's opprobrium may oppress me, woman's pity may desert me, suffering and wrong may still pursue me,—yet I am not desolate; for when all human charities have cast me off I know that a Diviner love will take me in."

To Paul's voice came the music of a fervent faith, in his eye burned the fire of a quenchless hope, and on his countenance there shone a pale serenity that touched it with the youth time cannot take away. Past and present faded from his sight, for in that moment his spirit claimed its birthright, and beyond the creature of his love, his heart beheld the aspiration of his life.

"Claudia, I never thought to know affection like your own; never thought I could deserve so great a blessing; but when it came to me in tenderest guise, pleading to be taken in, how could I bar the door to such a welcome visitant? I did not, and the strong sweet angel entered in to kindle on my lonely hearth a household fire that can never die. Heaven help me if the ministering spirit goes!"

Through all the story of his own despairs and griefs Paul had not faltered, but gone resolutely on, painting his sufferings lightly for Claudia's sake, but now when he remembered the affection she had cherished, the anguish she might feel, the confidence she might believe betrayed, a keen remorse assailed him, and his courage failed. He thought of Claudia lost, and with an exclamation of passionate regret paced the long room with restless feet—paused for a little, looking out into the magic stillness of the night, and came back calm again.

"When you first gave me the good gift you have a right to take again, I told you I was orphaned, friendless, poor; but I did not tell you why I was thus desolate, believing it was wiser to leave a bitter history untold. I thought I did no wrong, but I have learned that perfect peace is only found in perfect truth; and I accept the lesson, for I was too proud of my success, and I am cast down into the dust to climb again with steadier feet. I let you judge me as an equal, showing you my weaknesses, my wants, my passions, and beliefs, as any happier lover might have done; you found some spark of manhood there, for you loved me, and that act should have made me worthier of the gift—but it did not. Claudia, forgive me; I was weak, but I struggled to be strong; for in the blissful months that have gone by, you showed me all your heart, enriched me with your confidence, and left no sorrow of your life untold—this brave sincerity became a mute reproach to me at last, for far down in *my* heart was a secret chamber never opened to your eye, for there my lost youth lay so stark and cold I dared not show you its dead face. But as the time came nearer when you were to endow me with the name which should go hand in hand with innocence and truth, this vague remorse for a silent wrong determined me to make confession of my past. I wrote it all, believing I could never tell it, as I have done to-night, learning that love can cast out fear. I wrote it and brought it many times, but never gave it, for O, Claudia! O, my heart! I loved you more than honor, and I could not give you up!"

From sleeping garden and still night a breath of air sighed through the room, as mournful and as sweet as those impassioned words, but Claudia never lifted up her hidden face, or stirred to answer it, for she was listening to a more divine appeal, and taking counsel in the silence of her heart.

Paul watched her, and the shadow of a great fear fell upon his face.

"I brought this confession here to-night, resolved to give it and be satisfied; but you did not come to meet me, and while I waited my love tempted me; the strong moment passed, and I burned it, yielding the nobler purpose for the dearer peace. This single page, how dropped I cannot tell, betrayed me to that—woman, and her malice forced on me the part I was not brave enough to play alone.

"Now, Claudia, all is told. Now, seeing what I have been, knowing what I desired to be, remembering mercifully what I am, try my crime and adjudge my punishment."

There was no need of that appeal, for judgment had been given long before the prayer came. Pride, and fear, and shame had dropped away, leaving the purer passion free; now justice and mercy took love by the hand and led it home. On Claudia's face there came a light more beautiful than any smile; on cheek and forehead glowed the fervor of her generous blood, in eye and voice spoke the courage of her steadfast heart, as she flung down the barrier, saying only: "Mine still, mine forever, Paul!" and with that tender welcome took the wronged man to the shelter of her love.

Tears hot and heavy as a summer rain baptised the new born peace and words of broken gratitude sang its lullaby, as that strong nature cradled it with blessings and with prayers. Paul was the weaker now, and Claudia learned the greatness of past fear by the vehemence of present joy, as they stood together tasting the sweetness of a moment that enriched their lives.

"Love, do you remember what this gift may cost? Do you remember what I am henceforth to other eyes? Can you bear to see familiar faces growing strange to you, to meet looks that wound you with their pity, to hear words that sting you with their truth, and find a shadow falling on your life from me?"

As he spoke, Paul lifted up that face, "clear-shining after rain," but it did not alter, did not lose its full content, as Claudia replied with fervent voice: "I do remember that I cannot pay too much for what is priceless; that when I was loveless and alone, there came a friend who never will desert me when all others fail; that from lowly places poets, philosophers, and kings have come; and when the world sneers at the name you give me, I can turn upon it saying with the pride that stirs me now: 'My husband has achieved a nobler success than men you honor, has surmounted greater obstacles, has conquered sterner foes, and risen to be an honest man.' "

Paul proved that he was one by still arming her against himself, still warning her of the cruel prejudices which he had such sad cause to know and fear.

"Your generous nature blinds you to the trials I foresee, the disappointments I foretell. In your world there will be no place for me, when this is known, and I cannot ask you to come down from your high place to sit beside an outcast's fire. I have not lost your love,—that was the blow I feared; and still possessing it I can relinquish much, and yield the new title I was soon to know, if I may keep the dear old one of 'friend.' It is no longer in our power to keep this secret unknown, and strengthen our affection by it, as I once hoped. Think of this, Claudia, in a calmer mood, weigh well the present and the future cost, for you have the power to make or mar your happiness.

"No loss of yours must be my gain, and I had rather never look into this face again than live to see it saddened by a vain regret for any act I might have saved you from by timely pain."

"I will consider, I will prove myself before I take your peace into my hands; but, Paul, I know the answer that will come to all my doubts, I know I shall not change."

Claudia spoke steadily, for she knew herself; and when at length her lover went, her last words were, "Believe in me, I shall not change."

Slowly the clear flame of the lamp grew dim and died, softly Night sang her cradle hymn to hush the weary world, and solemnly the silence deepened as the hours went by, but Claudia with wakeful eyes trod to and fro, or sat an image of mute thought. She was not alone, for good and evil spirits compassed her about, making that still room the battle-field of a viewless conflict between man's law, and woman's love. All the worldy wisdom time had taught, now warned her of the worldly losses she might yet sustain, all the prejudices born of her position and strengthened by her education now assailed her with covert skill, all the pride grown with her growth now tempted her to forget the lover in the slave, and fear threatened her with public opinion, that grim ghost that haunts the wisest and the best. But high above the voice of pride, the sigh of fear, and the echo of "the world's dread laugh," still rose the whisper of her heart, undaunted, undismayed, and cried to her,—

"I was cold, and he cherished me beside his fire; hungry, and he gave me food; a stranger, and he took me in."

Slowly the moon climbed the zenith and dropped into the West, slowly the stars paled one by one, and the gray sky kindled ruddily as dawn came smiling from the hills. Slowly the pale shadow of all worldliness passed from Claudia's mind, and left it ready for the sun, slowly the spectral doubts, regrets and fears vanished one by one, and through the twilight of that brief eclipse arose the morning of a fairer day.

As young knights watched their arms of old in chapels haunted by the memory of warrior or saint, and came forth eager for heroic deeds, so Claudia in the early dawn braced on the armor consecrated by a night of prayerful vigil, and with valiant soul addressed herself to the duty which would bring her life's defeat or victory.

Paul found another Claudia than the one he left; for a woman steadfast and strong turned to him a countenance as full of courage as of cheer, when standing there again he looked deep into her eyes and offered her his hand as he had done on that betrothal night. Now, as then, she took it, and in a moment gave a sweet significance to those characters which were the only vestiges of his wrong, for bending she touched the scarred palm with her lips, and whispered tenderly, "My love, there is no anguish in that brand, no humiliation in that claim, and I accept the bondage of the master who rules all the world."

As he spoke, Paul looked a happier, more *contented* slave, than those fabulous captives the South boasts of, but finds it hard to show.

Claudia led him back into the lower world again by asking with a sigh—"Paul, why should Jessie Snowden wish to wound me so? What cause have I given her for such dislike?"

A swift color swept across her lover's face, and the disdainful smile touched his lips again as he replied, "It is not a thing for me to tell; yet for the truth's sake I must. Jessie Snowden wooed what Claudia won. Heaven knows I have no cause for vanity, yet I could not help seeing in her eyes the regard it took so long to read in these more maidenly ones. I had no return to make, but gave all the friendship and respect I could to one for whom I had a most invincible distaste. There was no other cause for her dislike, yet I believe she hated me, or why should she speak with such malicious pleasure where a more generous woman would have held her peace? I have no faith in her, and by tomorrow I shall see in some changed face the first cloud of the storm she once foretold. Claudia, let us be married quietly, and go away until the gossips are grown weary, and we are forgotten."

Paul spoke with the sudden impulse of a nature sensitive and proud, but Claudia's energy was fully aroused and she answered with indignant color, "No, nothing must be changed. I asked my friends to see me made a proud and happy wife; shall I let them think I am ashamed to stand before them with the man I love? Paul, if I cannot bear a few harsh words, a few cold looks, a little pain, for you, of what worth is my love, of what use is my strength, and how shall I prove a fit friend and help-meet to you in the heavier cares and sorrows heaven sends us all?"

"Claudia, you are the braver of the two! I should be stronger if I had much to give; but I am so poor, this weight of obligation robs me of my courage. I am a weak soul, love, for I cannot trust, and I am still haunted by the fear that I shall one day read some sorrowful regret in this face, grown so wan with one night's watching for my sake."

Claudia dropped on her knee before him, and lifting up her earnest countenance, said, "Read it, Paul, and never doubt again. You spoke once of atonement,—make it by conquering your pride and receiving as freely as I give; for believe me, it is as hard a thing greatly to accept, as it is bountifully to bestow. You are not poor, for there can be no mine and thine between us two; you are not weak, for I lean on your strength, and know it will not fail; you are not fearful now, for looking here, you see the wife who never can regret or know the shadow of a change." Paul brushed the brown locks back, and as he read it smiled again, for heart and eyes and tender lips confirmed the truth, and he was satisfied.

Jessie Snowden's secret haunted her like Lady Macbeth's, and like that strong-minded woman, she would have told it in her sleep, if she had not eased herself by confiding it to a single friend. "Dear Maria" promised an eternal silence, but "Dear Maria" was the well known "little bird" who gave the whisper to the air. Rumor sowed it broadcast, gossips nurtured it, and Claudia reaped a speedy harvest of discomforts and chagrins.

She thought herself well armed for the "war of words"; but women's tongues forged weapons whose blows she could not parry, and men's censure or coarse pity pierced her shield, and wounded deeper than she dared to tell. Her "dear five hundred friends" each came to save her from social suicide, and her peaceful drawing-room soon became a chamber of the Inquisition, where a daily "Council of Ten" tormented her with warnings, entreaties—and reproaches,—

harder trials for a woman to bear, than the old tortures of rack and thirst and fire.

She bore herself bravely through these troublous times, but her pillow received bitter tears, heard passionate prayers and the throbbing of an indignant heart, that only calmed itself by the power of its love. Paul never saw a tear or heard a sigh,—for him the steady smile sat on her lips, a cheerful courage filled her eye; but he read her pain in the meekness which now beautified her face, and silently the trial now drew them nearer than before.

There was no mother to gather Claudia to her breast with blessings and with prayers when the marriage morning dawned, no sister to hover near her, April-like, with smiles and tears, no father to give her proudly to the man she loved, and few friends to make it a blithe festival; but a happier bride had never waited for her bridegroom's coming than Claudia as she looked out at the sunshine of a gracious day, and said within herself, "Heaven smiles upon me with auspicious skies, and in the depths of my own heart I hear a sweeter chime than any wedding bells can ring,—feel a truer peace than human commendation can bestow. Oh father, whom I never knew! oh mother, whom I wholly loved! be with me now, and bless me in this happy hour."

Paul came at last, fevered with the disquiet of much sleepless thought, and still disturbed by the gratitude of a generous nature, which believed itself unworthy of the gift relenting Fortune now bestowed. He saw a fair woman crowned for him, and remembering his past, looked at her, saying with troubled and agitated voice— "Claudia, it is not yet too late." But the white shape fluttered from him to the threshold of the door, and looking back, only answered, "Come."

Music, the benignant spirit of their lives, breathed a solemn welcome as the solitary pair paced down the chancel, through the silken stir of an uprising throng. Down from the altar window, full of sacred symbols and rich hues, fell heaven's benediction in a flood of light, touching Paul's bent head with mellow rays, and bathing Claudia's bridal snow in bloom.

Silently that unconscious pair preached a better sermon than had ever echoed there, for it appealed to principles that never die, and made its text, "The love of liberty, the liberty of love."

Many a worldly man forgot his worldliness, and thinking of Paul's hard-won success, owned that he honored him. Many a frivolous woman felt her eye wet by sudden dew, her bosom stirred by sudden sympathy, as Claudia's clear, "I will," rose through the hush, and many a softened heart confessed the beauty of the deed it had condemned.

Stern bridegroom and pale bride, those two had come into the chapel's gloom; proud-eyed husband, blooming wife, those two made one, passed out into the sunlight on the sward, and down along that shining path they walked serenely into their new life.

The nine days' wonder died away and Paul and Claudia, listening to the murmur of the sea, forgot there was a world through all that happy month. But when they came again and took their places in the circle they had left, the old charm had departed; for prejudice, a sterner autocrat than the Czar of all the Russias, hedged them round with an invisible restraint, that seemed to shut them out from the genial intercourse they had before enjoyed. Claudia would take no hand that was not given as freely to her husband, and there were not many to press her own as cordially as they once had done. Then she began to realize the emptiness of her old life, for now she looked upon it with a clearer eye, and saw it would not stand the test she had applied.

This was the lesson she had needed, it taught her the value of true friendship, showed her the poverty of old beliefs, the bitterness of old desires, and strengthened her proud nature by the sharp discipline of pain.

Paul saw the loneliness that sometimes came upon her when her former pleasures ceased to satisfy, and began to feel that his forebodings would prove true. But they never did; for there came to them those good Samaritans who minister to soul as well as sense; these took them by the hand, and through their honor for her husband, gave to Claudia the crowning lesson of her life.

They led her out of the world of wealth, and fashion, and pretense, into that other world that lies above it, full of the beauty of great deeds, high thoughts and humble souls, who walk its ways, rich in the virtues that

"Smell sweet, and blossom in the dust."

Like a child in fairyland she looked about her, feeling that here she might see again the aspirations of her youth, and find those happy visions true.

In this new world she found a finer rank than any she had left, for men whose righteous lives were their renown, whose virtues their estate, were peers of this realm, whose sovereign was Truth, whose ministers were Justice and Humanity, whose subjects all "who loved their neighbor better than themselves."

She found a truer chivalry than she had known before, for heroic deeds shone on her in the humblest guise, and she discovered knights of a nobler court than Arthur founded, or than Spenser sang. Saint Georges, valiant as of old, Sir Guyons, devout and strong, and silver-tongued Sir Launcelots without a stain, all fighting the good fight for love of God and universal right.

She found a fashion old as womanhood and beautiful as charity, whose votaries lived better poems than any pen could write; brave Britomarts redressing wrongs, meek Unas succoring the weak, high-hearted Maids of Orleans steadfast through long martyrdoms of labor for the poor, all going cheerfully along the by-ways of the world, and leaving them the greener for the touch of their unwearied feet.

She found a religion that welcomed all humanity to its broad church, and made its priest the peasant of Judea who preached the Sermon on the Mount.

Then, seeing these things, Claudia felt that she had found her place, and putting off her "purple of fine linen," gave herself to earnest work, which is the strengthening wine of life. Paul was no longer friendless and without a home, for here he found a country, and a welcome to that brotherhood which makes the whole world kin; and like the pilgrims in that fable never old, these two "went on their way rejoicing," leaving the shores of "Vanity Fair" behind them, and through the "Valley of Humiliation" climbed the mountains whence they saw the spires of the "Celestial City" shining in the sun.

Slowly all things right themselves when founded on truth. Time brought tardy honors to Paul, and Claudia's false friends beckoned her to come and take her place again, but she only touched the little heads, looked up into her husband's face, and answered with a smile of beautiful content—"I cannot give the substance for the shadow,—cannot leave my world for yours. Put off the old delusions that blind you to the light, and come up here to me."

BIBLIOGRAPHY

The libraries in which rare books have been found are given after the titles of such books: Boston Athenaeum Library (B.A.L.); Boston Public Library (B.P.L.); Brown University Library (B.U.L.); Harper Memorial Library, of the University of Chicago (H.M.L.); Harvard College Library (H.C.L.); John Crerar Library, of Chicago (J.C.L.); Library of Congress (L.C.); Newberry Library, of Chicago (N.L.); New York Historical Society Library (N.Y.H.S.L.); New York Public Library (N.Y.P.L.); New York Public Library, 135th St. Branch, Schomburg Negro Collection (N.Y.P.L.S.); Library of the University of Pennsylvania (U.P.L.); Yale University Library (Y.U.L.).

GENERAL HISTORIES

Cambridge History of American Literature. Ed. by W. P. Trent [and others]. Vols. I and II. New York, 1917-1918.

Channing, Edward. A History of the United States. Vol. II. New York, 1908.

—— ——. Vol. III. New York, 1912.

—— ——. Vol. IV. New York, 1917.

—— ——. Vol. V. New York, 1921.

—— ——. Vol. VI. New York, 1925.

Rhodes, James Ford. History of the United States from the Compromise of 1850. Vols. IV and V. New York, 1904.

——. History of the United States from the Compromise of 1850 to the Final Restoration of Home Rule at the South in 1877. Vols. I, II, and III. New York, 1906.

Tyler, Moses C. Literary History of the American Revolution. Vol. I. New York, 1905.

Williams, George W. History of the Negro Race in America from 1619 to 1880. New York, 1883. 2 v.

HISTORIES OF THE ABOLITION MOVEMENT

Adams, Alice D. The Neglected Period of Anti-Slavery in America (1808-1831). Boston and London, 1908.

Birney, James G. James G. Birney and his Times. The Genesis of the Republican Party with Some Account of the Abolition Movement in the South before 1828. New York, 1890.

Clarkson, Thomas. The History of the Rise, Progress, and Accomplishment of the Abolition of the African Slave-Trade. Vol. I. Philadelphia, 1808.

DuBois, W. E. Burghardt. The Suppression of the African Slave-Trade to the United States of America, 1638-1870. New York, London, and Bombay, 1896.

Hart, Albert Bushnell. Slavery and Abolition. New York and London, 1906.

Helper, Hinton Rowan. The Impending Crisis of the South: How to Meet It. New York, 1857.

Locke, Mary Stoughton. Anti-Slavery in America from the Introduction of African Slaves to the Prohibition of the Slave Trade, 1619-1808. Boston, 1901.

Macy, Jesse. The Anti-Slavery Crusade. A Chronicle of the Gathering Storm. New Haven, 1919.

May, Samuel J. Some Recollections of our Anti-Slavery Conflict. Boston, 1869.

Poole, William Frederick. Anti-Slavery Opinions before the Year 1800. To which is appended a fac-simile Reprint of Dr. George Buchanan's Oration on the Moral and Political Evil of Slavery. Cincinnati, 1873.

Still, William. The Underground Railroad. A Record of Facts, Authentic Narratives, Letters, etc. Philadelphia, 1872.

Weeks, Stephen B. "Anti-Slavery Sentiment in the South; with Unpublished Letters from John Stuart Mill and Mrs. Stowe." (In the Publications of the Southern History Association. Vol. II. Washington, 1898.)

——. Southern Quakers and Slavery. A Study in Institutional History. Baltimore, 1896.

HISTORIES OF THE DRAMA AND THE STAGE

Brown, T. Allston. A History of the New York Stage From the First Performance in 1732 to 1901. Vol. I. New York, 1903.

Dunlap, William. A History of the American Theatre. New York, 1832.

Ireland, J. N. Records of the New York Stage from 1750 to 1860. Vol. I. New York, 1866.

Moses, Montrose J. The American Dramatist. 2nd ed. Boston, 1917.

Quinn, Arthur H. A History of the American Drama From the Beginning to the Civil War. New York and London, 1923.

NOVELS

Bigelow, Harriet Hamline. The Curse Entailed. Boston, 1857.

[Bird, Robert M.] Sheppard Lee. Written by Himself. New York, 1836. 2 v.

Brackenridge, Hugh H. Modern Chivalry: Containing the Adventures of a Captain, and Teague O'Regan, his Servant. Vol. I. Philadelphia and Richmond, 1815. Published originally in 1792.

——. Adventures of Captain Farrago. Philadelphia, 1856.

Brown, William Wells. Clotel; or The President's Daughter: A Narrative of Slave Life in the United States. London, 1853. (B.P.L.; H.C.L.; N.Y.P.L.S.)

——. Miralda; or, The Beautiful Quadroon. A Romance of American Slavery. Founded on Fact. (In the Weekly Anglo-African. Published by Thomas Hamilton. New York, 1860-1861.)

——. Clotelle: A Tale of the Southern States. Boston, 1864. (N.Y.P.L.S.)

——. Clotelle; or, The Colored Heroine: A Tale of the Southern States. Boston, 1867.

Bulfinch, Stephen G. Honor; or, The Slave-Dealer's Daughter. Boston, 1864.

[Carruthers, William A.] The Kentuckian in New York; or, The Adventures of Three Southerners. By a Virginian. New York, 1834. 2 v.

Creyton, Paul, pseud. (J. T. Trowbridge.) Neighbor Jackwood. Boston, 1857.

Delany, Martin R. Blake: or, The Huts of America. (Published in part in the Anglo-African Magazine. New York, February-July, 1859.)

Dickinson, Anna E. What Answer? Boston, 1868.

Griffith, Mattie. Madge Vertner. (In the National Anti-Slavery Standard. Vol. XX. New York, 1859-1860.) (N.Y.P.L.)

Hale, Sarah J. Northwood: A Tale of New England. Boston, 1827. 2 v. (L.C.)

——. Northwood; or, Life North and South: Showing the Character of Both. New York, 1852.

——. Liberia; or, Mr. Peyton's Experiment. New York, 1853.

Hardwick, J. P. Liberty or Death! or, The Mother's Sacrifice. Harrisburg, 1862. (L.C.)

Hildreth, Richard. The Slave: or Memoirs of Archy Moore. Boston, 1836. 2 v.

—— ——. Boston, 1840. 2 v.

Hosmer, H. L. Adela, The Octoroon. Columbus, 1860.

Imlay, Gilbert. The Emigrants; or, The History of an Expatriated Family. Vol. I. London, 1793. (H.M.L.)

[Jolliffe, John]. Belle Scott; or Liberty Overthrown! A Tale for the Crisis. Columbus and Cincinnati, 1856.

——. Chattanooga. Cincinnati, 1858.

Judd, Sylvester. Richard Edney and the Governor's Family. Boston, 1850.

Kirke, Edmund, pseud. (J. R. Gilmore). Among the Pines; or South in Secession Time. New York, 1862.

——. My Southern Friends. New York, 1863.

——. Down in Tennessee, and Back by Way of Richmond. New York, 1864.

Little, Sophia L. Thrice Through the Furnace; A Tale of the Times of the Iron Hoof. Pawtuckett, R.I., 1852.

Livermore, Elizabeth D. Zoë; or The Quadroon's Triumph. A Tale of the Times. Cincinnati, 1855. 2 v.

Logan, pseud. (Thomas Bangs Thorpe). The Master's House: A Tale of Southern Life. New York, 1854.

M'Keehan, Hattia. Liberty or Death; or, Heaven's Infraction of the Fugitive Slave Law. Cincinnati, 1859. (H.C.L.)

Melville, Herman. Mardi. New York, 1849. 2 v.

Morton, Sarah W. The Power of Sympathy; or, The Triumph of Nature. Founded in Truth. Boston, 1789. 2 v.

Pierson, Emily Catherine. Jamie Parker, the Fugitive. Hartford, 1851.

Pocahontas, pseud. (Emily Clemens Pearson). Cousin Franck's Household; or, Scenes in the Old Dominion. By Pocahontas. 4th ed. Boston, 1853.

Reid, Mayne. The Quadroon; or A Lover's Adventures in Louisiana. New York, 1856.

Roe, Elizabeth A. Aunt Leanna, or, Early Scenes in Kentucky. Chicago, 1855.

Rowson, Susanna H. The Inquisitor; or, Invisible Rambler. 2nd American ed. Philadelphia, 1794. 3 v. in 1. (H.M.L.)

Sargent, Epes. Peculiar: A Tale of the Great Transition. New York, 1864.

Sherburne, Henry. The Oriental Philanthropist; or, True Republican. Portsmouth, N.H., 1800.

Smith, M. B. My Uncle's Family; or, Ten Months at the South. Cincinnati, 1863.

Smith, William White. The Yankee Slave Driver; or, The Black and White Rivals. New York, 1860.

Story, Sidney A., Jr. Caste: Story of Republican Equality. Boston and New York, 1856.

Stowe, Harriet B. Uncle Tom's Cabin; or, Life Among the Lowly. Boston, 1852.

———. Dred; A Tale of the Great Dismal Swamp. Boston, 1856.

———. The Minister's Wooing. New York, 1859.

Trowbridge, J. T. Cudjo's Cave. Boston, 1892. Published originally in 1864.

Tyler, Royall. The Algerine Captive; or, The Life and Adventures of Doctor Updike Underhill. Hartford, 1816. Published originally in 1797.

Webb, Frank J. The Garies and Their Friends. London, 1857.

Anonymous. The Fanatic, or The Perils of Peter Pliant, the Poor Pedagogue. By the Author of Winona. Philadelphia, 1846. (L.C.)

PLAYS

Aiken, George L. Uncle Tom's Cabin; or, Life Among the Lowly. New York, 1852.

Bird, Robert M. "The Gladiator." (In C. E. Foust, Life and Dramatic Works of Robert Montgomery Bird. New York, 1919.)

Boucicault, Dion. "The Octoroon; or, Life in Louisiana." (In Arthur H. Quinn, Representative American Plays. New York, 1917.)

Brougham, John. Dred; or, The Dismal Swamp. New York, 1856.

Brown, William Wells. The Escape; or, A Leap for Freedom. A Drama in Five Acts. Boston, 1858. (H.M.L.)

Child, Lydia M. "The Stars and Stripes." (In the Liberty Bell. By Friends of Freedom. Boston, 1858.)

Clark, W. A. General Grant; or, The Star of Union and Liberty. New York, 1868.

Darling, David. Beaux Without Belles, or, Ladies We Can Do

Without You. A Musical Farce. Charlottesville, Va., 1820. (U.P.L.)

Dunlap, William. The Africans; or, War, Love, and Duty. Philadelphia, 1811. (N.Y.P.L.)

———. The Father of an Only Child. New York, 1807.

Ellison, James. The American Captive, or, Siege of Tripoli. A Drama in Five Acts. Boston, 1812. (H.M.L.)

Little, Sophia L. The Branded Hand: A Dramatic Sketch. Pawtucket, R.I., 1845. (B.U.L.)

Murdock, John. The Triumphs of Love; or, Happy Reconciliation. [Philadelphia, 1795]. (H.C.L.)

Ricord, Elizabeth. Zamba; or, The Insurrection. Cambridge, 1842.

Stowe, Harriet B. The Christian Slave. A Drama Founded on a Portion of Uncle Tom's Cabin. Boston, 1855.

Swayze, J. C. Ossawattomie Brown; or, The Insurrection at Harper's Ferry. New York, 1859.

Trowbridge, J. T. Neighbor Jackwood. New York, 1857.

[Whitney, Daniel S.]. Warren: A Tragedy. Boston, 1850.

POEMS

Adams, John Quincy. "Fragments from an Unfinished Manuscript." (In the Liberty Bell. By Friends of Freedom. Boston, 1847.)

Adelaide, Frances. "Columbia." (In the Emancipator and Free American. New York, 1842.) (Y.U.L.)

Alcott, L. M. "With a Rose, That Bloomed on the Day of John Brown's Martyrdom." (In the Liberator. Ed. by William Lloyd Garrison. Boston, January 20, 1860.)

Allinson, William J., ed. "A Plea for the Slave." (In the Non-Slaveholder. Philadelphia, 1853.)

[Armistead, Wilson]. The Garland of Freedom: A Collection of Poems, Chiefly Anti-Slavery. By a Friend of the Negro. London, 1853. Part III.

Baker, F. M. "The Spirit's Mission." (In the Anti-Slavery Bugle. Salem, Ohio, December 6, 1851.) (L.C.)

Barlow, Joel. "The Prospect of Peace." (In the Columbian Muse. New York, 1794.)

———. The Columbiad, A Poem. London, 1809.

Bell, James Madison. A Poem: Delivered August 1, 1862. San Francisco, 1862. (H.C.L.)

——. A Poem Entitled the Day and the War. San Francisco, 1864.

Bennison, D. M. Poems, Original and Selected. Boston, 1847.

Bigelow, Samuel. A Poem, Suitable For the Present Day. In Five Parts. Worcester, 1776.

Boker, George H. Poems of the War. Boston, 1864.

——. "Abraham Lincoln." (In the Liberator. Ed. by William Lloyd Garrison. Boston, September 22, 1865.)

Boulton, Thomas. The Voyage, A Poem in Seven Parts. Boston, 1773. (B.A.L.)

Bourne, William Oland. Poems of the Republic. New York, 1864.

Brainard, John G. C. "On the Project of Colonizing the 'Free People of Colour' in Africa." (In The Literary Remains of John G. C. Brainard. Hartford, 1832.)

Branagan, Thomas. Avenia; or a Tragical Poem. Philadelphia, 1805.

——. The Penitential Tyrant; or Slave Trader Reformed, a Pathetic Poem in Four Cantos. 2nd ed. New York, 1807.

Brown, William W., comp. The Anti-Slavery Harp: A Collection of Songs for Anti-Slavery Meetings. Boston, 1848.

Bruce, Helen. "The Sorrows of Yamba." (In the National Anti-Slavery Standard. New York, February 18, 1860.) (N.Y.P.L.)

Bryant, William Cullen. The Fountain and Other Poems. New York and London, 1842.

——. Thirty Poems. New York, 1864.

——. Poetical Works of William Cullen Bryant. Collected and Arranged by the Author. New York, 1878.

——. Poems. New York, 1890.

——. The Poetical Works of William Cullen Bryant. Roslyn Edition. Ed. by Henry C. Sturges. New York, 1903.

Bulkley, C. H. A. Niagara, A Poem. New York, 1848.

Burleigh, William H. "Emancipation in the West Indies." (In the Emancipator. New York, August 29, 1839.) (Y.U.L.)

——. Poems. Philadelphia, 1841.

Chandler, Elizabeth Margaret. The Poetical Works of Elizabeth Margaret Chandler: With a Memoir of Her Life and Character. By Benjamin Lundy. Philadelphia, 1836.

Channing, William Ellery [the Younger]. Poems. 2nd Series. Boston, 1847.

——. "To Kossuth." (In the Liberator. Ed. by William Lloyd Garrison. Boston, January 2, 1852.)

——. Near Home. A Poem. Boston, 1858.

Chapman, Maria Weston, comp. Songs of the Free and Hymns of Christian Freedom. Boston, 1836.

Child, David Lee. "Thoughts of a Stone-Splitter." (In the Liberty Bell. By Friends of Freedom. Boston, 1843.)

Child, Lydia M., ed. The Freedmen's Book. Boston, 1865.

Clark, George W., ed. The Liberty Minstrel. New York, 1845.

——. The Harp of Freedom. New York, 1856.

Cook, Martha W. "War Song:—Earth's Last Battle." (In the Continental Monthly. Vol. III. New York, May, 1863.)

——. "The Lady and Her Slave." (In the Continental Monthly. Vol. III. New York, March, 1863.)

Cowles, S. C., pub. Freedom's Gift: or, Sentiments of The Free. Hartford, 1840.

Cranch, Christopher Pearse. The Bird and the Bell, with Other Poems. Boston, 1875.

Denton, William. "The Advent of Freedom." (In Poems for Reformers. 2nd ed. Cleveland, Ohio, 1859.)

——. "Liberty's Star." (In Poems for Reformers. 2nd ed. Cleveland, Ohio, 1859.)

——. "On Being Asked to Take the Oath of Allegiance." (In Poems for Reformers. 2nd ed. Cleveland, Ohio, 1859.)

——. "Slavery." (In Poems for Reformers. 2nd ed. Cleveland, Ohio, 1859.)

Dwight, Timothy. The Conquest of Canaan; A Poem in Eleven Books. Hartford, 1785.

——. Greenfield Hill: A Poem in Seven Parts. New York, 1794.

Edwards, Bryant. "The Negro's Dying Speech." (In the Massachusetts Magazine or Monthly Museum. Vol. V. Boston, 1793.) (L.C.)

Ellis, Elsie. "Ennobled Bondmen." (In the Christian Recorder. Ed. by Elisha Weaver. Philadelphia, August 19, 1865.)

Emerson, Ralph W. "On Freedom." (In Autographs for Freedom. Ed. by Julia Griffiths. Auburn and Rochester, 1854.)

——. Poems. Ed. by Edward W. Emerson. Boston and New York, 1904.

Freneau, Philip. Poems of Philip Freneau. Vol. I. Ed. by F. L. Pattee. Princeton, N.J., 1902.

—— ——. Vol. II. Ed. by F. L. Pattee. Princeton, N.J., 1903.

—— ——. Vol. III. Ed. by F. L. Pattee. Princeton, N.J., 1907.

Garrison, William Lloyd. "Sonnets." (In A Brief Sketch of the Trial of William Lloyd Garrison for an Alleged Libel on Francis Todd of Newburyport, Mass. Boston, 1834.)

——. Sonnets and Other Poems. Boston, 1843. (H.C.L.)

——. "I am an Abolitionist." (In the National Anti-Slavery Standard. Vol. XXIII. New York, 1862.) (N.Y.P.L.)

Garrison, William Lloyd, ed. A Selection of Anti-Slavery Hymns, for the Use of the Friends of Emancipation. Boston, 1834. (B.P.L.)

——. Juvenile Poems for the Use of Free American Children of Every Complexion. Boston, 1835. (B.P.L.)

Gray, Iron, pseud. (Abel Charles Thomas). The Gospel of Slavery: A Primer of Freedom. New York, 1864.

Greenwood, Grace, pseud. (Sarah Jones Lippincott). "The Leap from the Long Bridge." (In Poems. Boston, 1851.)

Hale, Edward Everett. "Put It Through." (In Poems and Fancies. Boston, 1901.)

Hall, Louisa J. "Birth in the Slave's Hut." (In the Liberty Bell. By Friends of Freedom. Boston, 1849.)

Harper, Frances Ellen Watkins. Poems on Miscellaneous Subjects. Philadelphia, 1857.

——. "Bury Me in a Free Land." (In the National Anti-Slavery Standard. Vol. XIX. New York, December, 1858.) (N.Y.P.L.)

——. Poems. Philadelphia, 1871.

Hatfield, Edwin F., ed. Freedom's Lyre: or, Psalms, Hymns, and Sacred Songs, for the Slave and his Friends. 2nd ed. New York, 1840.

Hebbard, William Wallace. The Night of Freedom: An Appeal, in Verse, Against the Great Crime of Our Country, Human Bondage. Boston, 1857.

Higginson, Thomas Wentworth. "The Fugitives' Hymn." (In the Liberty Bell. By Friends of Freedom. Boston, 1848.)

Hill, Thomas. Christmas, and Poems on Slavery for Christmas, 1843. Cambridge, 1843. (H.C.L.)

Hine, Benjamin. "The Slave Holder." (In Miscellaneous Poetry: or, The Farmer's Muse. New York, 1835.)

Holmes, Daniel. Dialogue on Slavery, and Miscellaneous Subjects, Based on the Word of God. Dayton [Ohio], 1854.

Holmes, Oliver Wendell. Complete Poetical Works of Oliver Wendell Holmes. Cambridge Edition. Boston and New York, 1895.

Hoopes, John H. "Tell Me Not of the Sunny South." (In the National Era. Washington, D.C., April 5, 1855.)

[Horton, George M.]. Poems by a Slave. (In Memoir and Poems of Phillis Wheatley. Boston, 1838.) (H.C.L.)

Humphreys, David. Poems, on the Happiness of America. London, 1786.

——. A Poem on Industry. Philadelphia, 1794.

——. "A Poem on the Death of General Washington." (In The Miscellaneous Works of David Humphreys. New York, 1804.)

Jaques, D. H. "Your Brother is a Slave." (In the Emancipator and Weekly Chronicle. Boston, November 20, 1844.) (Y.U.L.)

Leland, Charles Godfrey. "Out and Fight." (In Poems of American History. Ed. by Burton E. Stevenson. Boston and New York, 1908.)

Levering, R. E. H. "Ho for Afric's Bounteous Clime." (In the African Repository. Published by the American Colonization Society. Vol. XXIX. Washington, 1853.)

Lewis, Alonzo. "Ode.—July 4, 1831." (In the Colored American. New York, July 8, 1837.)

Little, Sophia L. "The Autograph of Sims", 1851. (In the Liberty Bell. By Friends of Freedom. Boston, 1852.)

Lloyd, Elizabeth, Jr. An Appeal for the Bondwoman, to Her Own Sex. Philadelphia, 1846.

Longfellow, Henry Wadsworth. "Poems on Slavery." (In The Complete Poetical Works of Henry Wadsworth Longfellow. Boston, 1880.)

Lowell, James R. Class Poem. Cambridge, 1838. (H.C.L.)

——. The Poetical Works of James Russell Lowell. Household Edition. Boston, 1876.

——. Poetical Works of James Russell Lowell. Boston and New York, 1898.

Lowell, Maria. "The Slave Mother." (In The Poems of Maria Lowell. Cambridge, 1907. Published originally in 1855.)

MacFarlane, Isabella. "The Two Southern Mothers." (In the Continental Monthly. Vol. IV. New York, November, 1863.)

[Mann, Daniel]. The Virginia Philosopher, or Few Lucky Slave-Catchers. By Mr. Latimer's Brother. Boston, 1843.

Markham, M. Roland. Alcar, the Captive Creole; A Story of the South in Verse. Homer [N.Y.], 1857.

Martin, J. Selba. "The Sentinel of Freedom." (In the Anglo-African Magazine. Vol. I. New York, 1859.)

Matthews, J. Brander, ed. Poems of American Patriotism. New York, 1882.

McDougall, Frances H., ed. The Envoy From Free Hearts to the Free. Pawtucket, R.I., 1840.

Melville, Herman. Battle-Pieces and Aspects of the War. New York, 1866.

Moore, Henry D., ed. The Chaplet, A Collection of Poems. By E. H. C. Philadelphia, 1846.

Morton, Sarah W. Beacon Hill. A Local Poem, Historic and Descriptive. Book I. Boston, 1797.

——. "The African Chief." (In My Mind and Its Thoughts, in Sketches, Fragments, and Essays. Boston, 1823.)

Munford, Robert. "A Letter From the Devil to his Son." (In Collection of Plays and Poems. Petersburg, Va., 1797.)

Pierpont, John. The Anti-Slavery Poems of John Pierpont. Boston, 1843. (L.C.; H.C.L.)

Pike, Marshall S. Creola: or The Slave Minstrel. A Poetical Romance, in Five Parts. Boston, 1850. (L.C.)

Plato, Ann. "To the First of August." (In Essays; including Biographies and Miscellaneous Pieces, in Prose and Poetry. Hartford, 1841.) (N.Y.P.L.S.)

Putnam, George W. "Slavery in California." (In the National Era. Washington, D.C., September 20, 1849.)

Rand, Edward L., Jr. "A Song of Freedom." (In the Continental Monthly. Vol. I. New York and Boston, January, 1862.)

Reason, Charles L. "Freedom." (In A Eulogy on the Life and Character of Thomas Clarkson. By Alexander Crummell. New York, 1847.)

Reid, James. King Slavery's Council; or The Midnight Conclave: A Poem. Troy, 1844. (L.C.)

Rogers, E. P. A Poem on the Fugitive Slave Law. Newark, N.J., 1855.

——. The Repeal of the Missouri Compromise Considered. Newark, N.J., 1856. (N.Y.P.L.S.)

Rubeck, Sennoia, pseud. (John Burke.) The Burden of the South in Verse, or, Poems on Slavery. New York, 1864.

Sewall, J. M. "On Friendship." (In Miscellaneous Poems. Portsmouth, 1801.)

Sigourney, Lydia H. Zizendorff and Other Poems. New York, 1835.

——. Poems. New York, 1853.

Smith, Elihu H., ed. American Poems, Selected and Original. Vol. I. Litchfield, Conn., 1793.

Stacy, G. W., ed. Anti-Slavery Hymns, Designed to Aid the Cause of Human Rights. Hopedale, Mass., 1844.

Starbuck, Lucy C., ed. Seaweeds from the Shores of Nantucket. Boston, 1853.

Stedman, Edmund C. Poems, Lyrical and Idyllic. New York, 1860.

Stevenson, Burton E., ed. Poems of American History. Boston and New York, 1908.

Stoddard, Richard Henry. Abraham Lincoln. An Horatian Ode. New York, 1865.

——. "Men of the North and West." (In Poems of American History. Ed. by Burton E. Stevenson. Boston and New York, 1908.)

Story, William W. "Sonnet." (In the Liberty Bell. By Friends of Freedom. Boston, 1843.)

Stowe, Harriet Beecher. "Caste and Christ", 1852. (In Autographs for Freedom. Ed. by Julia Griffiths. Boston, 1853.)

Sumner, Charles P. The Compass. A Poetical Performance at the Literary Exhibition in September, 1795, at Harvard University. Boston, 1795.

Taylor, J. Bayard. "To Earth." (In the Liberty Bell. By Friends of Freedom. Boston, 1848.)

——. "The Continents." (In Poems of Home and Travel. Boston, 1855.)

Thompson, George. The Prison Bard, or Poems on Various Subjects. Hartford, 1848.

Tilton, Theodore. "A War Hymn." (In Douglass' Monthly. Ed. by Frederick Douglass. Rochester, N.Y., November, 1862.)

Very, Jones. Essays and Poems. Boston, 1839.

——. Poems and Essays. Boston, 1886.

Very, Lydia L. A. Poems. Andover, 1856.

——. Poems and Prose Writings. Salem, Mass., 1890.

Walker, James B. The Slaves: A Poem. Written by Appointment of the Faculty of the Western Reserve College, for the Commencement, in 1831. Hudson, Ohio, 1835.

Watkins, Frances Ellen. See Harper, Frances Ellen Watkins.

Wheatley, Phillis. Poems on Various Subjects, Religious and Moral. London, 1773.

Whitfield, J. M. America and Other Poems. Buffalo, 1853. (N.Y.P.L.S.)

[Whittier, John G.], ed. The North Star: The Poetry of Freedom, by her Friends. Philadelphia, 1840.

——. Voices of Freedom. 4th ed. Philadelphia, 1846.

——. The Poetical Works of John Greenleaf Whittier. Vol. III. Boston and New York, 1892.

Whitman, Walt. Complete Prose Works, pp. 339-340, 372-374. Philadelphia, 1892.

——. Leaves of Grass. Ed. by Emory Holloway. New York, 1924.

Willis, N. P. "Ode." (In the Pennsylvania Freeman. Philadelphia, August 22, 1839.) (N.Y.H.S.L.)

——. "The Pleasant Land We Love." (In The Liberty Minstrel. Ed. by George W. Clark. New York, 1845.)

Woodward, David. Slavery; Its Origin, Progress and Effects: A Poem. Boston, 1856.

Anonymous. The American in Algiers, or, The Patriot of Seventy-six in Captivity. A Poem, in Two Cantos. New York, 1797. (H.C.L.)

——. The Anti-Slavery Alphabet. Philadelphia, 1846.

——. "Corn is King." (In the Continental Monthly. Vol. II. Boston, August, 1862.)

——. "The Dying Negro." (In the Royal American Magazine, or Universal Repository of Instruction and Amusement. Boston, 1774.) (L.C.)

——. Hymns and Songs for the Friends of Freedom. Middletown, 1842. (L.C.)

——. "The Irrepressible Conflict." (In the Continental Monthly. Vol. I. New York and Boston, April, 1862.)

——. Lays of Liberty; or, Verses for the Times. Boston, 1854.

——. Lyrics for Freedom; and Other Poems. Under the Auspices of the Continental Club. New York, 1862.

——. Lyrics of a Day: or Newspaper Poetry. By a Volunteer in the United States Service. 2nd ed. New York, 1864.

——. "The Negro Boy." (In the Philadelphia Minerva. Vol. III. Philadelphia, 1797.) (L.C.)

——. "A Negro's Lamentation." (In the Monthly Magazine, and American Review. Vol. III. New York, 1800.)

——. A Poetical Epistle to the Enslaved Africans, in the Character of an ancient Negro, Born a slave in Pennsylvania, but liberated some years since, etc. Philadelphia, 1790. (H.C.L.)

——. "The Old Quadroon; or A National Version of the Virgin Martyr." (In the National Era. Vol. X. Washington, D.C., May 1-15, 1856.)

——. "The Slave." (In the New Haven Gazette and the Connecticut Magazine. New Haven, 1786.) (L.C.)

——. "The Slaveholder at the Bar of God." By W. M. T. (In the Emancipator and Free Soil Press. Boston, October 4, 1848.) (Y.U.L.)

——. "On Slavery, and the Slave Trade." (In the Christian's, Scholar's, and Farmer's Magazine. Vol. I. Elizabethtown, N.J., 1789.) (L.C.)

——. Songs of the Free, and Hymns of Christian Freedom, Boston, 1836.

——. "The Sorrows of Angola." (In Freedom's Journal. New York, June 8, 1827.) (N.Y.H.S.L.)

——. Star of Emancipation. For the Fair of the Massachusetts Female Emancipation Society. Boston, 1841.)

——. "Suggestions on Natural Rights." (In the Pennsylvania Freeman. Philadelphia, February 27, 1840.)

——. "The Tears of a Slave." By Africus. (In Freedom's Journal. New York, March 14, 1828.) (N.Y.H.S.L.)

ESSAYS

Bacon, Leonard Woolsey. Anti-Slavery before Garrison. An Address before the Connecticut Society of the Founders and Patriots of America. New Haven, 1903.

Benezet, Anthony. Some Historical Account of Guinea, Its Situation, Produce and the General Disposition of its Inhabitants, with An Inquiry into the Rise and Progress of the Slave-Trade, its Nature and Lamentable Effects. Philadelphia, 1771.

Boucher, Jonathan. A View of the Causes and Consequences of the American Revolution. London, 1797.

Carey, M. "African Civilization." (In A Short Account of the

Malignant Fever and Miscellaneous Essays. Philadelphia, 1830.)

———. "Emancipation of the Slaves in the United States." (In A Short Account of the Malignant Fever and Miscellaneous Essays. Philadelphia, 1830.)

Chandler, Elizabeth Margaret. Essays, Philanthropic and Moral, Principally Relating to the Abolition of Slavery in America. Philadelphia, 1836.

Channing, William E. Slavery. Boston, 1835.

Child, Lydia M. An Appeal in Favor of That Class of Americans Called Africans. New York, 1836.

Clark, James Freeman. Discourse on the Aspects of the War. Boston, 1863.

Cooper, James F. The American Democrat, or Hints on the Social and Civic Relations of the United States of America. Cooperstown, 1838.

Dew, Thomas R. Review of the Debate in the Virginia Legislature of 1831 and 1832. Richmond, 1832.

Edwards, Jonathan. The Injustice and Impolicy of the Slave Trade, and of the Slavery of the Africans. New Haven, 1791.

Emerson, Ralph Waldo. "Emancipation in the British West Indies." Address at Concord, August 1, 1844. (In The Complete Works of Ralph Waldo Emerson. Ed. by Edward Waldo Emerson. Vol. XI. Cambridge, 1904.)

———. "The Fugitive Slave Law." Address at Concord, May 3, 1851. (In The Complete Works of Ralph Waldo Emerson. Ed. by Edward Waldo Emerson. Vol. XI. Cambridge, 1904.)

———. "The Fugitive Slave Law." Lecture at New York, March 7, 1854. (In The Complete Works of Ralph Waldo Emerson. Ed. by Edward Waldo Emerson. Vol. XI. Cambridge, 1904.)

Faugeres, Margaretta V. "Fine Feelings Exemplified in the Conduct of a Negro Slave." (In The Posthumous Works of Ann Eliza Bleecker, in Prose and Verse, to which is added a Collection of Essays, Prose and Poetical. New York, 1793.)

Franklin, Benjamin. An Essay on the African Slave Trade. Philadelphia, 1790. (H.C.L.)

———. "An Address to the Public." (In The Works of Benjamin Franklin. Ed. by Jared Sparks. Vol. II. Boston, 1844.)

———. "On the Slave Trade." (In The Complete Works of Benjamin Franklin. Ed. by John Bigelow. Vol. X. New York, 1888.)

——. "Observations Concerning the Increase of Mankind and the Peopling of Countries." (In The Writings of Benjamin Franklin. Ed. by A. H. Smyth. Vol. III. New York, 1905.)

Frost, Maria G. Gospel Fruits: or, Bible Christianity Illustrated; A Premium Essay. Cincinnati, 1856.

Garnet, Henry Highland. Walker's Appeal, With a Brief Sketch of his Life. New York, 1848.

Garrison, William Lloyd. "First Anti-Slavery Address in Boston." (In Old South Leaflets. Vol. VIII. No. 180. Boston, 1829.)

Greeley, Horace. "Slavery at Home", June 3, 1845. (In Hints Toward Reform, in Lectures, Addresses, and Other Writings. New York, 1850.)

——. "The Dishonor of Labor", 1853. (In Autographs for Freedom. Ed. by Julia Griffiths. Auburn and Rochester, 1854.)

——. "The Prayer of Twenty Millions", August 19, 1862. (In the New York Daily Tribune, August 20, 1862.)

Grimke, A. E. Appeal to Christian Women of the South. [New York], 1836.

Hammon, Jupiter. An Address to the Negroes in the State of New York. New York, 1787. (H.C.L.)

Hopkins, Samuel. Timely Articles on Slavery. Boston, 1854.

Jefferson, Thomas. Notes on the State of Virginia. Second American Edition. Philadelphia, 1794.

Leland, C. G. "What to Do with the Darkies." (In the Continental Monthly. Vol. I. New York and Boston, 1862.)

Lowell, James Russell. Political Essays. Boston and New York, 1888.

——. The Anti-Slavery Papers of James Russell Lowell. Boston and New York, 1902. 2 v.

Mather, Cotton. Essays to Do Good. Glasgow, 1825. Published originally in 1710.

Mickley, Joseph J. "Some Account of William Usselinx and Peter Minuit." (In Historical and Biographical Papers of the Delaware Historical Society. Vol. I. No. III. Wilmington, Del., 1881.)

Morton, Sarah W. "Servants." (In My Mind and Its Thoughts in Sketches, Fragments, and Essays. Boston, 1823.)

Ossoli, Margaret Fuller. Life Without and Life Within; or, Reviews, Narratives, Essays, and Poems. Ed. by Arthur B. Fuller. New York, 1869.

Othello. "Essay on Negro Slavery." (In the American Museum. Vol. IV. Philadelphia, 1788.)

Paine, Thomas. "African Slavery in America." Published originally in 1775. (In The Writings of Thomas Paine. Vol. I. Ed. by Moncure D. Conway. New York, 1894.)

——. "Emancipation of Slaves." (In The Writings of Thomas Paine. Vol. III. Ed. by Moncure D. Conway. New York, 1894.)

Raymond, James. "A Prize Essay On the Comparative Economy of Free and Slave Labour in Agriculture." (In the African Observer. A Monthly Journal. Ed. by Enoch Lewis. Philadelphia, 1828.)

Rush, Benjamin. An Address to the Inhabitants of the British Settlements in America upon Slave-Keeping. 2nd ed. Philadelphia, 1773.

Sewall, Samuel. "The Selling of Joseph." (In the Massachusetts Historical Society Collections, 5th Series. Vol. VI, Boston, 1879.)

Thoreau, Henry David. "Civil Disobedience." (In A Yankee in Canada, with Anti-Slavery and Reform Papers. Boston, 1866.)

——. "A Plea for Captain John Brown." (In A Yankee in Canada, with Anti-Slavery and Reform Papers. Boston, 1866.)

——. "Slavery in Massachusetts." (In A Yankee in Canada, with Anti-Slavery and Reform Papers. Boston, 1866.)

Thurston, R. B. "The Error and the Duty in Regard to Slavery." (In Three Prize Essays on American Slavery. Boston, 1857.)

Trumbull, John. "The Correspondent, No. 8." (In the Connecticut Journal and New Haven Post-Boy. New Haven, July 6, 1770.) (Y.U.L.; L.C.)

Tucker, St. George. A Dissertation on Slavery with a Proposal for the Gradual Abolition of It, in the State of Virginia. New York, 1861. Reprinted. Published originally in 1796.

Tuckerman, Theodore. "Virginia." (In the Continental Monthly. Vol. IV. New York, December, 1863.)

Walker, David. Walker's Appeal. In Four Articles. Together with a Preamble to the Colored Citizens of the World. Boston, 1829. (H.C.L.)

—— ——. 2nd. ed. Boston, 1830. (L.C.)

—— ——. 3rd ed. Boston, 1830. (L.C.)

Whitman, Walt. "Slavers and the Slave Trade", 1846. (In The Uncollected Poetry and Prose of Walt Whitman. Vol. I. Ed. by Emory Holloway. New York, 1921.)

——. "New States: Shall They be Slave or Free?" 1847. (In The Uncollected Poetry and Prose of Walt Whitman. Vol. I. Ed. by Emory Holloway. New York, 1921.)

——. "American Workingmen, Versus Slavery", 1847. (In The Uncollected Poetry and Prose of Walt Whitman. Vol. I. Ed. by Emory Holloway. New York, 1921.)

——. "Slavery", 1857. (In The Uncollected Poetry and Prose of Walt Whitman. Vol. II. Ed. by Emory Holloway. New York, 1921.)

Whittier, John G. Justice and Expediency or Slavery Considered with a View to its Rightful and Effective Remedy, Abolition. Haverhill, 1833.

Williston, Timothy. "An Essay." (In Three Prize Essays on American Slavery. Boston, 1857.)

Anonymous. "An Answer to a Circumstance on which some Writers, in Defence of the Slave-Trade, have founded much of its Legality." (In the Columbian Magazine, or Monthly Miscellany. Vol. II. Philadelphia, 1788.) (L.C.)

——. "The Negro." (In the Weekly Magazine of Original Essays, Fugitive Pieces, and Interesting Intelligence. Vol. I. Philadelphia, 1798.) (L.C.)

——. "On Slavery." (In the Weekly Magazine of Original Essays, Fugitive Pieces, and Interesting Intelligence. Vol. III. Philadelphia, 1799.) (L.C.)

——. "A Plan for the Abolition of Slavery." By a North Carolinian. (In the National Era. Washington, D.C., April 22, 1847.)

——. "Slavery in the United States." (In Hints and Sketches.[1] By An American Mother. New York, 1839.)

——. "Treatment of the African Slaves in America." (In the Rural Magazine: or, Vermont Repository. Devoted to Literary, Moral, Historical, and Political Improvement. Vol. I. Rutland, 1795.) (L.C.)

[1] This book is in the Henry P. Slaughter Negro Collection, Washington, D.C.

——. "The True Character of Slavery." (In the Pennsylvania Freeman. Philadelphia, April 12, 1838.)

——. "True System of Emancipation." (In the Dial: A Monthly Magazine of Literature, Philosophy and Religion. Ed. by M. D. Conway. Cincinnati, 1860.)

——. "Views of the Benevolent Society of Alexandria for Ameliorating and Improving the Condition of the People of Color." (In Freedom's Journal. New York, May 25-June 22, 1827.) (N.Y.H.S.L.)

SHORT NARRATIVES AND SKETCHES

Alcott, Louisa M. "M. L." (In the Commonwealth. Boston, January 24-February 21, 1863.) (B.A.L.)

——. Hospital Sketches. Boston, 1863.

Brisbane, W. H. Amanda: A Tale for the Times. Philadelphia, 1848.

——. Narrative of Albert and Mary. (In Autographs for Freedom. Ed. by Julia Griffiths. Auburn and Rochester, 1854.)

Bruce, Helen. "Maud Clinton, The Planter's Daughter." (In the National Anti-Slavery Standard. Vol. XXI. New York, 1860.) (N.Y.P.L.)

Chapman, Maria Weston. "Pinda: A True Tale." (In the Monthly Offering. Ed. by John A. Collins. Boston, 1841.)

Child, Lydia M. "The Black Saxons." (In the Liberty Bell. By Friends of Freedom. Boston, 1841.)

——. "Slavery's Pleasant Homes: A Faithful Sketch." (In the Liberty Bell. By Friends of Freedom, Boston, 1843.)

——. "The Quadroons." (In Fact and Fiction: A Collection of Stories. New York and Boston, 1849.)

——. "The Kansas Emigrants." (In Autumnal Leaves: Tales and Sketches in Prose and Rhyme. New York, 1857.)

Colman, Julia. "Little Lewis—The Story of a Slave Boy." (In The Child's Anti-Slavery Book. New York, 1859.)

Dall, Caroline W. Healy. "Amy, A Tale." (In the Liberty Bell. By Friends of Freedom. Boston, 1849.)

Henshaw, Daniel. "Dialogue on Slavery." (In The Anti-Slavery Picknick. Ed. by John A. Collins. Boston, 1842.)

Jones, J. Elizabeth. The Young Abolitionist; or Conversations on Slavery. Boston, 1848.

Neal, John. "Instincts of Childhood." (In The Anti-Slavery Picknick. Ed. by John A. Collins. Boston, 1842.)

Parker, Theodore. "Socrates in Boston. A Dialogue between the Philosopher and a Yankee." (In the Liberty Bell. By Friends of Freedom. Boston, 1843.)

Richmond, Legh. "The Negro Servant." (In The Annals of the Poor. Philadelphia, n.d.)

[Rush, Benjamin]. "The Paradise of Negro-Slaves.—A Dream." (In the Columbian Magazine, or Monthly Miscellany. Vol. I. Philadelphia, 1787.) (L.C.)

Stowe, Harriet B. "The Freedman's Dream: A Parable." (In the National Era. Washington, D.C., August 1, 1850.)

——. The Two Altars; or, Two Pictures in One. New York, 1855. Published previously in Autographs for Freedom. Ed. by Julia Griffiths. Boston, 1853.

Thompson, Matilda G. "Aunt Judy's Story: A Story from Real Life." (In The Child's Anti-Slavery Book. New York, 1859.)

——. "Mark and Hasty." (In The Child's Anti-Slavery Book. New York, 1859.)

Anonymous. "African Resolution and European Infamy." (In the Observer. Vol. I. Ed. by Beatrice Ironside. Baltimore, 1807.)

——. "Duty and Safety of Emancipation." (In The Anti-Slavery Picknick. Ed. by John A. Collins. Boston, 1842.)

——. "Excalibur. A Story for Anglo-American Boys." (In the Dial: A Monthly Magazine of Literature, Philosophy and Religion. Ed. by M. D. Conway. Cincinnati, 1860.)

——. "A Few Words About American Slavery." (In The Child's Anti-Slavery Book. New York, 1859.)

——. Flora: A Tale for Children. New York, 1845.

——. "The Fugitives." (In The Star of Emancipation. Boston, 1841.)

——. "The Negro-Trade. A Fragment." (In the American Moral and Sentimental Magazine, consisting of a Collection of Select Pieces, in Prose and Verse, From the Best Authors, On Religious, Moral, and Sentimental Subjects. Vol. I. New York, 1797.)

——. "The Quadroon's Revenge." (In the National Anti-Slavery Standard. Vol. XIX. New York, 1858.) (N.Y.P.L.)

——. "The Slave." (In the American Museum, or Repository of Ancient and Modern Fugitive Pieces, Prose and Poetical. Vol. I. Philadelphia, 1787.)

——. "The Slaves. A Tale Too True." (In the New York Weekly Magazine; or, Miscellaneous Repository. Vol. I. New York, 1796.)

——. The Star of Freedom. New York, [184—?].

——. "Theresa,—A Haytien Tale." (In Freedom's Journal. Vol. I. New York, January 18-February 15, 1828.) (N.Y.H.S.L.)

PERIODICALS

The Abolitionist: or the Record of the New England Anti-Slavery Society. Vol. I. Edited by a Committee. Boston, 1833.

The African Observer. A Monthly Journal. Ed. by Enoch Lewis. Philadelphia, 1828.

The African Repository. Vol. XXIX. Published by the American Colonization Society. Washington, D.C., 1853.

The American Anti-Slavery Almanac. Comp. by L. M. Child. New York, 1843-1844.

The American Liberty Almanac. Hartford, 1846.

The American Moral and Sentimental Magazine, consisting of a Collection of Select Pieces, in Prose and Verse, From the Best Authors, On Religious, Moral, and Sentimental Subjects. Vol. I. New York, 1797. (L.C.)

The American Museum, or Repository of Ancient and Modern Fugitive Pieces, Prose and Poetical. Vol. I. Philadelphia, 1787.

——. Vol. IV. Philadelphia, 1788.

——. Vol. VI. Philadelphia, 1789.

The American Universal Magazine. Vols. I-II. Philadelphia, 1797. (L.C.)

The Anglo-African Magazine. Vol. I. New York, 1859.

The Anti-Slavery Bugle (L. C.). Salem, Ohio, 1850-1852.

The Atlantic Monthly. A Magazine of Literature, Art, and Politics. Vol. VIII. Boston, 1861.

——. Vols. IX and X. Boston, 1862.

——. Vol. XI. Boston, 1863.

——. Vol. XIV. Boston, 1864.

——. Vols. XV and XVI. Boston, 1865.

The Christian Recorder. Philadelphia, 1865.

The Christian's, Scholar's, and Farmer's Magazine. Vol. I. Elizabethtown, N.J., 1789. (L.C.)

The Colored American. New York, 1837. (N.Y.H.S.L.)

174 BIBLIOGRAPHY

The Columbian Magazine or Monthly Miscellany. Vol. II. Philadelphia, 1788. (L.C.)

The Columbian Muse. New York, 1794.

The Commonwealth. Boston, January 24-February 21, 1863. (B.A.L.)

The Connecticut Journal and New Haven Post-Boy. New Haven, 1770. (Y.U.L.; L.C.)

The Continental Monthly. Devoted to Literature and National Policy. Vol. I. New York and Boston, 1862.

——. Vols. II-VI. Boston, 1862-1864.

The Dial: A Monthly Magazine of Literature, Philosophy and Religion. Ed. by M. D. Conway. Cincinnati, 1860.

Douglass' Monthly.[1] Ed. by Frederick Douglass. Rochester, New York, 1862-1863.

The Emancipator. New York, 1838-1839. (Y.U.L.)

The Emancipator and Free American. New York, 1842. (Y.U.L.)

The Emancipator and Weekly Chronicle. Boston, 1844. (Y.U.L.)

The Emancipator and Free Soil Press. Boston, 1848. (Y.U.L.)

Freedom's Journal. New York, 1827-1828. (N.Y.H.S.L.)

The Genius of Universal Emancipation. Vol. II. 3rd Series. Ed. by Benjamin Lundy. Washington and Baltimore, 1831-1832. (H.C.L.)

The Harbinger. Devoted to Social and Political Progress. Vol. I. New York and Boston, 1845. (J.C.L.)

——. Vol. IV. New York and Boston, 1847. (J.C.L.)

——. Vol. VIII. New York and Boston, 1848-1849. (J.C.L.)

The Legion of Liberty and Force of Truth. New York, 1844.

The Liberator. Vols. I-XXXIV. Ed. by William Lloyd Garrison. Boston, 1831-1864. (B.P.L.)

The Liberty Almanac. New York, 1847-1852.

The Liberty Bell. By Friends of Freedom. Boston, 1839, 1841, 1843, 1848, 1849, 1851-1853, 1856, 1858. 15 v.

The Massachusetts Magazine, or Monthly Museum. Vol. V. Boston, 1793. (L.C.)

The Monthly Magazine and American Review. Vol. III. New York, 1800. (L.C.)

[1] Several numbers of this periodical, which is now very rare, are owned by Mr. Haley G. Douglass, of Washington, D.C., the grandson of Frederick Douglass.

The Monthly Offering. Vols. I-II. Ed. by John A. Collins. Boston, 1841-1842.

The National Anti-Slavery Standard. Vols. XIX-XXIII. New York, 1858-1862. (N.Y.P.L.)

The National Era. Ed. by Gamaliel Bailey. Washington, D.C., 1847-1860.

The New England Quarterly Magazine; Comprehending Literature, Morals and Amusement. No. III. Boston, 1802.

The New Haven Gazette, and the Connecticut Magazine. New Haven, 1786. (L.C.)

The New York Daily Tribune. Ed. by Horace Greeley. Vol. XXII. New York, 1862.

The New York Weekly Magazine; or, Miscellaneous Repository. Vol. I. New York, 1796. (L.C.)

The Non-Slaveholder. Ed. by William J. Allinson. Philadelphia, 1853.

The Observer. Vol. I. Ed. by Beatrice Ironside. Baltimore, 1807.

The Pennsylvania Freeman. Philadelphia, 1838-1841.

The Philadelphia Magazine: Containing a great variety of Important, Instructive and Entertaining Matter, chiefly Original, calculated to promote True Religion and Virtue. Vol. I. London, 1788. (L.C.)

The Philadelphia Minerva. Vol. III. Philadelphia, 1797. (L.C.)

The Royal American Magazine, or Universal Repository of Instruction and Amusement. Boston, 1774. (L.C.)

The Rural Magazine; or, Vermont Repository. Devoted to Literary, Moral, Historical and Political Improvement. Vol. I. Rutland, 1795. (L.C.)

The Slave's Friend. Vol. I. Published by R. G. Williams. New York, 1836.

The Weekly Magazine of Original Essays, Fugitive Pieces and Interesting Intelligence. Vols. I, III. Philadelphia, 1798-1799. (L.C.)

LETTERS, JOURNALS, DIARIES, AND BOOKS OF TRAVEL

Abbott, John S. C. South and North; or, Impressions Received during a Trip to Cuba and the South. New York, 1860.

Aughey, John H. The Iron Furnace: or, Slavery and Secession. Philadelphia, 1863.

Baldwin, A. C. "Friendly Letters to a Christian Slaveholder."

(In Three Prize Essays on American Slavery, Boston, 1857.)

Banneker, Benjamin. "An Appeal on Behalf of the African Race", August 19, 1791. (In The Negro's Friend. No. 17. London, n.d.) (B.P.L.)

Bryant, William Cullen. Letters of a Traveller; or, Notes of Things Seen in Europe and America. New York, 1851.

Byrd, William. "Letter to Lord Egmont." July 12, 1736. (In the American Historical Review. Vol. I. New York, 1896.)

Channing, William E. "Remarks on the Slavery Question, in a Letter to Jonathan Phillips, Esq." (In The Works of William E. Channing. Boston, 1886.)

Child, Lydia M. Letters from New York. 2nd Series. New York, 1846.

——. Correspondence between Lydia Maria Child and Governor Wise and Mrs. Mason, of Virginia. Boston, 1860.

[Cooper, James Fenimore]. Notions of the Americans; picked up by a Travelling Bachelor. London, 1828. 2 v.

Crèvecoeur, J. Hector St. John de. "Thoughts on Slavery." (In Letters from an American Farmer. London, 1782.)

Dwight, Timothy. Travels in New England and New York. Vol. IV. New Haven, 1822.

Emerson, Ralph Waldo. Journals of Ralph Waldo Emerson. With Annotations. Vols. I-IV, VI, VIII-IX. Ed. by Edward Waldo Emerson and Waldo Emerson Forbes. Boston and New York, 1909-1913.

Franklin, Benjamin. "Letter to Anthony Benezet." August 22, 1772. (In The Complete Works of Benjamin Franklin. Vol. IV. Ed. by John Bigelow. New York, 1887.)

——. "Letter to Dean Woodward." April 10, 1773. (In The Works of Benjamin Franklin. Vol. VIII. Ed. by Jared Sparks. Boston, 1839.)

——. "Letter to John Wright." November 4, 1789. (In The Works of Benjamin Franklin. Vol. X. Ed. by Jared Sparks. Boston, 1840.)

Grimke, A. E. Letters to Catherine E. Beecher, in Reply to An Essay on Slavery and Abolitionism. Boston, 1838.

Henry, Patrick. "Letter of Patrick Henry of Virginia, to Robert Pleasants, of the Society of Friends." January 18, 1773. (In The Evils of Slavery and the Cure of Slavery. By Lydia M. Child. Newburyport, 1839.)

Hitchcock, Enos. Memoirs of the Bloomgrove Family. In a Series of Letters to a Respectable Citizen of Philadelphia. Vol. II. Boston, 1790.

Hopkinson, Francis. "Translation of a Letter Written by a Foreigner on his Travels." (In The Miscellaneous Essays and Occasional Writings of Francis Hopkinson. Vol. I. Philadelphia, 1792.)

Imlay, Gilbert. A Topographical Description of the Western Territory of North America. London, 1793.

Jefferson, Thomas. "Letter to Dr. Price." August 7, 1785. (In The Writings of Thomas Jefferson. Vol. I. Ed. by H. A. Washington. New York, 1861.)

——. "Letter to M. Warville." February 12, 1788. (In The Writings of Thomas Jefferson. Vol. II. Ed. by H. A. Washington. New York, 1861.)

——. "Letter to Dr. Edward Bancroft." January 26, 1789. (In The Writings of Thomas Jefferson. Vol. V. Ed. by P. L. Ford. New York, 1904.)

——. "Letter to Governor Monroe." November 24, 1801. (In The Writings of Thomas Jefferson. Vol. IV. Ed. by H. A. Washington. New York, 1861.)

——. "Letter to Governor Monroe." June 2, 1802. (In The Writings of Thomas Jefferson. Vol. IX. Ed. by P. L. Ford. New York, 1905.)

——. "Letter to William A. Burwell." January 28, 1805. (In The Writings of Thomas Jefferson. Vol. X. Ed. by P. L. Ford. New York, 1905.)

——. "Letter to Dr. George Logan." May 11, 1805. (In The Writings of Thomas Jefferson. Vol. X. Ed. by P. L. Ford. New York, 1905.)

——. "Letter to Edward Coles." August 25, 1814. (In The Writings of Thomas Jefferson. Vol. XI. Ed. by P. L. Ford. New York, 1905.)

——. "Letter to Albert Gallatin." December 26, 1820. (In The Writings of Thomas Jefferson. Vol. XII. Ed. by P. L. Ford. New York, 1905.)

——. "Letter to William Short." September 8, 1823. (In The Writings of Thomas Jefferson. Vol. VII. Ed. by H. A. Washington. New York, 1861.)

——. "Letter to Jared Sparks." February 4, 1824. (In The

Writings of Thomas Jefferson. Vol. XII. Ed. by P. L. Ford. New York, 1905.)

Mather, Cotton. Diary of Cotton Mather (1681-1708). (In the Massachusetts Historical Society Collections, 7th Series. Vol. VII, Pt. I. Boston, 1911.)

———. Diary of Cotton Mather (1709-1724). (In the Massachusetts Historical Society Collections, 7th Series, Vol. VIII, Pt. II. Boston, 1912.)

Melville, Herman. Some Personal Letters of Herman Melville and A Bibliography. By Meade Minnigerode. New York, New Haven, and Princeton, 1922.

Olmsted, Frederick Law. A Journey in the Seaboard Slave States. With Remarks on their Economy. New York, 1856.

———. A Journey in the Back Country. New York, 1860.

Parker, Theodore. A Letter to the People of the United States Touching the Matter of Slavery. Boston, 1848.

[Paulding, James Kirke]. Letters from the South, Written During An Excursion in the Summer of 1816. New York, 1817.

Paxton, J. D. Letters on Slavery; Addressed to the Cumberland Congregation, Virginia. Lexington, Ky., 1833.

Philanthropos. "Letters on Liberty and Slavery: In answer to A Pamphlet, Entitled, 'Negro-Slavery Defended by the Word of God.'" (In the American Universal Magazine. Vols. I-II. Philadelphia, 1797.) (L.C.)

Rankin, John. Letters on American Slavery. Boston, 1833.

[Royall, Anne]. Sketches of History, Life, and Manners, in the United States. By a Traveller. New Haven, 1826.

Sewall, Samuel. Diary of Samuel Sewall. (In the Massachusetts Historical Society Collections, 5th Series. Vol. VII. Boston, 1882.)

———. Letter-Book of Samuel Sewall. (In the Massachusetts Historical Society Collections, 6th Series. Vol. I. Boston, 1886.)

Tappan, Lewis. "Letter to F. A. Packard." (In Letters Respecting a Book "Dropped from the Catalogue" of the American Sunday School Union in compliance with the Dictation of the Slave Power. New York, 1848.)

Thoreau, Henry D. The Writings of Henry David Thoreau. Journal. Vols. I-III, V, XII, XIV. Ed. by Bradford Torrey. Boston and New York, 1906.

Woolman, John. The Works of John Woolman. In Two Parts. Philadelphia, 1774.

——. The Journal of John Woolman. Ed. by John G. Whittier. Boston, 1871.

Anonymous. "Letter on Slavery." By a Free Negro. (In the American Museum. Vol. VI. Philadelphia, 1789.)

——. "Letters from a Man of Colour, on a late Bill before the Senate of Pennsylvania." (In Freedom's Journal. New York, February 22-March 21, 1928.) (N.Y.H.S.L.)

ORATIONS AND SERMONS

Beecher, Henry Ward. Patriotic Addresses. Ed. by John R. Howard, New York, 1887.

Buchanan, George. "An Oration upon the Moral and Political Evil of Slavery." (In Anti-Slavery Opinions Before the Year 1800. By William Frederick Poole. Cincinnati, 1873.)

Channing, William Henry. The Civil War in America: or, The Slaveholders' Conspiracy. Liverpool, England, 1861.

Clarke, James Freeman. Slavery in the United States. Boston, 1843.

——. The Rendition of Anthony Burns. Its Causes and Consequences. A Discourse on Christian Politics. Boston, 1854.

Douglass, Frederick. Oration. Delivered in Corinthian Hall, Rochester. Rochester, 1852.

Dwight, Theodore. An Oration Spoken before the Society of the Cincinnati, of the State of Connecticut. Hartford, 1792.

——. An Oration, Spoken before the Connecticut Society, for the Promotion of Freedom and the Relief of Persons Unlawfully Holden in Bondage. Hartford, 1794.

Miller, William. A Sermon on the Abolition of the Slave Trade. New York, 1810. (N.Y.P.L.S.)

Moore, Frank. Modern Eloquence: A Collection of Speeches and Addresses, by the Most Eminent Orators of America. Vol. I. New York, 1859.

Parker, Theodore. "The Dangers from Slavery." (In Old South Leaflets. Vol. IV. Boston, n.d.)

Parrott, Russell. An Address on the Abolition of the Slave Trade. Philadelphia, 1816. (B.P.L.)

Paul, Nathaniel. An Address, Delivered on the Celebration of the

Abolition of Slavery in the State of New York. Albany, 1827. (N.Y.P.L.S.)

Phillips, Wendell. "Sims Anniversary." (In Speeches, Lectures, and Letters. Boston, 1863.)

Sidney, Joseph. An Oration Commemorative of the Abolition of the Slave Trade in the United States. New York, 1809. (N.Y.H.S.L.)

Sumner, Charles. The Barbarism of Slavery: Speech of Hon. Charles Sumner, on the Bill for the Admission of Kansas as a Free State, in the United States Senate, June 4, 1860. New York, 1863.

Williams, Peter. An Oration on the Abolition of the Slave Trade. New York, 1808. (N.Y.P.L.S.)

Woodson, Carter G. Negro Orators and Their Orations. Washington, D.C., 1925.

Anonymous. "Speech of an American Quaker on African Slavery." (In the American Museum. Vol. IV. Philadelphia, 1788.)

BIOGRAPHIES AND AUTOBIOGRAPHIES

Binns, Henry Bryan. A Life of Walt Whitman. London, 1905.

Brownson, O. A. The Spirit-Rapper; An Autobiography. Boston and London, 1854.

Cabot, James Elliott. A Memoir of Ralph Waldo Emerson. Vol. II. Boston and New York, 1893.

Coad, O. S. William Dunlap, a Study of His Life and Works and of His Place in Contemporary Culture. New York, 1917.

Emerson, Edward Waldo. Emerson in Concord. A Memoir. Boston and New York, 1888.

Ford, Paul L. The Many-Sided Franklin. New York, 1899.

Foust, C. E. Life and Dramatic Works of Robert Montgomery Bird. New York, 1919.

Garrison, Francis J., and Wendell P. William Lloyd Garrison, 1805-1879. The Story of his Life told by his Children. Boston and New York, 1894. 4 v.

Goodwin, Parke. A Biography of William Cullen Bryant, with Extracts from his Private Correspondence. New York, 1833. 2 v.

Greeley, Horace. Recollections of a Busy Life. New York, 1868.

Hale, Edward E., ed. James Freeman Clarke. Autobiography, Diary and Correspondence. Boston and New York, 1899.

Hall, Arethusa. Life and Character of the Rev. Sylvester Judd. Boston, 1854.

Higginson, Mary Thacher. Thomas Wentworth Higginson; the Story of his Life. Boston and New York, 1914.

Lundy, Benjamin. The Life, Travels and Opinions of Benjamin Lundy, including his Journeys to Texas and Mexico; with a Sketch of Contemporary Events, and a Notice of the Revolution in Hayti. Compiled Under the Direction and on Behalf of his Children. Philadelphia, 1847.

Marble, Annie Russell. Thoreau. His Home, Friends and Books. New York, 1902.

Mather, Cotton. The Life and Death of the Renown'd Mr. John Eliot. 2nd ed. London, 1691. (N.L.)

McCray, Florine T. The Life-Work of the Author of Uncle Tom's Cabin. New York and London, 1889.

Morse, John T., Jr. Life and Letters of Oliver Wendell Holmes. Vol. I. Boston and New York, 1899.

Pickard, Samuel T. Life and Letters of John Greenleaf Whittier. Boston and New York, 1894. 2 v.

Sanborn, Frank B. Recollections of Seventy Years. Vol. II. Boston, 1909.

Sanborn, Frank B. and Harris, William T. A. Bronson Alcott. His Life and Philosophy. Vol. II. Boston, 1893.

Scott, Leonora Cranch. The Life and Letters of Christopher Pearse Cranch. Boston and New York, 1917.

Scudder, Horace E. James Russell Lowell: A Biography. Boston and New York, 1901. 2 v.

Stillman, William James. The Autobiography of a Journalist. Boston and New York, 1901. 2 v.

Weiss, John. Life and Correspondence of Theodore Parker. Vol. II. New York, 1864.

MISCELLANEOUS WRITINGS

Brawley, Benjamin. A Social History of the American Negro. New York, 1921.

Bryce, Ethel May. A Study of the Negro in American Drama. (Master's Thesis, University of Chicago, 1924.)

Byrd, William. Writings of Colonel William Byrd. Ed. by John S. Bassett. New York, 1901.

Channing, William E.   The Works of William E. Channing.   Boston, 1886.

Child, Lydia M.   The Oasis.   Boston, 1834.

——.   The Evils of Slavery and the Cure of Slavery.   2nd ed. Newburyport, 1839.

——.   The Freedmen's Book.   Boston, 1866.

Collins, John A.   The Anti-Slavery Picknick: A Collection of Speeches, Poems, Dialogues and Songs.   Boston, 1842.

Dodd, William E.   The Cotton Kingdom.   A Chronicle of the Old South.   New Haven, 1919.

Garrison, William Lloyd.   Selections from the Writings and Speeches of William Lloyd Garrison.   Boston, 1852.

Gilpin, Henry D., ed.   The Papers of James Madison.   Vol. I. Washington, 1840.

Griffiths, Julia, ed.   Autographs for Freedom.   Boston, 1853.

—— ——.   Auburn and Rochester, 1854.

Hart, Albert B., ed.   American History Told by Contemporaries.   Vol. II.   New York, 1898.

Keefer, Justus.   Slavery: Its Sin, Moral Effects, and Certain Death. Also the Language of Nature, Compared with Divine Revelation in prose and verse.   Baltimore, 1864.

Maclean, Grace Edith.   Uncle Tom's Cabin in Germany.   New York, 1910.

Newton, Pauline.   Anti-Slavery Poetry in America.   (Master's Thesis, Columbia University, 1928).

Redpath, James.   Echoes of Harper's Ferry.   Boston, 1860.

Stowe, Harriet B.   A Key to Uncle Tom's Cabin; Presenting the original Facts and Documents upon which the Story is Founded. Together with Corroborative Statements Verifying The Truth of the Work.   Boston, 1853.

INDEX

Abbott, John S. C., opposition of, to slave labor, 87.

Adams, A. B., *The Neglected Period of Anti-Slavery in America*, 33n., 35n., **44n.,** 45n.

Aiken, George L., dramatic version of *Uncle Tom's Cabin* by, 74.

Alcott, Louisa M., "M. L.," 111-112, 126-152.

American in Algiers, The, 15.

Anti-slavery societies: formation of, 26n., 32, 48; number of, between 1827 **and** 1837, 47-48.

"Appeal for the Slave, An," 61n.

Arguments, anti-slavery: moral and religious, 3-11, 33-36, 48-59, 71-86, 106-110; political, 87-88, 110-111; sentimental, 18-25, 37-44, 61-66, 89-100, 111-118; social and economic, 15-18, 36-37, 59-61, 86-88, 108-110; based upon natural and inalienable rights, 11-15, 32.

Aughey, John H. *The Iron Furnace; or, Slavery and Secession*, 107n.

Banneker, Benjamin, "An Appeal on Behalf of the African Race," 14, 15.

Barlow, Joel, argument based upon the theory of the natural rights of man, made by, 13.

Beard, Charles A., *The Economic Basis of Politics*, 11n.

Beecher, Henry Ward: views of, on slavery, 76n.-77n., 104; "Sermon on the Death of President Lincoln," 118n.

Bell, James Madison: *A Poem*, 114n.-115n.; *A Poem Entitled the Day and the War*, 117n.

Benezet, Anthony, 6, 26n., 29n.

Bennison, D. M., "The Slave's Musings," 61n.

Bibliography of anti-slavery literature, 153-182.

Bigelow, Harriet H. *The Curse Entailed*, 81, 103n.

Biographies and Autobiographies, 180-181.

Bird, Robert Montgomery: "The Gladiator," 41-42; *Sheppard Lee*, 50n.

"Body of Liberties," 3.

Boker, G. H., tribute of, in verse, to the martyred President, 117n.-118n.

Boucher, Jonathan, *A View of the Causes and Consequences of the American Revolution*, 16n.

Boucicault, Dion, *The Octoroon*, 89, 90-92.

Brackenridge, Hugh H., appeal of, for immediate emancipation, 30, 31, 32.

Bradley, Senator, notice of a bill to prohibit the introduction of slaves after 1808, given by, 25.

Branagan, Thomas, views of, on slavery, 17, 23-25.

Brougham, John, dramatic version of *Dred* by, 77.

Brown, William Wells, views of, on slavery, 79-81, 83-84, 104n.

Bryant, William Cullen: views of, on slavery, 38, 40-41, 60-61, 113-114; tribute of, in verse, to the martyred President, 117n.-118n.

Buchanan, George, "An Oration upon the Moral and Political Evil of Slavery," 14, 16.

Bulfinch, Stephen C., *Honor; or, The Slave-Dealer's Daughter*, 107.

Bulkley, C. H. A., *Niagara*, 61n.

Burleigh, W. H., "A Word to the South," 65-66.

Phillips, Wendell, views of, on slavery, 96.
Pierson, Emily Catherine, *Jamie Parker, the Fugitive*, 79n.
Pierpont, John: "Prayer for the Slave," 61n.; "Poem," 117n.
"Plan for the Abolition of Slavery, A," 68-69.
Plays, anti-slavery, 157-158.
Poems, anti-slavery, 158-166.
"Poetical Epistle to the Enslaved Africans, A," 19.
Political arguments. *See* Arguments, political.
Poole, W. F., *Anti-Slavery Opinions before the Year 1800*, 14n., 16n., 26n.
"President Lincoln's Proclamation of Emancipation," 116n.
Puritans, moral and religious arguments of the, 3-5, 32.

Quakers, moral and religious arguments of the, 5-7, 32.

Raymond, James, "A Prize Essay on the Comparative Economy of Free and Slave Labour in Agriculture", 36-37.
Reid, Mayne, *The Quadroon; or, A Lover's Adventures in Louisiana*, 90-91.
Rhodes, James Ford, *History of the United States*, 73n.
Ricord, Elizabeth, *Zamba; or the Insurrection*, 50n.
Ritchie, D. G., *Natural Rights*, 11n.
Rogers, E. P., *A Poem on the Fugitive Slave Law*, 99.
Rowson, Susanna, *The Inquisitor; or, Invisible Rambler*, 9-10.
Royall, Anne, *Sketches of History, Life, and Manners in the United States*, 34-35.
Rush, Benjamin, views of, on slavery, 9, 29.

Sandiford, Ralph, 6.
Sargent, Epes, views of, on slavery, 107, 108-111.
Scudder, H. E., quoted, 64.
Sentimental arguments. *See* Arguments, sentimental.
Sewall, Samuel, views of, on slavery, 1-2, 4-5, 11, 16, 32.
Sherburne, Henry, *The Oriental Philanthropist*, 20-21.
Short Narratives and Sketches, 171-173.
Sidney, Joseph, "An Oration Commemorative of the Abolition of the Slave Trade in the United States," 38n.
Sims, Thomas, remanding of, to slavery, 95.
Slave-Trade Act, 1, 3, 33, 46, 119.
Smith, M. B., *My Uncle's Family; or, Ten Months at the South*, 108.
Smith, William W., *The Yankee Slave Driver; or, The Black and White Rivals*, 99n.
Social and economic arguments. *See* Arguments, social and economic.
"Sorrows of Angola, The," 38n.
Stevens, Henry E., 74n.
Stoddard, Richard Henry: "Men of the North and West," 114; tribute of, in verse, to the martyred President, 117n.-118n.
Story, Sidney A., *Story of Republican Equality*, 104n.
Stowe, Harriet Beecher, views of, on slavery, 58-59, 71-79, 93-95, 103-105.
Sumner, Charles, economic argument of, against slavery, 86-87.